D1560016

Genealogical Research in Ohio

GENEALOGICAL
RESEARCH IN

OHIO

Kip Sperry

2nd Edition

Published by Genealogical Publishing Co., Inc.
1001 N. Calvert St., Baltimore, MD 21202
Library of Congress Catalogue Card Number 2002111726
International Standard Book Number 0-8063-1713-2
Made in the United States of America

Contents

Major Resources (continued)

Preface

Ohio has an abundance of sources available for genealogical research—statewide indexes and personal name finding aids, census indexes, biographies, county and other local histories, vital and church records, probate and court records, census and military records, land records, newspapers, naturalization records, gravestones and cemetery records, genealogical collections, and many others. In addition, numerous Ohio records have been published by genealogical and historical organizations, and many records and indexes are available on microfilm and microfiche. An increasing number of Ohio sources are also available on the Internet and compact discs (CD-ROM).

This research guide describes Ohio sources for family history and genealogical research. It also includes extensive footnotes and bibliographies, addresses of repositories that house Ohio historical and genealogical records and oral histories, and addresses of chapters of the Ohio Genealogical Society. Valuable Ohio maps conclude this work.

This second edition is an expanded and revised version of *Genealogical Research in Ohio*, published by Genealogical Publishing Company in 1997. This new edition describes many Ohio sources on the Internet and compact discs (CD-ROM), as well as additional genealogical and historical sources and bibliographies of Ohio sources.

The author wishes to express appreciation to the following colleagues and friends who assisted with providing updated material, helpful suggestions, and encouragement, for the first edition: K. Haybron Adams, Orem, Utah; Carol Willsey Bell, Youngstown, Ohio; Mary L. Bowman, Athens, Ohio; Petta Khouw, Columbus, Ohio; Phyllis Brown Delaney; Joy Wade Moulton, FSG, Columbus, Ohio; and William Bart Saxbe, Jr., M.D., CG, FASG, Williamstown, Massachusetts.

For this second edition, I wish to especially thank Amy Johnson Crow, CG, Reynoldsburg, Ohio; Diane VanSkiver Gagel, Perrysburg, Ohio; Marian Hoffman, Genealogical Publishing Company, Baltimore, Maryland; and Thomas Stephen Neel, Library Director, Ohio Genealogical Society, Mansfield, Ohio, who assisted with reading the manuscript and confirming details. Tom Neel helped confirm OGS Library holdings and information regarding OGS chapters.

Also helpful for verifying their library holdings was Elaine Hasleton, Family History Library, Salt Lake City; Paul Immel, Genealogy Services Librarian, State Library of Ohio, Columbus; Louise T. Jones, Head, Research Services, Archives/Library Division, Ohio Historical Society, Columbus; David Lincove, William O. Thompson Memorial Library, Ohio State University, Columbus; Glenn V. Longacre, National Archives and Records Administration—Great Lakes Region, Chicago, Illinois; James C. Marshall, Local History and Genealogy Department, Toledo-Lucas County Public Library, Toledo; Ann Sindelar, Western Reserve Historical Society, Cleveland; Patricia Van Skaik, History and Genealogy Department, Public Library of Cincinnati and Hamilton County, Cincinnati; and Christy Wiggins, Fairview Park Regional Library, Fairview Park, Ohio. Their assistance is greatly appreciated; however, they are not responsible for any errors in this book.

Reference librarians and archivists have provided a great deal of assistance—particularly those at Brigham Young University, Harold B. Lee Library, Provo, Utah; Case Western Reserve University, Kelvin Smith Library, Cleveland, Ohio; Cleveland Public Library, Cleveland, Ohio; Columbus Metropolitan Library, Columbus, Ohio; Cuyahoga County Public Library, Fairview Park Regional Library, Fairview Park, Ohio; Family History Library, Salt Lake City, Utah; Morley Library, Painesville, Ohio; New England Historic Genealogical Society, Boston, Massachusetts; Ohio Genealogical Society, Mansfield, Ohio; Ohio Historical Society, Columbus, Ohio; Public Library of Cincinnati and

Hamilton County, History and Genealogy Department, Cincinnati, Ohio; State Library of Ohio, Columbus, Ohio; Toledo-Lucas County Public Library, Toledo, Ohio; and Western Reserve Historical Society Library, Cleveland, Ohio.

Special thanks to Brigham Young University, Provo, Utah, for providing secretarial and editorial services, especially Kirsha Johnson and Marci Anne Purnell; cartography assistance; and research support. Professor Don E. Norton and Maria Ilieva of Brigham Young University's English Department were especially helpful reading the manuscript and offering editing suggestions. Research for this volume was partially funded by Brigham Young University's Religious Studies Center and Brigham Young University's Department of Church History and Doctrine.

—Kip Sperry

ABBREVIATIONS

ACPL	Allen County Public Library, Fort Wayne, IN
ALAO	Academic Library Association of Ohio
ALICE	Ohio University's online library catalog
AO	Auditor's Office
APG	Association of Professional Genealogists
BBS	Bulletin Board System
BCG	Board for Certification of Genealogists, Washington, DC
BGSU	Bowling Green State University, Bowling Green, OH
BLM	Bureau of Land Management
BLM-ESO	Bureau of Land Management, Eastern States Office
BLW	Bounty Land Warrant
CAAO	County Auditors' Association of Ohio
CAC	Center for Archival Collections, Bowling Green, OH
CAGG	Computer Assisted Genealogy Group (e.g., Cleveland Area)
CALICO	Columbus Area Library and Information Council of Ohio, Columbus, OH
CAMLS	Cleveland Area Metropolitan Library System
CAR	Cleveland Archival Roundtable
CC	Clerk of Courts
CCAO	County Commissioners Association of Ohio
CCOGS	Colorado Chapter, Ohio Genealogical Society
CCPL	Cuyahoga County Public Library
CH	county courthouse
CHS	Cincinnati Historical Society, Cincinnati, OH
CINCH	Computerized Information Network for Cincinnati and Hamilton County (online catalog)

CLIO	County Library Information Online
CML	Columbus Metropolitan Library, Columbus, OH
CO	company, county, county office, county officer
COIN	Central Ohio Interlibrary Network
comp.	compiler
CONSORT	Combined online library catalog of College of Wooster, Denison University, Kenyon College, and Ohio Wesleyan University
COSI	Center of Science and Industry, Toledo, OH
CP	Common Pleas Court
CPCt	Common Pleas Court (record)
CR	criminal, criminal court case
CPL	Cleveland Public Library, Cleveland, OH
CRL	Center for Research Libraries
CSU	Cleveland State University, Cleveland, OH
CW	*Ohio Civil War Genealogy Journal*
CWRT	Civil War Roundtable
CWRU	Case Western Reserve University, Cleveland, OH
DAR	National Society Daughters of the American Revolution, Washington, DC
DMC	Digital Media Center (i.e., OhioLINK)
EFIC	Early Families of Cleveland (Ohio)
EOA	*Encyclopedia of Ohio Associations*
ERC	Educational Resources Center
FFO	First Families of Ohio (Ohio Genealogical Society, Mansfield, OH)
FGS	Federation of Genealogical Societies
FHL	Family History Library, Salt Lake City, UT
FHLC	Family History Library Catalog
FPR	Fairview Park Regional Library, Fairview Park, OH
GAR	Grand Army of the Republic

GC	General Code of Ohio
GCLC	Greater Cincinnati Library Consortium
GIS	Geographic Information System
GLO	General Land Office
GRC	Genealogical Records Committee(s), National Society Daughters of the American Revolution
GSC	Genealogy Services Collection, State Library of Ohio, Columbus, OH
GTTW	*Gateway to the West*
HCCOGS	Hamilton County Chapter, Ohio Genealogical Society
HCGL	Historical Collections of the Great Lakes
HRS	Historical Records Survey
HUC	Hebrew Union College, Cincinnati, OH
ICAPGen	International Commission for the Accreditation of Professional Genealogists
IGI	International Genealogical Index
IGLR	Institute for Great Lakes Research (Bowling Green State University)
JP	Justice of the Peace
KSL	Kelvin Smith Library, Case Western Reserve University, Cleveland, OH
KSU	Kent State University, Kent, OH
LC	Library of Congress, Washington, DC
LDS	The Church of Jesus Christ of Latter-day Saints
LEECA	Lake Erie Educational Computer Association
LGR	local government records
LRS	Library Research Service, Western Reserve Historical Society, Cleveland, OH
MAC	Midwest Archives Conference, Toledo, OH
MAGIC	Mohican Area Genealogists Interested in Computers
MC	Municipal Court

MG	Minister of the Gospel
MILO	Miami Valley Library Organization
ML	Morley Library, Painesville, OH
MLW	Military Land Warrant
MM	Monthly Meeting (Society of Friends/Quakers)
MOLO	Regional Library System (Eastern Ohio)
MS/MSS	manuscript/manuscripts
MVAR	Miami Valley Archival Roundtable
MVGI	Miami Valley Genealogical Index
MVL	Miami Valley Libraries
NA	naturalized, naturalization
NARA	National Archives and Records Administration, Washington, DC
n.d.	no date(s)
NEOCAG	Northeast Ohio Computer-Aided Genealogy
NGS	National Genealogical Society, Arlington, VA
NOECA	Northern Ohio Educational Computer Association
NOLA	Northeastern Ohio Library Association
NORWELD	Northwest Library District
NSDAR	National Society Daughters of the American Revolution, Washington, DC
NUCMC	*National Union Catalog of Manuscript Collections*
NW	Northwest
NWOCA	Northwest Ohio Computer Association
NWT	Northwest Territory
OA	*Ohio Archivist*
OAC	Ohio Administrative Code
OAH	Ohio Academy of History, Delaware, OH
OAHQ	*Ohio Archaeological and Historical Quarterly*
OAHSM	Ohio Association of Historical Societies and Museums
OANG	Ohio Air National Guard

OCA	Oberlin College Archives, Oberlin, OH
OCA	Ohio College Association
OCA	Ohio Court of Appeals Reports
OCC	Online Collections Catalog (Ohio Historical Society's online catalog)
OCLC	Online Computer Library Center, Dublin, OH
OCP	Ohio Company Purchase
OCPS	Ohio Cemetery Preservation Society
OCWGJ	*Ohio Civil War Genealogy Journal* (Ohio Genealogical Society, Mansfield, OH)
OD	Ohio Decisions
ODCI	Ohio Death Certificate Index (Ohio Historical Society, Columbus, OH)
ODH	Ohio Department of Health, Columbus, OH
ODNR	Ohio Department of Natural Resources
OFD	Ohio Federal Decisions
OFDA	Ohio Funeral Directors Association
OFL	Ohio Friends of the Library
OGN	*OGS Genealogy* News (Ohio Genealogical Society, Mansfield, OH)
OGQ	*Ohio Genealogical Quarterly*
OGS	Ohio Genealogical Society, Mansfield, OH
OGSQ	*Ohio Genealogical Society Quarterly* (formerly *The Report*)
OGS REP	Ohio Genealogical Society, *The Report*
OGSRP	Ohio Genealogical Society, *The Report*
OH	Ohio
OH	*Ohio History*
OHC	Ohio Humanities Council
OhioLINK	Ohio Library and Information Network
OHLF	*Ohio's Last Frontier* (newsletter)

OHN	Ohio History Network
OHO	*Ohioana*
OHP/OHPO	Ohio Historic Preservation Office, Columbus, OH
OHQ	*Ohio Historical Quarterly*
OHQ	*Ohio State Archaeological and Historical Quarterly*
OhR	Ohio River
OHRAB	Ohio Historical Records Advisory Board
OHRPF	*Ohio Records and Pioneer Families* (Ohio Genealogical Society, Mansfield, OH)
OHS	Ohio Historical Society, Columbus, OH
OhSL	State Library of Ohio, Columbus, OH
OhU	Ohio State University, Columbus, OH
OI	Ohio Infantry
OIB	Ohio Independent Battery
OL	Laws of Ohio; Ohio Laws
OLA	Ohio Law Abstract
OLA	Ohio Library Association
OLC	Ohio Library Council
OLJ	*Ohio Law Journal*
OLR	*Ohio Law Reporter*
OLTA	Ohio Library Trustees Association
OMA	Ohio Museum Association
OML	Ohio Municipal League
ONAHRC	Ohio Network of American History Research Centers
ONGQ	*Old Northwest Genealogical Quarterly*
ONU	Ohio Northern University, Ada, OH
OO	Ohio Opinions
OPAC	Online Public Access Catalog
OPAL	Ohio Private Academic Libraries
OPC	Ohio Preservation Council
OPLIN	Ohio Public Library Information Network

OR	*Ohio Records and Pioneer Families*
OR	Ohio Roster of Soldiers of 1812
ORC	*Ohio Revised Code*
ORPF	*Ohio Records and Pioneer Families* (Ohio Genealogical Society, Mansfield, OH)
ORVF	Ohio River Valley Families
OS	Ohio State Reports
OSAHQ	*Ohio State Archaeological and Historical Quarterly*
OSCAR	Ohio State University Libraries online catalog
OSL	State Library of Ohio, Columbus, OH
OSU	Ohio State University, Columbus, OH
OSU	Ohio Supreme Court Decisions
OTA	Ohio Township Association
OU	Ohio University, Athens, OH
OVA	Ohio Volunteer Artillery
OVAL	Ohio Valley Area Libraries
OVC	Ohio Volunteer Cavalry
OVHA	Ohio Volunteer Heavy Artillery
OVI	Ohio Volunteer Infantry
OVIL	Ohio Vital Information for Libraries Center
OVLA	Ohio Volunteer Light Artillery
OVM	Ohio Volunteer Militia
OVSS	Ohio Volunteer Sharpshooters
Pal-Am	Palatines to America, Columbus, OH
PC	Probate Court
PERSI	*Periodical Source Index*
PLCH	Public Library of Cincinnati and Hamilton County, Cincinnati, OH
PRF	Pedigree Resource File
RLS	Regional Library Systems (Ohio)
RS	Revised Statutes of Ohio

SBO	Settlers and Builders of Ohio
SCDL	Stark County District Library, Canton, OH
SCWFO	Society of Civil War Families of Ohio (Ohio Genealogical Society, Mansfield, OH)
SEO	Southeastern Ohio Regional Library Center, Caldwell, OH
SLO	State Library of Ohio, Columbus, OH
SOA	Society of Ohio Archivists
SOLO	Southeastern Ohio Regional Library Center
TAGS	Toledo Area Genealogical Society
TCGC	Theological Consortium of Greater Columbus
TIGER	Toledo's Information Gateway to Electronic Resources (Toledo-Lucas County Public Library, Web browser-based electronic catalog, Toledo, OH)
TPL	Toledo Public Library, Toledo, OH
TR	*The Report* (Ohio Genealogical Society)
TWP	Township
UA	University of Akron, Akron, OH
UC	University of Cincinnati, Cincinnati, OH
UCLID	University of Cincinnati Libraries online catalog
UGRR	Underground Railroad
USGS	United States Geological Survey
UTMOST	University of Toledo online catalog
VMD	Virginia Military District (Ohio)
WCTU	Woman's Christian Temperance Union of Ohio
WINSLO	State Library of Ohio, Columbus, OH
WPA	Works Progress Administration
WRHS	Western Reserve Historical Society, Cleveland, OH
WSU	Wright State University, Dayton, OH
YHCIL	Youngstown Historical Center of Industry & Labor
YSU	Youngstown State University, Youngstown, OH

For Further Reference

Evans, Barbara Jean. *A to Zax: A Comprehensive Dictionary for Genealogists and Historians.* 3rd ed. Alexandria, Va.: Hearthside Press, 1995.

Internet. See especially Google (www.google.com).

Sperry, Kip, comp. *Abbreviations and Acronyms: A Guide for Family Historians.* 2nd revised edition. Orem, Utah: Ancestry, 2003.

Note:
While some of these abbreviations are found in this book, additional abbreviations are included in this list since they may be useful to Ohio genealogical and historical researchers, reference librarians, and others.

Ohio Capsule

Capital:	Columbus (since 1816)
Cities (largest):	Akron, Canton, Cincinnati, Cleveland, Columbus, Dayton, Lorain, Toledo, and Youngstown
Counties:	88 (largest, Ashtabula County; smallest, Lake County)
Crops:	soybeans, corn, wheat, others
Economy:	agriculture, manufacturing, mining
Land area:	41,328 square miles
Libraries (largest):	Cleveland Public Library, Cleveland; Columbus Metropolitan Library, Columbus; Ohio Historical Society, Columbus; Ohio State University, Columbus; Public Library of Cincinnati and Hamilton County, Cincinnati; State Library of Ohio, Columbus; Toledo-Lucas County Public Library, Toledo; Western Reserve Historical Society, Cleveland
Local government:	Approximately 1,311 townships, 701 villages, 239 cities
Migration to Ohio:	Ohio River and other rivers, canals, Lake Erie, National (Cumberland) Road, Zane's Trace, railroads
Motto:	With God, All Things Are Possible
Natural resources:	coal and limestone

Newspapers (major):	*Akron Beacon Journal*
	The Cincinnati Enquirer
	The Cincinnati Post
	The Columbus Dispatch
	Dayton Daily News
	Plain Dealer (Cleveland)
	Springfield News-Sun
	The Toledo Blade
	The Vindicator (Youngstown)
Nickname:	The Buckeye State
Population (2000):	11,353,140 (www.census.gov)
	277.3 persons per square mile in 2000
Postal abbreviation:	OH
Presidents:	seven former U.S. presidents were born in Ohio
Religions (major):	Baptist, Congregational, Episcopal, Jewish, Lutheran, Methodist, Presbyterian, and Roman Catholic
Rivers (major):	Cuyahoga, Grand, Great Miami, Hocking, Huron, Little Miami, Maumee, Muskingum, Ohio, Portage, Sandusky, Scioto, Vermilion
Statehood granted:	1 March 1803, the 17th state and the first state admitted in the Northwest Territory

CHRONOLOGY

1669-70	The first exploration in what is now Ohio is made by the French between Lake Erie and the Ohio River. The French later claim the entire Ohio Valley.
1744	King George II charters the first Ohio Company which was organized by Virginians and London merchants who traded with Virginia.
1747	Ohio Company of Virginia is organized to settle the Ohio River Valley.
1748	Ohio Land Company is organized.
1750	Christopher Gist, from Virginia's Ohio Company, explores Ohio.
1754	The Ohio Company constructs a fort at the forks of the Ohio River.
1754-63	French and Indian War.
1763	Treaty of Paris ends French and Indian War. France gives Great Britain most of its lands east of the Mississippi River.
1772	A Moravian settlement is established near present-day New Philadelphia; it is abandoned in 1776.
1773	First school in Ohio opens for Indians at Schoenbrunn, near New Philadelphia.
1775-83	Revolutionary War.
1778	First American Army post in Ohio territory built at Fort Laurens.
1780	George Rogers Clark defeats the Shawnee Indians.
1781	New York cedes its claims to Ohio to the United States government.
1783	3 September. Treaty of Paris ends the American

	Revolution. Great Britain formally relinquishes its right and interest in the Northwest Territory. Ohio Valley is given to the United States.
1784	Virginia cedes its claims to Ohio and other western lands to the United States.
	Congress passes an ordinance designed to guide the development of government of the Northwest Territory (Ordinance of 1784).
1784-86	Native Americans sign treaties giving up southern Ohio.
1785	Massachusetts grants its western claims, including Ohio, to the United States government.
	Congress passes the Land Ordinance of 1785. Townships are established. A section of each township is reserved for school development.
	Seven Ranges in Ohio are surveyed.
	Fort Harmar established at the mouth of the Muskingum River.
1786	Connecticut relinquishes its western land claims, including Ohio, to the United States (except the Connecticut Western Reserve in northeastern Ohio).
	Ohio Company of Associates established at Boston to settle lands along the Ohio River.
1787	13 July. The United States Congress enacts the Northwest Ordinance of 1787, establishing a government in the area north of the Ohio River. It encourages education; freedom of speech, press, and assembly; and prohibition of slavery. It becomes the basic instrument of government in the Northwest Territory. Ohio becomes part of the Northwest Territory. Connecticut and Virginia retain title to Ohio

land—the Connecticut Western Reserve and the Virginia Military District.

Congress authorizes the Ohio Company Purchase.

Scioto Company is created.

1788   The first territorial government is formed at Marietta. Ohio Company of Associates establishes settlement at Marietta at the Muskingum and Ohio rivers.

Marietta is the first permanent white settlement in Ohio. It is the first capital of the Northwest Territory.

Campus Martius is built as a fortress against the Indians.

Washington County, with its seat at Marietta, is established.

25 July. Ohio National Guard organized at Marietta.

1789   The Symmes Company is organized at Cincinnati. Fort Washington established at Cincinnati.

1790   Hamilton County, with its seat at Cincinnati, is established.

A large French settlement is established at Gallipolis.

1793   The first newspaper north and west of the Ohio River, *The Centinel of the Northwestern Territory*, is published at Cincinnati (it was published 1793-96).

Fort Recovery built by General Anthony Wayne.

1794   Battle of Fallen Timbers ends the Indian Wars in Ohio. Indians are defeated by General Anthony Wayne.

1795   Treaty of Greenville ends Native American wars and opens two-thirds of Ohio to settlers. Greenville Treaty Line separates Native American lands in northwest Ohio from settlers' lands in the east and south.

Connecticut Land Company created.

A subscription library opens at Belpre.

1796	Chillicothe established in the Virginia Military District. General Moses Cleaveland leads a group of settlers from Connecticut and founds the city of Cleveland at the mouth of the Cuyahoga River.
	Freeman's Journal published at Cincinnati, 1796-99.
	Youngstown established.
	Land act creates Pittsburgh and Cincinnati land offices and the United States Military Tract.
	Zane's Trace, which extends from Wheeling, Virginia (now West Virginia), to Zanesville and Lancaster, Ohio, and Limestone (now Maysville), Kentucky, on the Ohio River opens for migrants.
1797	Adams and Jefferson counties established.
	Migrants continue to use Zane's Trace.
	Muskingum Academy (now Marietta College) established (the first institution of higher learning in the Northwest Territory).
1798	Ross County created.
1799	Territorial government established in Ohio with Cincinnati as the capital.
	The *Western Spy and Hamilton Gazette* is published at Cincinnati.
1800	First territorial census taken in Ohio; population 45,365 people.
	Clermont County, with its seat at Batavia, is created.
	Fairfield County, with its seat at Lancaster, is established.
	Trumbull County established.
	Land office opens at Steubenville.
	Connecticut gives up jurisdiction of the Western Reserve in northeastern Ohio.

The Scioto Gazette begins publication at Chillicothe. Chillicothe is the capital of the Territory of Ohio. Congress passes the Division Act, which creates Indiana Territory.

1801   Belmont County created.

1802   45,028 people residing in the Northwest (Ohio and Michigan).

Ohio University is chartered as American Western University in Athens, renamed Ohio University in 1804.

Constitutional convention held at Chillicothe.

1803   1 March. Ohio admitted to the Union as the 17th state. Edward Tiffin is the first governor.

State capital is at Chillicothe from 1803 to 1810.

Butler, Columbiana, Franklin, Gallia, Greene, Montgomery, Scioto, and Warren counties created.

Louisiana Purchase lands purchased by the United States from France.

Ohio population approximately 50,000 people.

1804   18 February. Ohio University established at Athens. Muskingum County created.

Coonskin Library organized at Ames (Amesville); books are distributed on horseback.

1805   Athens, Champaign, and Highland counties created. Many settlers migrate to Ohio.

1806   Geauga County established.

1807   Miami County created.

1809   Miami University established as a state-supported university at Oxford; first classes held in 1824.

1810   Population: 230,760 people in Ohio (U.S. census). State capital temporarily moved from Chillicothe to

	Zanesville (until 1812). Partial 1810 census survives.
1811	The *New Orleans* is the first steamboat to travel down the Ohio River.
1812	Capital transferred from Zanesville back to Chillicothe (until 1816).
1812-15	War of 1812. Ohio militia mobilizes in 1812. 26,280 Ohioans take an active part in this conflict.
1813	Commodore Oliver Hazard Perry wins a significant naval victory during the War of 1812, the Battle of Lake Erie, on the Ohio side of the boundary line defeating the British fleet on Lake Erie.
1815	Thousands of settlers arrive in Ohio, often known as the "Great Migration" [to Ohio].
1816	State capital established at Columbus, Franklin County.
1817	Treaty of Maumee Rapids allows many settlers into northwest Ohio. State Library of Ohio established at Columbus. Zoar Village organized near New Philadelphia by a group of Germans. *The Philanthropist*, the country's first antislavery newspaper, is published at Mount Pleasant.
1818	National Road reaches Wheeling, (West) Virginia. *Walk-in-the-Water*, the first steamboat on Lake Erie, stops at Cleveland and Sandusky on route from Buffalo, New York, to Detroit, Michigan.
1819	University of Cincinnati established at Cincinnati as a municipal college. Cincinnati receives its city charter.
1817/1819	Society of Separatists at Zoar (German separatists in Tuscarawas County) is an experiment in communal living which lasts until 1898.

1820	Population: 581,434 (U.S. census).
	Federal census of Ohio taken and is now indexed.
	Ohio is the fifth most populous state.
	Land Act changes purchase of land from federal government to a cash basis.
1823	Decline in sales of western Ohio lands.
	First Methodist mission established at Upper Sandusky.
1824	*Rufus Putnam*, the first steamboat on the Muskingum River, travels from Marietta to Zanesville.
	Kenyon College (Gambier) organized by Episcopalians (the first denominational college in Ohio).
1825	New York state's Erie Canal connects the Hudson River with Lake Erie. Western migration to Ohio and other Midwestern states increases.
	Work begins on the Miami and Erie Canal in Ohio.
	State law requires counties to fund education. Ohio public school system begins.
1826	Western Reserve Academy established by Congregationalists at Hudson.
1827	Akron-Cleveland branch of Ohio and Erie Canal opened. *Daily Gazette*, the first daily newspaper west of Philadelphia, begins publication at Cincinnati.
1829	Boat service on the Miami and Erie Canal begins with the arrival of the *Governor Brown* from Cincinnati to Dayton.
1830	Population: 937,903 (U.S. census).
1830-60	Many mills and factories are built in Ohio.
1831	Joseph Smith, Jr., arrives in Kirtland, Ohio, and begins a settlement for the Latter-day Saints (Mormons).
	Xavier University created by Jesuit Order at

	Cincinnati.
1831-38	Kirtland, Geauga Co. (now Lake Co.) serves as headquarters of The Church of Jesus Christ of Latter-day Saints. LDS Church units are established in northeastern Ohio and elsewhere.
1832	Ohio and Erie Canal completed. Its route extends from Cleveland (Lake Erie) to Portsmouth near the Ohio River and links Lake Erie and the Ohio River.
1833	Ottawa Indians removed by Maumee Treaty.
	Oberlin College established—the first college in the U.S. to admit African Americans and women. It is the first coeducational college in the U.S. for both men and women and is a center of the antislavery movement.
	National (Cumberland) Road opens to Columbus.
	Cholera epidemic in Columbus claims some 200 lives.
1836	The Erie and Kalamazoo, Ohio's first railroad, is completed from Toledo to Adrian, Michigan.
	Ohio-Michigan boundary dispute settled.
	Kirtland Temple dedicated by Joseph Smith, Jr., leader of the Latter-day Saints in Kirtland, Ohio. The Kirtland Temple is now owned by the Community of Christ.
1837	Oberlin College becomes coeducational after opening its doors to women.
	Muskingum College established by United Presbyterian Church at New Concord.
1838	National Road completed to Vandalia.
	Latter-day Saints leave Kirtland for western Missouri.
1840	Population: 1,519,467 (U.S. census).
	Census of pensioners for Revolutionary War or military services taken.
	Ohio is one of the leading corn and wheat producing

	states.
1842	Ohio Wesleyan University established in Delaware, Ohio, by the Methodists.
1843	Wabash and Erie Canal links Lafayette, Indiana, to Toledo, Ohio.
1845	Miami and Erie Canal, connecting Toledo and Cincinnati, is completed.
	20 December. Baldwin-Wallace College is chartered as Baldwin Institute at Berea. Founded by Methodists, it becomes Baldwin University in 1854 and granted its first degrees in 1858. The Institution joins with German Wallace College in 1914 to form Baldwin-Wallace College.
	Wittenberg University (Springfield) established by Lutherans.
1846	Mount Union College established at Alliance by members of the Methodist Episcopal Church.
1846-48	Mexican War. Many Ohioans serve in this conflict.
1847	Otterbein University established by United Brethren Church at Westerville (now Otterbein College).
1848	Oxford College for Women established at Oxford.
	Ohio's African American laws repealed.
1849	Cholera kills about 7,500 people in Cincinnati during the years 1849-50. Cholera spreads across Ohio.
	Cholera kills about 400 people at Sandusky.
1850	Population: 1,980,329 (U.S. census).
	Many Ohio residents in 1850 are foreign born—Germany, Ireland, England, France, Wales, Canada, Scotland, Switzerland, and other foreign countries (source: 1850 U.S. census).
	Catholic Archdiocese created at Cincinnati.

Heidelberg College created at Tiffin by the Ohio Synod of the Reformed Church in the United States.

Dayton-Sandusky railroad begins.

Capital University (Columbus) established.

University of Dayton established.

1851   Probate Court assumes responsibility for recording probate and estate matters.

New Constitution of Ohio adopted.

1852   The railroad reaches Cleveland from Pittsburgh.

Virginia relinquishes and cedes to the U.S. government its claim to any unsettled land in the Virginia Military District in Ohio.

1853   Public high schools in Ohio authorized.

1856   Wilberforce University becomes the nation's first college for African Americans.

1856-57   Some county registration of births and deaths recorded.

1859   Ohio has 22 colleges and universities.

1860   Population: 2,339,511 (U.S. census).

Ohio is the third most populous state in the U.S.

1861-65   Civil War. Over 310,000 Ohio men serve for the Union.

The Underground Railroad in Ohio helps slaves from the southern states migrate to Canada.

1862   Homestead Act.

1863   July. Some 3,000 Confederate soldiers, under the command of General John Morgan, enter south-western and southern Ohio.

1867   County-level registration of civil births and deaths (some county birth and death records begin in 1868).

1869	G.A.R. (Grand Army of the Republic) establishes the Ohio Soldiers' and Sailors' Orphans Home at Xenia.
1870	Population: 2,665,260 (U.S. census).
	Buchtel College established, later the University of Akron, Akron, Ohio.
	Ohio Agricultural and Mechanical College established at Columbus (later Ohio State University), a land-grant college.
	University of Cincinnati incorporated as a municipal university.
	John D. Rockefeller organizes Standard Oil Company in Cleveland.
1872	University of Toledo established at Toledo.
1873	Ohio Agricultural and Mechanical College in Columbus (later Ohio State University) opens for students.
1876	Ohio has 6,400 churches and 35 church-supported colleges.
1880	Population: 3,198,062 (U.S. census).
1884	Western Reserve University chartered in Cleveland.
1886	American Federation of Labor organized at Columbus.
	College of Wooster, Wooster, established by Presbyterians.
1890	Population: 3,672,329 (U.S. census; later destroyed).
	Special Union Veterans and Widows Census taken.
1890s	Akron becomes a major tire manufacturing center.
1898	Spanish-American War. 14,255 Ohioans contribute to this conflict.
	Zoarites abandon their communal lifestyle.
1899	Bluffton College, Bluffton, organized by Mennonites.
1900	Population: 4,157,545 (U.S. census).
	There are approximately 11,000 one-room school-

	houses in Ohio.
1908	20 December. Birth and death records kept on a state level.
	Youngstown State established.
1910	Population: 4,767,121 (U.S. census).
	Kent State University established at Kent.
	Bowling Green State University established.
1913	Many Ohioans suffer from severe floods, which kill over 400 people.
1917-18	World War I. Over 240,000 Ohioans serve in the first World War; some 7,000 are killed.
1917	Selective Service Act.
1919	Ohio ratifies the 19th Amendment providing for women's suffrage.
1920	Population: 5,759,394 (U.S. census).
1921	School becomes mandatory for youth between the ages of 6 and 18 years.
1930	Population: 6,646,697 (U.S. census).
1938	Ohio has about 1,674 one-room schoolhouses.
1939-45	World War II. Many Ohioans serve in this war.
1940	Population: 6,907,612 (U.S. census).
1949	7 September. Marriage records are kept on a state basis. Abstracts of Ohio marriage records after 7 September 1949 are available from the Ohio Department of Health, Columbus, OH. Many marriage records are also available at the Ohio Historical Society, Columbus, OH.
1950	Population: 7,946,627 (U.S. census).
1960	Population: 9,706,397 (U.S. census).
1970	Population: 10,657,423 (U.S. census).
1980	Population: 10,797,624 (U.S. census).

1990   Population: 10,847,115 (U.S. census).
2000   Population: 11,353,140 (U.S. census).

Chronology References

Academic American Encyclopedia. Danbury, Conn.: Grolier, Inc., 1998, 14:356-62.

Brown, Jeffrey P. and Andrew R.L. Cayton, eds. *The Pursuit of Public Power: Political Culture in Ohio, 1787-1861*. Kent, Ohio: Kent State University Press, 1994.

Burke, Thomas Aquinas. *Ohio Lands: A Short History*. 9th ed. Columbus: Auditor of State, 1997.
(http://freepages.history.rootsweb.com/~maggie/ohio-lands/ohlands.html)

The Encyclopedia Americana. Danbury, Conn.: Grolier, 2000.

Knepper, George W. *The Official Ohio Lands Book*. Columbus: Auditor of State, 2002. (www.auditor.state.oh.us)

The Ohio Almanac. Wilmington, Ohio: Orange Frazer Press, 1992/93.

U.S. Bureau of the Census. *Census of Population*. Ohio. Washington, DC: U.S. Government Printing Office, 1900-2001.

U.S. Bureau of the Census. *U.S. Census of Populations, 1950: Volume II, Characteristics of the Population, Part 35, Ohio*. Washington, DC: U.S. Government Printing Office, 1952.

U.S. Census Bureau. Internet:
(http://factfinder.census.gov/servlet/BasicFactsServlet).

Vexler, Robert I. and William F. Swindler, eds. *Chronology and Documentary Handbook of the State of Ohio*. Dobbs Ferry, N.Y.: Oceana Publications, 1978.

Writers' Program (Ohio). *The Ohio Guide*. New York: Oxford University Press, 1940; reprinted 1973.

EARLY SETTLEMENT

Ohio, historically known as the Gateway to the West, is an important state for westward migration in America. Although there were explorations and settlements in the Ohio country as early as the seventeenth century, principally by French Canadians, the earliest permanent white settlement in the present bounds of this state occurred late in the eighteenth century. Following the creation of the Northwest Territory in 1787, land companies were formed by various Anglo-American groups and the settlement of the Ohio country began in earnest.[1]

Marietta, the territory's first permanent white settlement, was established in 1788 under the direction of General Rufus Putnam, who arrived there from New England.[2] Marietta was named in honor of Marie Antoinette, then queen of France. Early settlements were clustered in the southern and northeastern areas of the state and along the many waterways. As frontier settlement advanced in Ohio, the northwestern counties were the last to be settled.

Washington County was created in 1788, with Marietta as the county seat. As the first county to be organized in the Northwest

1. An indispensable history treating the American frontier, with maps and bibliographies, is Ray Allen Billington and Martin Ridge, *Westward Expansion: A History of the American Frontier*, 5th ed. (New York: Macmillan, 1982). A valuable collection of U.S. maps is contained in *Atlas of American History*, 2nd rev. ed. (New York: Charles Scribner's Sons, 1984). See also R. Douglas Hurt, *The Ohio Frontier: Crucible of the Old Northwest, 1720-1830* (Bloomington, Ind.: Indiana University Press, 1996), the basic reference, *History of the Ordinance of 1787 and the Old Northwest Territory* (Marietta, Ohio: Northwest Territory Celebration Commission, 1937), and Peter S. Onuf, "From Constitution to Higher Law: The Reinterpretation of the Northwest Ordinance," *Ohio History* 94 (Winter-Spring 1985): 5-33.
2. Julia P. Cutler, *The Founders of Ohio* (Cincinnati: Robert Clarke & Co., 1888). This work includes historical background and a brief biographical sketch of Rufus Putnam and others.

Territory, it covered all the eastern limits of present Ohio as far west as the Scioto River. Hamilton County was established in 1790, Adams and Jefferson counties in 1797, and Ross County in 1798. The formation of other counties soon followed.

Ohio was admitted to the Union in 1803 as the seventeenth state and the first state created from the Northwest Territory. Soon new settlers poured into the region. The 1825 completion of New York State's Erie Canal, a mostly man-made waterway, linked New England and New York to Lake Erie. Settlers could travel to Ohio's northern shores and west to Michigan and beyond on New York's Erie Canal. In the 1830s the opening of the National Road, which originated in Maryland and crossed westward through Columbus and central Ohio, provided a similarly convenient highway to Ohio, Indiana, and Illinois. In addition, by 1832 Ohio created its own network of canals linking Lake Erie and Ohio towns with the Ohio River.

Beginning where the Allegheny and Monongahela rivers converge in southwestern Pennsylvania, the Ohio River was one of the major waterways in America, connecting Pennsylvania and Ohio with the Mississippi River. Travelers on the Ohio River could connect to the Muskingum, Scioto, and Miami rivers, and later Ohio's canals—Ohio and Erie Canal, Miami and Erie Canal, and other smaller canals in the state. Within the Ohio country, settlers traveled the Ohio and Erie Canal, which extended from Cleveland to Portsmouth, and the Miami and Erie Canal, which connected Toledo with Cincinnati.

Migration studies of early Ohio show considerable diversity among the early heterogeneous population. Many settlers came from the New England states, especially Connecticut, Massachusetts, and Vermont. A significant number were also from the Middle Atlantic states of New York, Pennsylvania (particularly western Pennsylvania), and New Jersey. Virginia, Kentucky, Maryland, the Carolinas, and other southern states also provided early settlers to Ohio. Immigrants from foreign countries came principally from England, Ireland, Wales, Scotland, Germany, eastern and southern Europe, and Canada, mostly as a result of industrial development and urbanization. A large group of Manx, from the Isle of Man in the Irish Sea, settled in northeastern Ohio. Larger Ohio cities attracted Italians, French, and other Europeans. Cleveland is ethnically diverse and once had a large population of Hungarians. Many African Americans migrated to Ohio beginning in the nineteenth century.

Five major early nineteenth-century migration routes into Ohio were: (1) by Lake Erie's shores and on Lake Erie, (2) across western Pennsylvania, (3) through southeastern Ohio to Marietta and up the Muskingum River, (4) through south-central Ohio and up the Scioto River, and (5) into Cincinnati and up the Great and Little Miami rivers.[3] Some migration from Michigan, Indiana, and other Midwestern states also occurred later in the nineteenth century. The Ohio River, which comprises the state's southern border, was the most important migration route into southern Ohio, while Lake Erie was an important migration route in northern Ohio. Migrants passed through the state using roads, canals, railroads, and the Ohio River as they moved west, north, and south. Ohio is bordered by Pennsylvania on the east, West Virginia on the southeast (Virginia before 1863), Michigan and Lake Erie on the north, Indiana on the west, and Kentucky on the southwest. Leonard Peacefull's *A Geography of Ohio* is an important geographical resource for Ohio genealogists and historians.[4]

---

3. "How We Came to Ohio." *The Report* 19 (Summer 1979): 61. This article includes an excellent map of major migration routes to Ohio; see the map section at the end of this volume. See also pp. 62-67 of this same issue of *The Report*.

4. Leonard Peacefull, ed., *A Geography of Ohio*, rev. ed. (Kent, Ohio: Kent State University Press, 1996). Consult also Andrew R.L. Cayton, *The Frontier Republic: Ideology and Politics in the Ohio Country, 1780-1825* (Kent, Ohio: Kent State University Press, 1986) and Norris Franz Schneider, *The National Road: Main Street of America* (Columbus: Ohio Historical Society, 1975).

HISTORICAL GUIDES

Numerous histories and guides exist for the genealogist who seeks to understand the early settlement of Ohio and the development of the various counties from which records must be sought. George W. Knepper's *Ohio and Its People*, 2nd edition, is an impressive and well illustrated work that includes several maps of interest to genealogists; it is a scholarly historical treatise.[5] Another valuable history is Henry Howe's *Historical Collections of Ohio,* a popular state history with social and political background describing Ohio's counties, together with maps, illustrations, population statistics, and biographical sketches of many early Ohio settlers.[6] See Henry Howe's work on the Internet (www.hti.umich.edu/cgi/b/bib/bibperm?q1=aja2910).

The Newberry Library's *Historical Atlas and Chronology of*

---

5. George W. Knepper, *Ohio and Its People*, 2nd ed. (Kent, Ohio: Kent State University Press, 1997). See especially the bibliographical essay therein.

6. Henry Howe, *Historical Collections of Ohio*, 2 vols. (Cincinnati: State of Ohio, 1888, 1900); this work is indexed separately. Several other Ohio state histories of general interest are John Stevens Cabot Abbott, *The History of the State of Ohio from the Discovery of the Great Valley to the Present Time*, 2 vols. (Detroit: Northwestern Publishing Co., 1875); Simeon D. Fess, *Ohio: A Four-Volume Reference Library on the History of a Great State*, 5 vols. (Chicago: Lewis Publishing Co., 1937) [note that Fess' series actually contains more volumes than the title states]; Charles Burleigh Galbreath, *History of Ohio*, 5 vols. (Chicago: American Historical Society, 1925), separately indexed by Robertalee Lent (Post Falls, Idaho: Genealogical Reference Builders, 1969); Emilius Oviatt Randall and Daniel J. Ryan, *History of Ohio: The Rise and Progress of An American State*, 6 vols. (New York: Century History Co., 1912-15); Eugene H. Roseboom and Francis P. Weisenburger, *A History of Ohio* (Columbus: Ohio Historical Society, 1986), and Carl Frederick Wittke, ed., *The History of the State of Ohio*, 6 vols. (Columbus: Ohio Archaeological and Historical Society, 1941-44). Two useful general histories of the Buckeye State are Walter Havighurst, *Ohio: A Bicentennial History* (New York: W.W. Norton & Co., 1976), and George W. Knepper, *An Ohio Portrait* (Columbus: Ohio Historical Society, 1976). Also valuable is R. Carlyle Buley, *The Old Northwest: Pioneer Period, 1815-1840*, 2 vols. (Bloomington, Ind.: Indiana University Press, 1978), which provides historical background of the Northwest Territory.

County Boundaries, 1788-1980, is an important reference source, that shows Ohio's interior and exterior boundary changes and offers an excellent collection of state maps.[7] A valuable guide to Ohio's counties is *Jurisdictional Histories for Ohio's Eighty-Eight Counties, 1788-1985.*[8] Additionally, *Evolution of Ohio County Boundaries* gives the historical background of boundary changes and includes maps of Ohio county-boundary lines.[9] A valuable study of nineteenth-century migration into the Ohio country is Hubert G.H. Wilhelm's *The Origin and Distribution of Settlement Groups: Ohio, 1850.*[10] Wilhelm offers

7. Newberry Library, *Historical Atlas and Chronology of County Boundaries, 1788-1980,* John H. Long, ed. and Stephen L. Hansen, comp. (Boston: G.K. Hall, 1984), pp. 275-383. This scholarly work, arranged by counties, shows the date on which each area was created or changed and includes regional history maps along with a boundary history of Illinois, Indiana, and Ohio. The Ohio boundary chronology section is especially helpful. This is an essential reference source for American genealogists, historians, and demographers. A state atlas for the Buckeye State is Henry Francis Walling, *Atlas of the State of Ohio* (1868; reprint, Knightstown, Ind.: Bookmark, 1983), which includes a section describing the evolution of Ohio counties. Another valuable map reference is William Thorndale and William Dollarhide, *Map Guide to the U.S. Federal Censuses, 1790-1920* (Baltimore: Genealogical Publishing Co., 1987), which shows Ohio county boundaries at the time of each federal census superimposed over modern county lines. In addition to the above titles, Ohio place-name directories can be obtained from the Department of Natural Resources, Division of Geological Survey, Fountain Square, Columbus, OH 43224. A catalog of publications is available. A useful early gazetteer is *The 1833 Ohio Gazetteer,* 11th ed. (1833; reprint, Knightstown, Ind.: Bookmark, 1981).

8. W. Louis Phillips, *Jurisdictional Histories for Ohio's Eighty-Eight Counties, 1788-1985* (Bowie, Md.: Heritage Books, 1986), shows the names of current counties and governing counties as well as significant dates. Two additional references are Lawrence J. Marzulli, *The Development of Ohio's Counties and Their Historic Courthouses* (Columbus: County Commissioners Association of Ohio, n.d.), and John Clements, *Ohio Facts: A Comprehensive Look at Ohio Today, County by County* (Dallas: Clements Research II, 1988).

9. Randolph C. Downes, *Evolution of Ohio County Boundaries* (1927; reprint, Columbus: Ohio Historical Society, 1970). Errors in this work have been corrected by Phillips in his *Jurisdictional Histories for Ohio's Eighty-eight Counties, 1788-1985.*

10. Hubert G. H. Wilhelm, *The Origin and Distribution of Settlement Groups: Ohio, 1850* (Athens, Ohio: Ohio University, 1982). This well-illustrated work should be carefully studied by genealogists doing nineteenth century Ohio migration research.

tabular statistics to show the birthplace of non-native Ohioans and establishes regional patterns of ethnic settlements in the state based on the 1850 U.S. census.

LIBRARIES AND ARCHIVES

Ohio has an exceptional array of genealogical libraries, historical societies, and archives of major importance. Principal among these are the Ohio Historical Society and State Library of Ohio, both in Columbus; the Ohio Genealogical Society Library, Mansfield; the Western Reserve Historical Society Library, Cleveland; and the Cincinnati Historical Society Library. The Cleveland Public Library and the Public Library of Cincinnati and Hamilton County are the two largest public libraries in the state, although large genealogical collections may be found in the libraries in Akron, Columbus, Dayton, Toledo, Xenia, and elsewhere. The public library at Toledo has a particularly strong New England collection. Academic libraries also house significant collections, particularly Ohio State University's Thompson Library, among others, and Campus Martius Museum at Marietta. Regional libraries with strong genealogical collections are available, for example, Fairview Park Regional Branch, Cuyahoga County Public Library, Fairview Park, Ohio.

The state provides an abundance of library services, including computer catalogs and OhioLINK (Ohio Library and Information Network). OhioLINK is a statewide library and information network that links universities, colleges, academic libraries, and other institutions. A state-funded consortium of university and college libraries and the State Library of Ohio, this online catalog provides access to research databases in many subject areas and gateways to the Internet through numerous search engines. It offers access to millions of library items statewide. Digital images include historic Ohio city maps. Access to research databases is restricted to OhioLINK member users. In summary, it is an online computer catalog of the holdings of member libraries and is available from the Internet, OhioLINK Central Catalog:

(www.ohiolink.edu) and (http://olc1.ohiolink.edu/search). OhioLINK e-mail address for questions (info@ohiolink.edu). Various government records, as well as more general genealogical aids, are available throughout the state. As in most states, the county courthouse is the basic repository of genealogical records. Cuyahoga, Delaware, Geauga, Montgomery, and other counties have their own county record centers (county archives) where local records are housed.

Some of the most valuable genealogical and historical records for Ohio have been centralized in eight regional network centers, known as the Ohio Network of American History Research Centers (ONAHRC), which serve contiguous Ohio counties. Organized by the Ohio Historical Society in 1970, network libraries house a variety of Ohio records, and may include historically valuable local government records, vital records, deeds, census schedules, court records, militia rolls, soldiers' discharges and other military records, naturalization records, church records, newspapers, Court of Common Pleas records (civil and criminal dockets, apprenticeship books, etc.), Probate Court records (births, marriages, and deaths, estate records, naturalization records, wills, ministers' licenses, etc.), County Coroner (morgue) records, County Sheriff's (jail) registers, microfilmed records, publications of county and municipal governments, printed materials, finding aids, record inventories, photographs, genealogical and historical manuscripts, guides, biographies, city directories, DAR records (transcriptions of Ohio records), periodicals, tax lists, and many other resources.[11]

---

11. See, for example, Ohio Historical Society, *Guide to Local Government Records at the Ohio University Library,* rev. ed. (Athens, Ohio: Ohio University Library, 1992). The records at Ohio University cover eighteen counties. See also Jeanne Lacy Pramaggiore, "The Ohio Historical Society: American History Research Centers," *The Report* 33 (Spring 1993): 2-4, and *Ohio County Government Microfilm: Microfilm Available from the Ohio Historical Society* (Columbus: Ohio Historical Society, 1987). Ohio inventories identify court, land, military, probate, and other local government records.

Regarding the Ohio Network of American History Research Centers, two relevant Web sites of interest are:

Ohio Historical Society Online:
(www.ohiohistory.org/textonly/resource/lgr/network1.html)

Ohio County Information:
(http://homepages.rootsweb.com/~maggieoh/ohionet.html)

Many early Ohio records have been transferred to regional network centers, such as county government records, vital records, university records, and many others. Regional centers also have original newspapers or microfilm copies of newspapers for the counties in their region. As an example of local records, many genealogical records for Cincinnati and Hamilton County have been computerized and are available at the University of Cincinnati.

Counties included in each Ohio Network of American History Research Center are listed on a map available from the Ohio Historical Society in Columbus and included at the end of this volume. Addresses and Internet sites for each research center are shown on the following chart.

Ohio Network of American History Research Centers

Bowling Green State University, Center for Archival Collections, Jerome Library, Bowling Green, OH 43403-0175 (www.bgsu.edu/colleges/library/cac/cac.html)

Ohio Historical Society, Archives/Library Division, 1982 Velma Avenue, Columbus, OH 43211-2497 (www.ohiohistory.org/resource/archlib)

Ohio University, Archives and Special Collections, Alden Library, Athens, OH 45701-2978   (www.library.ohiou.edu)

University of Akron, Archival Services, Polsky Bldg., Akron, OH 44325-1702   (www3.uakron.edu/archival/home1.htm)

University of Cincinnati, Archives and Rare Books Department, Blegen Library, Cincinnati, OH 45221-0113 (www.archives.uc.edu)

Western Reserve Historical Society, 10825 East Boulevard, Cleveland, OH 44106-1788   (www.wrhs.org)

Wright State University, Archives and Special Collections, Paul Laurence Dunbar Library, Dayton, OH 45435-0001 (www.libraries.wright.edu/special)

Youngstown Historical Center of Industry and Labor, Archives/ Library, P.O. Box 533, Youngstown, OH 44501-0533 (www.ohiohistory.org/youngst/arch_lib.html)

Family History Library

The largest repository of Ohio records outside the state is the Family History Library (FHL) of The Church of Jesus Christ of Latter-day Saints (LDS). It is the world's largest genealogical research library. Ohio records housed in this library are listed in the Family History Library Catalog (FHLC), available on compact disc, on computer at the main library in Salt Lake, and on the Internet (www.familysearch.org). An older version of FHLC is also on microfiche, along with another older compact disc version, at LDS Family History Centers and at many other libraries.

Three useful guidebooks describe the services and holdings of the Family History Library and its branches are Paula Stuart Warren and James W. Warren, *Your Guide to the Family History Library*; Johni Cerny and Wendy Elliott, eds., *The Library: A Guide to the LDS Family History Library;* and a brief guide by J. Carlyle Parker, *Going to Salt Lake City to Do Family History Research.*[12]

Some of the records on microfilm at the Family History Library for each of Ohio's eighty-eight counties include census schedules for the years 1820-1930 (taken every ten years); Soundex census indexes for 1880, 1900, 1910 (Soundex and Miracode index for some states), 1920, and 1930 (Soundex index for some states);[13] civil vital records of births,

---

12. Paula Stuart Warren and James W. Warren, *Your Guide to the Family History Library* (Cincinnati: Betterway Books, 2001); Johni Cerny and Wendy Elliott, eds., *The Library: A Guide to the LDS Family History Library* (Salt Lake City: Ancestry Publishing, 1988); and J. Carlyle Parker, *Going to Salt Lake City to Do Family History Research*, 3rd ed. (Turlock, Calif.: Marietta Publishing Co., 1996).

13. Readers who are not familiar with the phonetic indexes known as Soundex and Miracode, as well as genealogically valuable federal government records, should consult *Guide to Genealogical Research in the National Archives*, 3rd. ed., edited by Anne Bruner Eales and Robert M. Kvasnicka (Washington, DC: National Archives and Records Administration, 2000). This is a major reference source for American genealogists, historians, and reference librarians.

marriages, and deaths; death certificates; church records for many denominations; wills and other probate records; deeds and other land records; tax lists; copies of gravestones and other cemetery records; naturalization records; township records; military records (federal, state, and local); court records; voting records; school records; and various genealogical collections, many of which are discussed in greater detail throughout this work. Many of the DAR records housed at the State Library of Ohio in Columbus and at the DAR Library in Washington, DC, have been microfilmed. The Ohio Genealogical Society's statewide Ancestor Card File and other indexes have been filmed.

Most Family History Library microfilms may be loaned to over 3,800 Family History Centers throughout the world.[14] Family History Centers are located throughout Ohio; a current list is available from the Family History Library in Salt Lake City (800-346-6044) and on the Internet under "Library" at (www.familysearch.org).

Carol Bell's *Ohio Guide to Genealogical Sources* identifies many of Ohio's microfilmed records available at the Family History Library.[15] Ohio records continue to be microfilmed by the Genealogical Society of Utah (GSU), the microfilming division of the Family and Church History Department of the LDS Church in Salt Lake City, and on the county level by local governments, the eight regional network centers, and several OGS chapters. Consult the Family History Library Catalog (FHLC) for an updated description of library holdings.

Printed sources for Ohio at the Family History Library in Salt Lake City (which are not available on loan to Family History Centers, unless they are on microfilm or microfiche), include family histories (compiled

---

14. A current list of LDS Family History Centers is available on the Internet (www.familysearch.org), by writing to the Family History Library, 35 North West Temple Street, Salt Lake City, UT 84150, or by contacting an LDS Family History Center (branch library). There are over 3,800 Family History Centers worldwide.

15. Carol Willsey Bell, *Ohio Guide to Genealogical Sources* (Baltimore: Genealogical Publishing Co., 1988).

genealogies), county and other local histories, published vital records, church records, military records, and other sources described in this guidebook. Numerous Ohio titles at the Family History Library are also available on microfilm and microfiche.

Two major genealogical databases for Ohio, and other localities as well, are (1) Pedigree Resource File (PRF), consisting of lineage-linked pedigrees, many with notes and sources, and (2) Ancestral File. They are two of several computer databases that comprise FamilySearch™ Internet Genealogy Service, a computerized system available on the Internet (www.familysearch.org). An older version is available on compact discs at LDS Family History Centers and some other libraries (and on computer network at the Family History Library, Brigham Young University, Provo, Utah, and elsewhere).

Ancestral File is a lineage-linked database linking individuals into pedigrees, showing their ancestors and descendants. Pedigree Resource File and Ancestral File should be searched for clues for all American pedigrees; however, Ancestral File does not contain documentation or source references. The Pedigree Resource File (PRF) is updated periodically and contains names and addresses of individuals who contributed the information (and sometimes their e-mail address). PRF databases are generally more reliable than the Ancestral File, more up to date, and sometimes show notes and sources. Research should be performed in other records after computer databases are searched.

Also part of FamilySearch™, International Genealogical Index (IGI) indexes many thousands of nineteenth-century Ohio marriages (civil and church marriages) and also many Ohio birth and baptism (christening) records. The IGI may be searched on the Internet (www.familysearch.org); it contains over 750 million names of deceased individuals. Research into more reliable sources, such as original records, is needed after locating information of interest in any compiled source, including the International Genealogical Index (IGI), Pedigree

Resource File (PRF), Ancestral File, and similar computer databases. U.S. Social Security Death Index, U.S. Military Index, and Scottish Church Records are other valuable files found in FamilySearch™.

The Family History Library publishes research outlines and user guides describing genealogical sources in Ohio and other states, as well as several foreign countries and specialized topics. They are available in paper copy, on compact disc, and on FamilySearch Internet online (www.familysearch.org). These publications will help genealogists use the Family History Library, Family History Centers, and locate records in other repositories as well. *Ohio Research Outline* is an overview to sources for the state and is arranged by Family History Library Catalog (FHLC) subject headings.[16] An updated version is available on the Internet (www.familysearch.org) under "Research Helps."

Many early Ohio settlers (and other early Americans as well) are identified in *Vital Records Index: North America* (available on CD-ROM from the Family and Church History Department in Salt Lake City, Utah).

The e-mail address for reference questions concerning the Family History Library is (fhl@ldschurch.org).

The Family History Library's mailing address is:

Family History Library
35 North West Temple Street
Salt Lake City, UT 84150-3400

---

16. *Ohio Research Outline* (Salt Lake City: Family and Church History Department, 2001). See also *United States Research Outline* (Salt Lake City: Family History Department, 2001). Research outlines for other localities and subjects are also available from the Family History Library.

The Family and Church History Department in Salt Lake City maintains one of the largest genealogical Web sites on the Internet. A summary of databases and sources available at this Web site follows:

FamilySearch™ Internet Genealogy Service

(www.familysearch.org)

- Ancestral File
- Census Records (1880 U.S. census and other census records)
- International Genealogical Index (IGI)
- Pedigree Resource File (PRF)
- U.S. Social Security Death Index
- Vital Records Indexes
- Links to Family History Web Sites
- Family History Library Catalog (FHLC)
- Research Guidance
- Research Helps
- Family History Library information (address, hours, etc.)
- Family History Centers (addresses, telephone numbers, and hours open)
- Education and Training (conferences and institutes)
- Collaboration E-mail Lists
- Share My Genealogy
- General Product Support
- Order/Download Products (Online Distribution Center)
- Other databases and genealogical information

Ohio Genealogical Society

The Ohio Genealogical Society (OGS) in Mansfield, the largest state genealogical organization in the United States, maintains an expanding library of Ohio source materials that is open to the public. OGS members may use the library at no cost. Here researchers will find a valuable collection of family histories (compiled genealogies), county and other local histories, atlases, census indexes, family Bible records, cemetery records, genealogical periodicals, city directories, First Families of Ohio (FFO) and Society of Civil War Families of Ohio (SCWFO) application papers, published Ohio genealogical source materials, and some manuscript material. Collection emphasis includes Ohio, the thirteen colonies, and states surrounding Ohio. OGS maintains an extensive Ancestor Card File with over two hundred thousand cards (submitted by OGS members), ancestor charts, Bible records, and a growing microfilm collection. The Ancestor Card File is a major statewide research aid and should be searched for all early Ohio families. A selected listing of OGS library holdings follows.

The Society will answer correspondence or e-mail that relates to its holdings and general Ohio reference questions. They provide a research and copy service into their library holdings for OGS members and also the public. OGS publishes Ohio source material and periodicals and sponsors a large annual genealogy conference and annual meeting each spring and an annual OGS chapter management seminar. OGS chapters are found in most Ohio counties as well as outside the state. An OGS chapter directory is published periodically by the Society; the current edition is titled *2003 Ohio Genealogical Society Chapter Directory & Publications List*.[17] Chapters are also listed in Elizabeth Petty Bentley's

---

17. Ohio Genealogical Society, *2003 Ohio Genealogical Society Chapter Directory & Publications List* (Mansfield, Ohio: The Society, 2003).

The Genealogist's Address Book.[18] A current list of OGS chapters and their addresses is published in *Ohio Genealogical Society Quarterly* (formerly *The Report*), *OGS Genealogy News*, and the OGS Web site. Most OGS chapters publish records for their respective geographical areas, such as ancestor charts, family Bible records, newspaper obituaries, gravestone inscriptions and cemetery records, military records, and many other local Ohio records for their particular region.

OGS created First Families of Ohio in 1964 for its members to honor their Ohio pioneer ancestors. As a result, the published annual FFO rosters are useful research aids for locating early Ohioans.[19] A major genealogical reference source for the state is *First Families of Ohio Roster, 1964-2000*. Rosters are regularly listed in the *Ohio Genealogical Society Quarterly* (formerly *The Report*) and are published separately by the Society. To be eligible for membership in FFO, OGS members must prove direct descent and residence of an ancestor who resided in Ohio before 1821and submit documented application papers and a fee.

OGS also sponsors for its members the Society of Civil War Families of Ohio (SCWFO), a lineage society with the purpose of honoring participants in the Civil War, 1861-65. Either Union or Confederate service is acceptable, but the ancestor must have lived, served in Ohio, or died there; the applicant must be a direct descendant

---

18. Elizabeth Petty Bentley, *The Genealogist's Address Book*, 4th ed. (Baltimore: Genealogical Publishing Co., 1998). This is a major reference source for locating addresses of genealogical and family interest.

19. Ohio Genealogical Society, *First Families of Ohio Roster, 1964-2000*, edited by Sunda Anderson Peters and Kay Ballantyne Hudson (Mansfield, Ohio: Ohio Genealogical Society, 2001). Names of OGS members accepted into FFO are also identified in *The Report*, along with name of Ohio pioneer, FFO number, county, date, birth and death dates, spouse's name, name of FFO member, and membership numbers. These rosters provide indispensable references for Ohio genealogists. See, for example, Amy Johnson Crow, "First Families of Ohio Roster, 2001-2002," *The Report* 42 (Summer 2002): 64-71. First Families of Ohio genealogical collection is on microfilm at the Family History Library, Salt Lake City.

or a collateral relative. SCWFO rosters are published annually in *Ohio Genealogical Society Quarterly* (formerly *The Report*). As a result of the interest in Ohio and the Civil War, OGS publishes the quarterly *Ohio Civil War Genealogy Journal*, which features Civil War-related material pertaining to Ohio soldiers and their units. Ohio's portion of the Civil War Soldiers System, a national database, is complete: (www.itd.nps.gov/cwss).

OGS also publishes the quarterly *Ohio Records and Pioneer Families*, which includes Bible records, vital records, gravestone inscriptions, tax lists, military records, newspaper abstracts, queries, and other published Ohio records of genealogical value (surname indexes).

Society information, genealogical indexes, links to other Ohio Web sites, OGS library catalog, and much more are available on the OGS home page. OGS has a Lending Library of duplicate books for its members available for a small fee, and a Lending Library catalog is available. A history of OGS was compiled by Hartien S. Ritter, *History of the Ohio Genealogical Society, 1959-1984*.[20] OGS projects include collecting ancestor cards and pedigree charts from its members, obtaining copies of family Bible records, statewide church records survey, publishing Ohio records, identifying Ohio cemeteries, and posting data to their Web site.

The OGS e-mail address for reference queries is (ogs@ogs.org).

The Society's Web site is (www.ogs.org).

The address of the OGS Library and headquarters is:

Ohio Genealogical Society
713 South Main Street
Mansfield, OH 44907-1644

---

20. Hartien S. Ritter, *History of the Ohio Genealogical Society, 1959-1984* (Mansfield, Ohio: Ohio Genealogical Society, 1984).

Ohio Genealogical Society Library: Selected Holdings[21]

Ancestor Card File—200,000 card index to ancestors on member charts: ancestral cards submitted by OGS members giving name, birth, death, and marriage information for each person (microfilmed)

Bible Records Card Index (every-name index to Bible records at OGS)

Biographies (for Ohio counties and other localities in the U.S.)

Card Catalog—entered by author, title, subject, and county

Census schedules (Ohio), 1820-1930, and many census indexes

Church and religious records

City and county directories for Ohio, 1820 to date

Compact discs (CD-ROMs) of genealogical records

Court records for many Ohio counties

Ethnic records (African American, Native American, and others)

Family Bible Records—photocopies of actual Ohio family Bible records of births, marriages, and deaths, plus an every-name index

Family Card Catalog—cross-referenced by family name if the genealogy covers surnames additional to those found in the title

Family Group Records—notebooks alphabetically arranged by surname

Family Vertical File List—alphabetical roster of family files at OGS

Family Vertical Files—pamphlets, newsletters, correspondence, clippings, short articles, arranged alphabetically by family surname

First Families of Ohio (FFO) roster—index by pioneer name of over 3,300 packets on some 10,000 pre-1820 ancestors; indexed by OGS member

21. This information is adapted from a handout available from the Ohio Genealogical Society, Mansfield, Ohio, and from research by the author at the OGS Library in Mansfield, Ohio (see www.ogs.org). Appreciation is extended to Thomas Stephen Neel, OGS Library Director, for his valuable assistance and suggestions.

Genealogies: over 4,000 published family histories (compiled
    genealogies), alphabetically arranged on open shelves by surname
Local histories and biographies, with emphasis on Ohio localities
Maps and atlases, cadastral maps for Ohio counties
Military records and rosters, especially for the Civil War
Newspaper abstracts
Periodicals (Ohio emphasis) and OGS chapter newsletters
Society of Civil War Families of Ohio application files
Tax records, 1801-1814 (and for other years) for Ohio localities
Transcriptions of wills, cemeteries, marriages, births, and deaths for
    Ohio counties
Vital records (births, marriages, and deaths for Ohio counties for various
    time periods)
Yearbooks—high school, college, alumni directories, annuals

Manuscripts available at the Ohio Genealogical Society Library
include the following (refer to the "OGS Manuscript Register" for
further details): family Bible records, cemetery records, church records,
correspondence, court records, diaries, family papers, funeral home
records, genealogy charts, marriage records, military records, newspaper
clippings and newspaper obituaries, photographs, and others. Most of
the OGS manuscript collections pertain to Ohio families.

Ohio Genealogical Society online searchable databases include the
following at the OGS Web site (www.ogs.org). OGS online databases
are available to Society members and several are available to
nonmembers:

- OGS Bible Records Index
- 1880 Ohio Federal Census Index
- Miami Valley Genealogical Index (Computerized Heritage
  Association, Miami County, Ohio)
- Online OGS Library catalog
- Online OGS Lending Library catalog

Ohio Historical Society

One of the finest collections of genealogical and historical records in the state is available at the Ohio Historical Society Library (OHS). OHS is responsible for preserving historically valuable records of the state and serves as the archives for the state of Ohio as well. Manuscripts, books, microfilms, microfiche, newspapers, periodicals, maps and atlases, are available for researchers   at OHS. Online databases include Ancestry Plus. The research services staff at the library will examine indexed and alphabetically arranged materials and perform limited research by correspondence or by e-mail. OHS administers the State Archives for Ohio regarding accession of records, determining their value, and custody:

(www.ohiohistory.org/resource/statearc/index.html).

In addition to a magnificent collection of Ohio newspapers, OHS has large holdings of compiled genealogies (family histories), county and other local histories, Ohio vital records, deeds and other land records, tax lists, city directories, atlases and maps, military records, manuscript collections, federal census records and census indexes, mortality schedules (1850-80; not complete for all Ohio counties), genealogical and historical periodicals, biographies, divorce records, DAR transcriptions, immigration records, local government records, naturalization records, quadrennial enumerations, FamilySearch™, and many other resources.

Researchers should begin their ancestral search with the Online Collections Catalog (OCC) which provides access to the collections at OHS, including printed materials (books, pamphlets, serials, and newspapers), manuscripts, microforms, and other resources. The OCC describes the entire newspaper collection. A newspaper catalog, manuscript catalog, and government records catalog, as well as a catalog of books and pamphlets, are also available at the OHS Library. The Ohio County History Surname Index (also known as the Ohio Surname Index) and Graves Registration File (an alphabetical listing of veterans buried in Ohio) are useful to Ohio genealogists as general statewide finding aids. Consult also published and unpublished materials of the Work Projects Administration (WPA), microfilm copies of many early Ohio county records, and regional archival records, which are subsequently described in greater detail.[22] WPA surveys describe church, county, and other local records; they provide valuable background material for researchers. Other areas collected are Northwest Territory history, women's history, Jewish history, Native Americans in Ohio, African American sources, and Ohio political and military history.

Updated guides, reference sources, and finding aids are published on the Society's Web page (www.ohiohistory.org). Although partially dated, several important guides published by the Ohio Historical Society and by others may be used to access their holdings. *Genealogical Researcher's Manual with Special References for Using the Ohio Historical Society Library* describes many Ohio sources among the genealogical and historical holdings of the society.[23] Although published some years ago, *A Guide to Manuscripts at the Ohio Historical Society* provides a catalog of collections of mostly private papers as of 1972.[24] For more current information, consult OCC and the manuscripts catalog

---

22. Carol Willsey Flavell [Bell], "Research at the Ohio Historical Society," *Genealogical Journal* 6 (June 1977): 55-58. This article describes many genealogical sources available at OHS; however, it is now partially outdated.

23. Suzanne Wolfe Mettle, et al., comps., *Genealogical Researcher's Manual with Special References for Using the Ohio Historical Society Library* (Columbus: Franklin County Chapter, Ohio Genealogical Society, 1981). This volume is also useful for locating Ohio sources in other libraries. County township maps are included, as well as other illustrations. This guide is now partially outdated.

24. Ohio Historical Society, *A Guide to Manuscripts at the Ohio Historical Society*, edited by Andrea D. Lentz and Sara S. Fuller (Columbus: The Society, 1972). Although this guide is dated, it gives useful descriptions of many manuscript collections at the Ohio Historical Society.

at the library. *Ohio County Records Manual* describes many local government records for the state.[25] *Ohio Municipal Records Manual* is an informative guidebook for municipal officials and will help genealogists understand records created and maintained at this level.[26] The OHS Library has a copy of the *Abstract of County Archives Inventory, 1803-1977*, an inventory of county records housed by regional research centers in Ohio. A brief summary of OHS holdings is:

- Audiovisuals, 8,500 cubic feet (1 million photo images)
- Books, over 142,000 volumes (84,500 titles)
- Local government records, 13,500 cubic feet
- Manuscripts, 10,700 cubic feet
- Maps, over 15,000
- Micrographics, 85,000 rolls of microfilm; 12,000 microfiche
- Newspapers, 4,500 titles; 20,000 volumes; 47,000 rolls
- State Archives, 20,000 cubic feet

The Ohio Historical Society has an outstanding homepage on the Internet which includes research guides, finding aids, indexes, and also describes many of its holdings and services (www.ohiohistory.org). See also the Ohio Memory Project (www.ohiomemory.org).

The OHS e-mail address for reference questions is: (ohsref@ohiohistory.org).

The OHS mailing address is:

Ohio Historical Society
Archives/Library Division
1982 Velma Avenue
Columbus, OH 43211-2497

---

25. Ohio Historical Society, *Ohio County Records Manual,* rev. ed. (Columbus: Ohio Historical Society, 1983).
26. *Ohio Municipal Records Manual,* rev. ed., editor David Levine, comp. George Bain (Columbus: Ohio Historical Society, 1986).

State Library of Ohio

Researchers will find in the Genealogy Services Collection of the State Library of Ohio, Columbus, an extensive collection of over 25,000 open-stack volumes, some 13,000 microfiche, over 7,200 microfilm rolls, many genealogical sources on compact discs (CD-ROM), as well as typescripts of many Ohio genealogical records. Major materials of interest to genealogists include compiled genealogies, county and other local histories, Ohio county atlases, cemetery records, genealogical periodicals, city directories, military rosters and other military records, pension indexes, Ohio regimental histories, guidebooks, vital records (especially marriages and deaths), census indexes, tax records, OGS chapter publications, and FamilySearch™.

The State Library has a growing collection of Ohio source materials, including microfilms of Ohio census schedules, mortality schedules (1850-80), Ohio agricultural schedules, and many other records. The State Library is the depository for all transcribed records generated by the Ohio Society of the Daughters of the American Revolution (DAR), including copies of vital records, church records, family Bibles, gravestone inscriptions, wills, military records, and many other records. The State Library is a major reference and interlibrary loan source for other Ohio libraries, although the genealogy collection of books, microfilms, and microfiche is non-circulating.

The genealogy staff at the State Library has compiled an essential reference book, *County by County in Ohio Genealogy*, which lists genealogical materials available at this library for each Ohio county.[27] This volume is arranged alphabetically by county and indicates whether titles are on microfilm. Petta Khouw compiled *Genealogy: Helping You Climb Your Family Tree*, which is a useful, but partially outdated, overview of Ohio sources and a description of the genealogical holdings at the State Library of Ohio.[28]

One of the State Library's special collections are books, microfiche, and compact discs of the Ohio Huguenot Society housed in a special bookcase. A detailed inventory of the histories, genealogies, and Huguenot Society publications is available (some 250 volumes and 300 microfiche).

Online genealogical resources include the Internet and the State Library's online catalog; AncestryPlus; Civil War Research Database; Everton Online; Genealogy.com; Genealogy and Local History Online (ProQuest); New England Ancestors (New England Historic Genealogical Society); and Sanborn Fire Insurance Maps for Ohio, 1867-1970.

In addition to Ohio materials, the State Library also houses sizable collections of resources for most states that preceded Ohio into the Union, notably the New England states (early Connecticut vital records indexed in the Barbour Collection), Virginia, Kentucky, Maryland, New York, Pennsylvania, and other states as well, including West Virginia. An article by the library's staff, published in *The Report,* describes the

---

27. Petta Khouw, et al., *County by County in Ohio Genealogy*, rev. ed. (Columbus: State Library of Ohio, 1992). Although partially dated, this guide serves as a listing of some 16,000 volumes and 15,000 microforms in the non-circulating genealogy collection of the State Library of Ohio and identifies many DAR titles. The State Library's Web site should be searched for updated information regarding their holdings and services.

28. Petta Khouw, *Genealogy: Helping You Climb Your Family Tree*, Occasional Paper, series 3, no. 2 (Columbus: State Library of Ohio, 1990). This is a valuable summary of Ohio genealogical sources. See also Petta Khouw, "Finding Roots at the State Library of Ohio," *Ohio Libraries* 9 (1996): 4-7.

holdings of the State Library.[29] The genealogy staff at the State Library offers limited research service by correspondence. They will check their indexes if a researcher will provide an ancestor's name and county of residence. There is a fee for photocopies.

The Web version computerized catalog of the State Library of Ohio is available on the Internet (http://slonet.state.oh.us). The State Library of Ohio is an OhioLINK member.

The State Library of Ohio Web site is (http://winslo.state.oh.us).
The State Library's Online Catalog is (http://slonet.state.oh.us).
The State Library of Ohio's Genealogy Services Web site is:
    (http://winslo.state.oh.us/services/genealogy/index.html).
Online Genealogical Subscription Services:
    (http://winslo.state.oh.us/services/genealogy/geneonline.html)
Their e-mail address for reference assistance is:
    (genhelp@sloma.state.oh.us)

Genealogy librarians at the State Library will respond to brief queries sent by email or regular mail:
    (http://winslo.state.oh.us/services/genealogy/slogenecorr.html).

Their location and mailing address is:

State Library of Ohio
274 East First Avenue
Columbus, OH 43201

---

29. "The State Library of Ohio," *The Report* 23 (Winter 1983): 187-88. See also Petta Khouw, "The State Library of Ohio," *Genealogy* 82-83 (January-February 1984): 20-22. Both of the articles are now partially outdated.

Western Reserve Historical Society

With some 235,000 books, 25,000 volumes of newspapers, over 31,000 microfilm rolls, one million prints and photographs, and over 3,000 manuscript collections, the Western Reserve Historical Society Library (WRHS) houses one of the largest genealogical collections in America. It is particularly strong in original records of northeastern Ohio counties, but also holds records for all Ohio counties, a fine book collection, family and local histories, many newspapers, maps and atlases, periodicals, genealogical indexes, FamilySearch™, Family Registry, microfilm copies of the 1790 through 1930 census population schedules, census indexes, city directories, military records and regimental histories, passenger lists, and many other resources. A large microfilm and microfiche collection and several valuable card files are available.

WRHS manuscript collections include original vital, church, township, military records, land records; gravestone inscriptions; school records; genealogical collections; personal and family papers; account books; diaries and journals; local government records; photographs (including a major Civil War collection); correspondence; local histories; maps; land surveys, plats, and field notes; newspaper clippings; among numerous other genealogical and historical materials. These records are identified in the Manuscripts Card Catalog, the online catalog, manuscript guides available at WRHS, and printed guides. Many collections emphasize Cleveland, Cuyahoga County, Ohio, and especially northeastern Ohio, but the collection is statewide in scope.

In addition to collecting records for Ohio counties, the WRHS Library houses many New England materials (especially for Connecticut), British records, and genealogical records for other localities. It houses the largest Shaker manuscript collection in America, covering the years 1723 through 1952, together with a membership card file. (Shakers are also known as the United Society of Believers in the Second Appearing of Christ.) A descriptive published guide to the Shaker collection is available.[30] Two other helpful publications for using this library are Kermit Pike's *A Guide to the Manuscripts and Archives of the Western Reserve Historical Society*, which gives a description of many voluminous manuscript collections found there; and the *Western Reserve Historical Society Genealogical Committee Bulletin*, a quarterly newsletter that describes many of the genealogical collections at the WRHS Library and which is available by subscription from the society.[31] The Society's mailing address is:

Western Reserve Historical Society Library
ATTN: Reference Division
10825 East Boulevard
Cleveland, OH 44106-1788

---

30. Kermit J. Pike, comp., *A Guide to Shaker Manuscripts in the Library of the Western Reserve Historical Society* (Cleveland: Western Reserve Historical Society, 1974). The Shaker Collection is available on microfilm from University Microfilms International, Ann Arbor, MI.

31. Kermit J. Pike, comp., *A Guide to the Manuscripts and Archives of the Western Reserve Historical Society* (Cleveland: Western Reserve Historical Society, 1972). Two related guides to the WRHS Library are available: Kermit J. Pike, comp., *A Guide to Major Manuscript Collections Accessioned and Processed by the Library of the Western Reserve Historical Society Since 1970* (1987), and Bari Stith, comp., *A Guide to Local Government Records in the Library of the Western Reserve Historical Society* (1987). An excellent history of the Western Reserve is Harlan Hatcher's *The Western Reserve: The Story of New Connecticut in Ohio*, rev. ed. (Cleveland: World Publishing Co., 1966). For an overview of genealogical sources, consult Meredith B. Colket, Jr., *The Widely Known "Western Reserve" in Ohio* (Cleveland: Western Reserve Historical Society Genealogical Committee, 1976), and George R. Griffiths, "The Western Reserve," *The Report* 17 (Spring 1977): 30-36. A major biographical and historical reference for Western Reserve researchers is Mary Lou Conlin's *Simon Perkins of the Western Reserve* (Cleveland: Western Reserve Historical Society, 1968).

Western Reserve Historical Society's Internet address:
(www.wrhs.org).

Western Reserve Historical Society Library's Web address:
(www.wrhs.org/sites/library.htm).

Western Reserve Historical Society online catalog:
(www.wrhs.org/searchme.htm).

E-mail address for Western Reserve Historical Society reference
questions:
(reference@wrhs.org).

Other Major Genealogical Collections

Allen County Public Library
900 Webster Street
P.O. Box 2270
Fort Wayne, IN 46801-2270
(www.acpl.lib.in.us)
(www.acpl.lib.in.us/genealogy)
Compiled genealogies; local histories; a large collection of genealogical and historical periodicals; gravestone inscriptions; U.S. census schedules, 1790-1930; many U.S. city directories; published vital records; military records; immigration records; and many other printed sources and microfilms. Emphasis is on Indiana, Ohio, and other Midwestern states, but the genealogy library collection is national in scope.

Brigham Young University
Harold B. Lee Library
Provo, UT 84602
(www.lib.byu.edu)
(http://uvrfhc.lib.byu.edu)
The Harold B. Lee Library, and the Utah Valley Regional Family History Center (the largest Family History Center of the Family History Library in Salt Lake City), house one of the largest genealogical and historical collections in America—many of these resources pertain to Ohio and other Midwestern states. Here researchers will find over 650,000 rolls of microfilm (including the U.S. census, 1790-1930), over 2 million microfiche, over 3 million books, many compact discs, some 250,000 maps, electronic databases, newspapers, genealogical reference books, indexes, manuscripts, and many other resources.

Cleveland Public Library
325 Superior Avenue, N.E.
Cleveland, OH 44114-1271
(www.cpl.org)
An excellent collection of Ohio local histories and biographies, compiled genealogies, city directories, newspapers, vertical files, and other resources. Especially valuable is CPL's Cleveland Necrology File database, taken from an alphabetical card file (with records dating from the early 1800s to ca. 1975). For necrology data after 1975 refer to the *Cleveland News Index* (www-catalog.cpl.org/CLENIX). Many genealogical sources at the CPL have been placed on microfiche.

Columbus Metropolitan Library
96 South Grant Avenue
Columbus, OH 43215-4781
(www.cml.lib.oh.us)
(www.columbuslibrary.org)
A large collection of compiled genealogies, local histories, military unit histories, Civil War sources, and many printed Ohio genealogical sources, especially for Franklin County and other central Ohio counties.

Cuyahoga County Public Library
Fairview Park Regional Library
21255 Lorain Road
Fairview Park, OH 44126-2120
(http://clio1.cuyahoga.lib.oh.us/home/locations/FPR.html)
This regional library has a strong collection of compiled genealogies, Ohio local histories, periodicals, printed Ohio genealogical records, indexes and abstracts of some Ohio vital records (such as the Cleveland

Necrology File and Cuyahoga County Marriage License Index), general interest biographies, city directories for major U.S. cities, microfilms and microfiche (census schedules and other records), genealogical indexes, and many other resources. Emphasis is on Cleveland and northeastern Ohio, but they also have sources for other areas of the state as well. A Genealogy/Local History Source File is a subject index to books, periodical articles, and microfilms available in the collection (however, this file is no longer maintained). This library is an example of one of the larger regional libraries in the state. See the "Addresses— Ohio" section later in this volume for additional addresses of other libraries in Ohio.

National Archives and Records Administration—
Great Lakes Region
7358 South Pulaski Road
Chicago, IL 60629-5898
(www.archives.gov/facilities/il/chicago.html)
(www.archives.gov/facilities/great_lakes_region.html)
Original federal records for Ohio and other states in the region (Illinois, Indiana, Michigan, Minnesota, and Wisconsin); microfilms of genealogical records; U.S. census population schedules (1790-1930); census indexes; military service and pension records; immigration records, historical records received by federal agencies and courts in Ohio and other states; records of District Courts of the United States (bankruptcy, civil—law, equity, and admiralty) and criminal cases; naturalization records of the U.S. District Courts in Ohio from ca. 1850s to 1960s (Cincinnati, Cleveland, Dayton, and Toledo); naturalization papers (declarations of intention, petitions for naturalization, depositions, naturalization stubs); records of the Bureau of Land Management for land offices in Ohio, ca. 1800-1828; records of the Veterans

Administration; records of the U.S. Customs Service; records of the U.S. Courts of Appeals; and other federal records. They do not house pension or service records for the twentieth century, and only limited pension and service records for the nineteenth century. See their Web site for descriptions of their holdings and finding aids. Consult also National Archives and Records Administration, *Guide to Records in the National Archives—Great Lakes Region*, compiled by Glenn Longacre and Nancy Malan (Chicago: National Archives and Records Administration, 1996).

Ohioana Library
274 East First Avenue
Columbus, OH 43201
(www.oplin.lib.oh.us/index.cfm?ID=773)
A large collection of Ohio local histories, biographies, and other printed sources relating to Ohio, as well as many books written by Ohio authors.

Ohio State University Libraries
1858 Neil Avenue Mall
Columbus, OH 43210-1286
(www.lib.ohio-state.edu)
One of the largest libraries in the state, Ohio State University's Thompson Library houses many genealogical and historical resources and indexes, electronic databases, guides, bibliographies, Ohio local and regional histories, city directories, newspapers, published genealogical sources, periodicals and periodical indexes, biographies, legal references, and many other sources of interest to genealogists and historians. See their Web site for online research tools and online catalog. OSU's libraries are primarily academic libraries and not genealogical resources. The Thompson Library is the main library on

campus, although there are other libraries as well. OSCAR is OSU's online electronic catalog.

Public Library of Cincinnati and Hamilton County
History and Genealogy Department
800 Vine Street
Cincinnati, OH 45202-2071
(www.cincinnatilibrary.org)
(www.cincinnatilibrary.org/info/main/hi)
One of the largest public libraries in the state, this library houses one of the largest genealogy collections in a public library in the country. Emphasis is on Ohio and the surrounding states, including Virginia, but the collection covers all states and several foreign countries as well. With an extensive book and microform collection, the History and Genealogy Department houses over 100,000 genealogy books, including 11,000 compiled genealogies, state and local histories, a large newspaper collection with some 10,000 bound volumes, over 45,000 bound periodicals, city directories, church and cemetery records, published vital records, military histories, maps and atlases, and many others. The map and atlas collections are particularly valuable and include nineteenth-century land ownership maps. The collection at the main library includes some 100,000 rolls of microfilm (over 50,000 genealogy rolls and some 50,000 reels of newspapers), some 200,000 microfiche; U.S. census schedules, 1790-1930; passenger lists; and other sources. The Civil War collection, U.S. pension application indexes, regimental histories, Civil War narratives and diaries, are particularly strong for both Union and Confederate units. Newspapers are housed in the Magazines and Newspapers Department. For a description of their holdings, begin by searching the CINCH online library catalog (author, title, subject, and keyword) and the Family

Surname (genealogy) index—a surname index to many printed compiled genealogies housed in this public library. Also useful is NEWSDEX (index to local newspapers).

Toledo-Lucas County Public Library
Local History and Genealogy Department
325 North Michigan Street
Toledo, OH 43624-1628
(www.toledolibrary.org)
(www.toledolibrary.org/gen.htm)
A large genealogical book collection of some 35,000 volumes, including compiled genealogies, state and local histories, periodicals, newspapers and newspaper indexes, city directories, genealogical reference books, microfilms (census schedules and many other records on microfilm), census indexes, electronic databases, biographies, published genealogical sources, vital records, church and cemetery records, military records, ancestor charts, maps, and many other resources. The Toledo-Lucas County Public Library houses many printed sources for northwest Ohio, for other areas of Ohio, and also for the six New England states, but also has records for other states as well. TIGER, Toledo's Information Gateway to Electronic Resources, is a Web browser based electronic catalog and includes access to the library's online catalog.

Guides to Repositories

Numerous guides exist on both the state and national levels to help researchers explore Ohio repositories. The *American Library Directory* is the standard reference on the subject for the United States and Canada and includes addresses of Ohio libraries.[32] Addresses of historical and genealogical societies, museums, and similar organizations in Ohio are listed in the *Directory of Historical Organizations in Ohio*, 5th edition (1996).[33] Addresses of genealogical societies exclusively, both in Ohio and in other states, are listed in *Meyer's Directory of Genealogical Societies in the U.S.A. and Canada*,[34] although this work is partially outdated. *Guide to Manuscripts Collections and Institutional Records in Ohio* lists the addresses of many church archives, college archives, public libraries, historical societies, and other libraries in the state.[35]

Other references of value are Paul D. Yon's *Guide to Ohio County and Municipal Records for Urban Research*, which can be used to identify many of the municipal records in Ohio, provide inclusive dates

32. *American Library Directory*, 2 vols., 54th ed. (New Providence, N.J.: Bowker, 2001).

33. Ohio Historical Society, *Directory of Historical Organizations in Ohio*, 5th ed. (Columbus: Ohio Historical Society, 1996). This is a significant reference source for identifying Ohio historical societies, museums, and similar libraries and societies in the state. See also American Association for State and Local History, *Directory of Historical Organizations in the United States and Canada*, 15th ed. (Walnut Creek, Calif.: Alta Mira Press, 2002).

34. Mary Keysor Meyer, ed., *Meyer's Directory of Genealogical Societies in the U.S.A. and Canada*, 10th ed. (Mt. Airy, Md.: Libra Publications, 1994). See also Dina C. Carson, ed., *Directory of Genealogical and Historical Societies in the U.S. and Canada* (Niwot, Colo.: Iron Gate Publishing, 1992).

35. David R. Larson, ed., *Guide to Manuscripts Collections and Institutional Records in Ohio* (Columbus: Society of Ohio Archivists, 1974). This work is now partially outdated.

for them, and give their location.[36] Elizabeth Bentley's two reference guidebooks, *County Courthouse Book* and *The Genealogist's Address Book*, are valuable for locating addresses of interest to genealogists.[37] The above guides are available at major libraries in Ohio and elsewhere.

Guides to regional and local libraries are also available for the state. See, for example, Dorothy Smith and Maggie Yax, *A Guide to Manuscripts, Special Collections and Archives, Paul Laurence Dunbar Library*, revised edition, a fine example of an Ohio regional archive inventory.[38]

---

36. Paul D. Yon, *Guide to Ohio County and Municipal Records for Urban Research* (Columbus: Ohio Historical Society, 1973). This guide gives the location of many local Ohio records, although it is partially outdated.

37. Elizabeth Petty Bentley, *County Courthouse Book*, 2nd ed. (Baltimore: Genealogical Publishing Co., 1995) and *The Genealogist's Address Book*, 4th ed. (Baltimore: Genealogical Publishing Co., 1998).

38. Dorothy Smith and Maggie Yax, comps., *A Guide to Manuscripts, Special Collections, and Archives, Paul Laurence Dunbar Library*, rev. ed. (Dayton, Ohio: Special Collections and Archives, Wright State University Libraries, 1996).

MAJOR RESOURCES

Birth and Death Records

County-level registration of civil births and deaths in Ohio date from 1867 (record of births and record of deaths reported to the Probate Court), although some earlier records are sometimes available but are incomplete. Less systematic recording for some counties occurred as early as the 1850s (1856-57), and a few such registrations may be found for even earlier years in the records of townships or other local governing bodies. Early Ohio vital records are incomplete, however, even after mandated by law. The obligatory recording of Ohio's births and deaths on the state level began 20 December 1908.

Pre-1908 civil vital records on the county level—births, marriages, and deaths—are found in the Probate Court at each county courthouse, or they may be housed at the responsible Ohio regional network center, and several counties have county archives. Most early Ohio vital records are available on microfilm at the Family History Library or they are available on loan to LDS Family History Centers. Many vital records are available at the Ohio Historical Society. Virginia E. McCormick's article in *The Report* provides a useful discussion of death-related sources in Ohio.[39]

Ohio death certificates for the period 20 December 1908 through 31 December 1944 are housed at the Ohio Historical Society and may be accessed by mail. An index to deaths on microfiche and microfilm is also housed at OHS. The Family History Library (Genealogical Society of Utah) has microfilmed indexes to Ohio death certificates for the

---

39. Virginia E. McCormick, "Sources of Information about Death: A Strategy for Searching by Mail," *The Report* 22 (Fall 1982): 125-29.

period 1908-44, and Ohio death certificates, 1908-44. *Ohio Death Certificate Index* online database for the period 1913-1937, may be searched on the Internet at the Ohio Historical Society site (www.ohiohistory.org/dindex). This Web site is one of the major personal name indexes for the state.

State level recording of birth certificates since 20 December 1908 and death certificates since 1 January 1945 are available from the Ohio Department of Health (Vital Statistics Office) in Columbus. Most government offices in Ohio respond to mail requests, and most records are open to the public.[40] See "Marriage Records" later in this volume.

Family Bibles are another rich genealogical source for researchers looking for birth, marriage, and death information. Many family Bibles and Ohio vital records have been transcribed by the DAR, and copies may be found at the DAR Library in Washington, DC, State Library of Ohio, the Family History Library, and many libraries in Ohio. Because of some transcription and typing errors, however, DAR records should be used with some caution. The Ohio Genealogical Society Library in Mansfield also has many family Bible records. Sometimes Bibles and family records were taken outside the state by family members or others who moved and took family records with them—this may make them more difficult to locate. However, when family Bibles and other family records are located, the effort may well be worth it. Information found in home sources—scrapbooks, newspaper clippings, correspondence, photographs, genealogies, and in published sources—should be verified by performing research into original records.

---

40. "Court Rules on Ohio Open Records Law," *National Genealogical Society Newsletter* 18 (1992): 159-60. Also helpful for a discussion of Ohio's records is Ann Fenley, *The Ohio Open Records Law and Genealogy: Researching Ohio Public Records* (Dayton, Ohio: Ohio Connection, 1989), although it is partially outdated. See also *Ohio Public Information Laws* (Columbus: Ohio Attorney General, n.d.) for a study of court rulings.

Cemetery Records

Gravestones and cemetery records are an important source for birth and death dates, names of spouses and children, and (sometimes) age, birthplace, parents' names, relationships, references to military service, and other genealogical and family history information. Occasionally a place of birth is given on a gravestone, for example, if the birth was in another state or a foreign country.

Many of the state's gravestones have been copied by the DAR, by local genealogical organizations, and by interested individuals. Additionally, the records of sextons, morticians, churches, and coroners may prove helpful in locating burial information in township, city, denominational, family, or private cemeteries. A variety of transcribed cemetery records are available at the Ohio Genealogical Society Library, Ohio Historical Society, State Library of Ohio, Western Reserve Historical Society Library, public and other libraries in the state, as well as the Family History Library in Salt Lake City.

Ohio genealogists and OGS chapter volunteers have done an exceptional job of providing published records of cemeteries and guides to the location of such records. The major reference guidebook, *Ohio Cemeteries, 1803-2003*, identifies the location of cemeteries throughout the state and indicates whether the inscriptions have been published.[41] This guidebook does not, however, include individual gravestone inscriptions or names of people who are buried in the state. The Ohio Genealogical Society has an active Cemetery Committee that continues

---

41. Ohio Genealogical Society, Cemetery Committee, comp., *Ohio Cemeteries, 1803-2003* (Mansfield, Ohio: Ohio Genealogical Society, 2003). Earlier titles were Ohio Genealogical Society, *Ohio Cemeteries*, ed. Maxine Hartmann Smith (Mansfield, Ohio: The Society, 1978) and *Ohio Cemeteries Addendum* (Baltimore: Gateway Press, 1990).

to survey cemeteries in the state and works with local OGS chapters. A comprehensive and updated directory of Ohio cemeteries, 1803-2003, was an OGS Ohio Bicentennial project.

Another useful work, *Ohio Cemetery Records*, provides actual inscriptions, conveniently bringing together those previously published over the years in *The "Old Northwest" Genealogical Quarterly*.[42] These records may prove helpful to researchers working in northeastern and central Ohio counties.

Other gravestone inscriptions have been published in genealogical periodicals and elsewhere. One fine example is the enormous cemetery compilation entitled *A Monumental Work: Inscriptions and Interments in Geauga County, Ohio, through 1983*, a 732-page indexed volume that includes maps of cemeteries and townships in Geauga County located in northeastern Ohio.[43]

Several Internet sites are useful for locating cemeteries in Ohio:

Ohio Cemeteries (Interment.net):
    (www.interment.net/us/oh/index.htm)
Ohio Cemeteries (OPLIN):
    (www.oplin.lib.oh.us/index.cfm?ID=3-56-2287)
Ohio Cemeteries (Tombstone Transcription Project):
    (www.rootsweb.com/~cemetery/ohio.html)
Ohio Cemetery Preservation Society:
    (www.rootsweb.com/~ohcps).

---

42. *Ohio Cemetery Records Extracted from the "Old Northwest" Genealogical Quarterly* (Baltimore: Genealogical Publishing Co., 1984). This work comprises all the cemetery records in the fifteen volumes of the cited quarterly and is a companion to Marjorie Smith's *Ohio Marriages*. *Ohio Cemetery Records* has an excellent every-name index compiled by Elizabeth P. Bentley.

43. Violet Warren and Jeannette Grosvenor, comps., *A Monumental Work: Inscriptions and Interments in Geauga County, Ohio, through 1983* (Evansville, Ind.: Whipporwill Publications, 1985).

Census Records and Census Substitutes

United States census population schedules are one of the basic sources American genealogists use. For Ohio, the first extant federal census is 1820. A collection of federal population schedules from 1790 through 1930 is widely accessible on microfilm at the National Archives and Records Administration and its regional archives, Allen County Public Library, Brigham Young University's Harold B. Lee Library, Family History Library, Ohio Historical Society, State Library of Ohio, Western Reserve Historical Society Library, and other major research libraries throughout the country. The Ohio Genealogical Society Library has Ohio census schedules on microfilm for the years 1820-1930.

A useful microfiche publication compiled by the National Archives, *Federal Population and Mortality Schedules, 1790-1910, in the National Archives and the States*, identifies institutions that house microfilm copies of the population schedules and mortality schedules.[44] Researchers using the Ohio federal census schedules may wish to consult William Thorndale and William Dollarhide's *Map Guide to the U.S. Federal Censuses, 1790-1920.*[45]

An early "1790 Census" listing heads of households, mainly in Hamilton, Washington, and other early Ohio counties was published by Accelerated Indexing Systems.[46] Also by the same publisher are the census reference works, *Early Ohio Census Records* and *Ohio Early*

---

44. *Federal Population and Mortality Schedules, 1790-1910, in the National Archives and the States*, Special List 24 (Washington, DC: National Archives and Records Administration, 1986). Microfiche.

45. Thorndale and Dollarhide, *Map Guide*.

46. Ronald Vern Jackson, *First Census of the United States, 1790, Ohio North West Territorial Census Index* (North Salt Lake: Accelerated Indexing Systems, 1984). See also *Ohio, 1790, Volume Two* (North Salt Lake: Accelerated Indexing Systems, 1986).

Census Index covering various years before 1820.[47]

A *Census of Pensioners of the Revolutionary War or Military Services* was taken in 1840 and is published.[48] It shows the name of the pensioner, age, name of head of family with whom the pensioner resided on 1 June 1840, and town and county of residence. Remnants of the 1890 census, which suffered general destruction by fire in Washington, DC, in 1921, include the special schedule of surviving Union Civil War veterans or their widows and are available for Ohio counties at the Ohio Historical Society, Family History Library, and other libraries as well.

Statewide indexes to the federal population schedules of Ohio have been published for the years 1820 through 1880. Census indexes serve as major research aids for locating heads of households, although they do not index all names in households. Several large cities—notably Akron, Cincinnati, Cleveland, Columbus, Dayton, and Toledo—and an increasing number of counties have printed 1870 census indexes.

Family Quest Archives, part of Heritage Quest, in Bountiful, Utah, has produced *Ohio 1870 Census Index* on compact disc, an index to heads of households for the state of Ohio. See also *Ohio 1870 Census Index*, edited by Raeone Christensen Steuart, 6 volumes.[49] Some local 1870 census schedules are also indexed. For example, *1870 Census Index to Hamilton County, Ohio, Including Cincinnati.*[50] Many United States federal census and related census indexes, such as the year 1870,

---

47. Ronald Vern Jackson, Gary Ronald Teeples, and David Schaefermeyer, eds., *Early Ohio Census Records*, 2nd ed. (Bountiful, Utah: Accelerated Indexing Systems, 1975-80), and Ronald Vern Jackson, et al., eds., *Ohio Early Census Index*, 2 vols. (Salt Lake City: A.G.E.S., 1980).

48. *A Census of Pensioners for Revolutionary or Military Services* (Washington DC: Blari and Rives, 1841). Ohio pensioners are listed on pp. 168-81. This work is indexed separately.

49. Raeone Christensen Steuart, ed., *Ohio 1870 Census Index*, 6 vols. (Bountiful, Utah: Heritage Quest, 1999).

50. Pamela Miller and Richard Rees, *1870 Census Index to Hamilton County, Ohio, Including Cincinnati* (San Francisco: Egeon Enterprises, 1988).

are available on the Internet (see "Ohio Census Indexes Summary" later in this volume), such as HeritageQuest Online (ProQuest).

The most complete index and transcription of the 1880 U.S. federal census is online at FamilySearch Internet (www.familysearch.org); it has also been published on compact disc (CD-ROM) by the Family and Church History Department in Salt Lake City. It is one of the major finding aids for the United States for this time period. An exhaustive printed index to the Ohio 1880 United States census was compiled by members of the Ohio Genealogical Society and was published by Precision Indexing.[51] An 1880 Ohio census index is available on compact disc, produced by Automated Archives. These are major finding aids for the state. In addition, the microfilmed 1880 Soundex index, prepared by the federal government, identifies families that have children age ten years old and younger in 1880; it is on microfilm and is widely available at many libraries.[52]

The more comprehensive 1900, 1910 (Soundex index for some states and Miracode index for Ohio and some states), 1920, and 1930 Soundex indexes (1930 for some states), are also valuable statewide census indexes, available on microfilm at many libraries throughout the country. Ohio 1930 census indexes are available online, not the micro-filmed Soundex index. Ohio is one of only a few states with a 1910 statewide (Miracode) census index (similar to a Soundex index). Thomas Jay Kemp identifies in-print and online census indexes, arranged by county and by census year, for Ohio and other states in *The*

---

51. Ohio Genealogical Society, *Ohio 1880 Census Index*, 3 vols. (Bountiful, Utah: Precision Indexing, 1991). Also available on microfiche and compact disc (Automated Archives). OGS has the original census duplicate books which were used to create this index. This is one of the major OGS indexing projects.

52. For a discussion of Soundex indexes see Willis I. Else, *The Complete Soundex Guide* (Apollo, Penn.: Closson Press, 2002). This illustrated work includes a history of soundexing federal records and tips for using Soundex indexes.

American Census Handbook.[53] For 1910, see HeritageQuest Online (ProQuest).

In addition to the more commonly known federal population census schedules, several auxiliary schedules were taken in early years— principally schedules of mortality (1850-80), agriculture, commerce and industry, and mining. All have genealogical significance, even though they do not intrinsically identify relationships.

The most frequently used of these auxiliary enumerations, the mortality schedules, identify persons who died during the twelve months immediately preceding the official census date of 1 June. Although some Ohio mortality schedules have not survived, they are extant for the years 1850 (Ohio counties alphabetically H-W), 1860 (all Ohio counties), 1870 (incomplete), and 1880 (counties A through Geauga County only). They are available on microfilm at the State Library of Ohio, the Family History Library, and other libraries, and some are published.[54] Original mortality schedules and the microfilm copies are housed at the Ohio Historical Society. Various Ohio auxiliary census schedules are discussed by Dr. William B. Saxbe, Jr., in a useful article in *The Report.*[55]

Although Ohio did not take an official state census (as did Illinois, Massachusetts, Michigan, New Jersey, New York, and several other states), some local census substitutes are extant. Quadrennial enumerations listing adult males over twenty-one years of age as eligible voters were taken by township. Lists were compiled by county assessors

---

53. Thomas Jay Kemp, *The American Census Handbook* (Wilmington, Del.: Scholarly Resources, 2001).
54. See for example, Ronald Vern Jackson, ed., *Mortality Schedule: Ohio, 1850* [counties H-W] (Bountiful, Utah: Accelerated Indexing Systems, 1979), and Jeanne Britton Workman, *1880 Ohio Mortality Records: Counties Adams through Geauga* (North Olmsted, Ohio: S&J Workman, 1991), as two examples. Some Ohio mortality schedules have also been published in periodicals.
55. William B. Saxbe, Jr., "Non-population Census Schedules, 1850-1880," *The Report* 24 (Spring 1984): 1-2.

at the same time that they assessed taxable property; they cover various years from approximately 1803 to 1911.[56] Prior to 1863 they recorded white males only. Quadrennial enumerations are records of potential voters—they are not complete for all Ohio townships but are very valuable when extant.

Valuable census substitutes do exist, principally tax records and tax duplicates, city directories (especially for large cities), school records, and land records. *The 1812 Census of Ohio: A Statewide Index of Taxpayers* serves as a statewide finding aid for Ohio for this time period.[57] Pre-1850 school records are particularly valuable as a genealogical source in Ohio. Most of these records give the name of the head of the family, and the names, ages, and sex of school-aged children.[58] School enumeration records are housed in public and other local libraries, as well as historical societies throughout the state; some are on microfilm at the Family History Library. Random school records have been transcribed and published. School attendance books may also be helpful in locating names of ancestors. City and county directories also help locate people in large cities and may be useful as census substitutes.

56. Ann S. Lainhart, *State Census Records* (Baltimore: Genealogical Publishing Co., 1992). See also Ronald Vern Jackson, et al., eds., *Early Ohio Census Records* (Bountiful, Utah: Accelerated Indexing, 1974), an introduction by K. Haybron Adams; and Ronald Vern Jackson, et al., eds., *Ohio Early Census Index*, 2 vols. (Salt Lake City: A.G.E.S., 1974-80).

For a discussion of quadrennial enumerations see *Ohio Laws* 25 v 16 (1827) and Kenneth J. Winkle, *The Politics of Community: Migration and Politics in Antebellum Ohio* (Cambridge: Cambridge University Press, 1988), p. 189.

57. *The 1812 Census of Ohio: A Statewide Index of Taxpayers* (Miami Beach, Florida: T.L C. Genealogy, 1992).

58. School records have been beneficial for the author in compiling Ohio genealogies. See, for example, Kip Sperry, "The Harrison Family: Manx Immigrants to the Western Reserve in Ohio," *The Genealogist* 5 (Fall 1984): 240-55.

Useful Ohio and U.S. census Web sites include the following:

Ancestry.com, Ohio Census, 1820-1930:
   (www.ancestry.com)
Census Images—Ohio (USGenWeb Archives):
   (www.rootsweb.com/~usgenweb/cen_o.htm#OH)
Census Links (Ohio) (http://censuslinks.com)
Census Online, Ohio:
   (www.census-online.com/links/OH)
Cyndi's List: U.S. Census:
   (www.cyndislist.com/census.htm)
Genealogy.com (www.genealogy.com)
HeritageQuest Online (www.heritagequestonline.com)
   (www.heritagequest.com/html/censushq.html)
Ohio Federal Census:
   (www.rootsweb.com/~census/states/ohio)
Ohio 1910 Census Miracode Index (www.ancestry.com)
RootsWeb.com (www.rootsweb.com)
U.S. Census Bureau Quick Facts:
   (http://quickfacts.census.gov/qfd/states/39000.html)
USGenWeb Project
   (www.usgenweb.org)
1930 Census Enumeration Districts (select state, city, street):
   (http://home.pacbell.net/spmorse/census)

Ohio Census Indexes Summary

Census Years	Notes
1790 (partial index)	Published (incomplete) *Early Ohio Census Records*
1800, 1803, 1810	Published (partial indexes and years vary; incomplete)
1820	Published census index
1830	Published census index
1840	Published census index
1820-50	Online (www.ancestry.com)
1850	Published census index
1850	*1850 U.S. Federal Census Index (AIS): Ohio*, CD-ROM (Ancestry.com)
1850	*U.S. Census Index, 1850, Indiana, Ohio*, CD-ROM (Automated Archives)
1860	Published census index
1870	Published census indexes
1870	Online (HeritageQuest Online)

Census Years	Notes
1870	Statewide census index on CD-ROM (Family Quest Archives) (Heritage Quest)
1870	Several Ohio counties and cities are published (for example, Columbus and Dayton, Cuyahoga County, Hamilton County, Lucas County, Stark and Summit counties)
1870	CD-ROM (Generations Archives by Heritage Quest)
1870	Online (www.genealogy.com)
1880	Online census and national index (www.familysearch.org)
1880	CD-ROM (Family and Church History Department) (national in scope). Includes a national name index.
1880	Printed census index (compiled by Ohio Genealogical Society and published by Precision Indexing, Bountiful, Utah)
1880	OGS Online (www.ogs.org) Online for OGS members

Census Years	Notes
1880	Census index on CD-ROM (Automated Archives)
1880	Soundex index on microfilm (partial index to all households with children age 10 years and younger)
1890 (Union veterans and their widows)	Published schedules
1890	Online (www.genealogy.com)
1900	Statewide Soundex index (microfilm and CD-ROM)
1900	Online (www.genealogy.com)
1910	Statewide Miracode index on microfilm (similar to Soundex index)
1910	Miracode Index (www.ancestry.com)
1910	Miracode Index: Ohio, CD-ROM (Ancestry.com)
1910	Online (HeritageQuest Online)
1910	Online (www.genealogy.com)

Census Years	Notes
1920	Statewide Soundex index (microfilm and CD-ROM)
1920	Online (www.ancestry.com)
1930	Online (www.ancestry.com)

Notes:

Additional digitized U.S. census schedules and census indexes are continually being posted online. For updates, consult:
- Internet sites listed above for updated information
- Google Search Engine (www.google.com) under the locality of interest
- Check other Internet Search Engines

Many Ohio and other U.S. census schedules, census extracts, and census indexes are being posted or linked from the USGenWeb Project pages under each state and county (www.usgenweb.org).

Church Records

Ohio's religious heritage is rich and panoramic. Major denominations in the state before 1900 included Baptist, Congregational, Episcopal, Lutheran, Methodist, Presbyterian, and Roman Catholic. Other religious groups in the state are African Methodist Episcopal, Amish, Brethren in Christ, Church of God, Church of the Brethren, Church of Christ Scientist, Disciples of Christ, The Church of Jesus Christ of Latter-day Saints (Mormon), Mennonite, Moravian, Quaker (Society of Friends), Reformed, Seventh-day Adventist, Seventh-day Baptist, Shakers, Unitarian, and United Brethren, among others.[59] Jewish congregations in Ohio began to increase during the nineteenth century.

Church inventories exist, particularly those compiled by the Work Projects Administration, which describe many surviving church records in the state. Of the WPA titles, one of the most significant is *Inventory of the Church Archives of Ohio Presbyterian Churches.*[60] This inventory is available at the Presbyterian Historical Society in Philadelphia, the Ohio Historical Society in Columbus, and the Family History Library in Salt Lake City.

Church records are among the most useful of primary sources available for genealogical research in Ohio—although it must be remembered that not all Ohioans regularly attended church. The records created by the various denominations can substitute for nonexistent civil vital records, and in some cases they provide even better information than civil vital records. Church records usually contain minutes of

---

59. *Churches in the Buckeye Country* (Religious Participation Committee, Ohio Sesquicentennial Commission, 1953).

60. Work Projects Administration, *Inventory of the Church Archives of Ohio Presbyterian Churches*, T.W. Marshall, comp. (Columbus: Ohio Historical Records Survey, 1940).

church meetings and records of births, baptisms, marriages, deaths or burials, and other events. A place of previous residence is sometimes given; therefore, church records are useful in tracing migration of individuals and families to Ohio and within the state. The breadth and genealogical value of such records vary widely; some denominations or congregations kept better records than others, and some records have been preserved better than others.

Although church records are sometimes difficult to locate, a number of Ohio church records have been microfilmed, and many have been transcribed or published in books or periodicals. Some may be found on the Internet. Good collections of church records are available at the Western Reserve Historical Society Library, regional network centers in Ohio, and other libraries in Ohio; many are also on microfilm at the Family History Library in Salt Lake City. Local churches may still have custody of the original records, or they may be housed in denominational archives. For example, many Presbyterian Church records are available at the Presbyterian Historical Society in Philadelphia. Early Mennonite records are located at Bluffton College in Bluffton, Ohio.

Some Ohio church records have been published, most notably those of the Society of Friends (Quakers), which appear in Hinshaw's *Encyclopedia of American Quaker Genealogy.*[61] Church histories are also available for some congregations; they contain historical background as well as information on early church members and leaders. A useful historical overview of church groups in Ohio is *Advent*

---

61. William Wade Hinshaw, *Ohio Quaker Genealogical Records*, vols. 4-5 of *Encyclopedia of American Quaker Genealogy*, 6 vols. (Ann Arbor, Mich.: Edwards Brothers, 1946). These volumes are indexed. Consult also Willard Heiss, "Migrations of Quakers in the Late 18th Century," *National Genealogical Society Quarterly* 65 (March 1977): 35-44, which discusses Quaker migrations to the Old Northwest; and Corinne Hanna Diller, "Quaker Migrations," *The Report* 23 (Winter 1983): 196-97.

of Religious Groups into Ohio.[62]

Many early Ohio church records, mostly christenings (baptisms) and marriages before about 1895, are indexed in the International Genealogical Index (IGI) available on the Internet, known as IGI Internet (www.familysearch.org). An older version of the IGI is available on compact discs (CD-ROM) at some libraries. Family History Centers have an older version on microfiche, but the most up-to-date information is available at IGI Internet (www.familysearch.org). The IGI serves as a statewide index to many early Ohio vital records, but it indexes records of other localities as well.

The Ohio Genealogical Society in Mansfield, Ohio, has an ongoing church records survey project that identifies church records in the state; this survey is being expanded and revised. Researchers should contact OGS regarding the status of this project for their area of research interest.

---

62. Ferne Reedy Lubbers and Margaret Dieringer, eds., *Advent of Religious Groups into Ohio* (Mansfield, Ohio: Clark County Chapter, Ohio Genealogical Society, 1978).

Court Records

Court records contain an abundance of primary source materials of interest to genealogists and historians. Within Ohio, the various judicial levels that need to be searched include the Chancery Court, Circuit Court, Court of Common Pleas, District Court, Probate Court, Supreme Court, as well as other state and local courts. Court records commonly include record books, court dockets (a listing of cases held each term), bonds, petitions, minutes, journals, final records, case files (loose papers), adoption records, guardianships, appearance dockets, civil dockets, civil journals, Chancery records, criminal journals, execution dockets, jury books, ministers' license records, record of bonds, Sheriff's returns, Justice of the Peace dockets, trial lists, witness records, and related indexes. Ownership of land may suggest that a case was generated in Chancery records, and these records often provide names of family members, relationships, residence, and other valuable genealogical information. Occasionally, family information may be found in criminal and similar court records.

Ohio's court records may be found in county courthouses and in regional network centers in the state; many court records are on microfilm at the Family History Library in Salt Lake City. Several Ohio counties have a county archives which house court and other local records (Cuyahoga and Geauga counties are two examples).

Records of recent adoptions handled by the court systems are generally restricted from public use (records after 1964 must be searched under the direction of the Probate Judge). Records of some nineteenth-century adoptions are available in county courthouses.

Since the history of Ohio's court system is quite complex,

researchers are advised to study David Levine's article in *The Report*[63] and Carrington Tanner Marshall's detailed study of the state's court system, *A History of the Courts and Lawyers of Ohio*.[64] *Baldwin's Ohio Revised Code: Annotated Ohio Administrative Code*, available on compact disc (CD-ROM) at the Ohio Historical Society and other libraries, is a standard legal reference source that includes biographical sketches of many Ohio attorneys.[65] A useful Ohio court reference manual, though partially dated, is *A Digest of All Reported Decisions of the Courts of Ohio from the Earliest Period to Date*.[66] Transcriptions of early Ohio federal court records, 1803-1807, are published in *Ohio Federal Court Orders, 1803-1807*.[67] A useful Ohio court reference manual, though dated, is *A Digest of All Reported Decisions of the Courts of Ohio from the Earliest Period to Date*.[68]

63. David Levine, "Ohio's Court System," *The Report* 20 (Winter 1980): 171-74. See also, Diane VanSkiver Gagel, *Ohio Courthouse Records*, Ohio Genealogical Society Research Guide No. 1 (Mansfield, Ohio: The Society, 1997).

64. Carrington Tanner Marshall, ed., *A History of the Courts and Lawyers of Ohio*, 4 vols. (New York: American Historical Society, 1934). This work includes many detailed biographies. See also Henry R. Timman, "Undiscovered Treasures in Ohio Court Houses," *The Report* 18 (Fall 1978): 93-98; Edward N. McConnell, "Ohio County Court Records: A Genealogical Research Tool," *Genealogy* 37 (May 1978): 1-5; and Frank R. Levstik, "A Guide to Ohio County Records for Genealogical Research," *Genealogy* 55 (August 1980): 6-7.

65. *Baldwin's Ohio Revised Code: Annotated Ohio Administrative Code* (Banks-Baldwin Law Publishing Co., 1996). Indexed. CD-ROM.

66. *A Digest of All Reported Decisions of the Courts of Ohio from the Earliest Period to Date* (Cincinnati: W.H. Anderson Co., 1952).

67. TLC Genealogy, *Ohio Federal Court Orders, 1803-1807* (Miami Beach, Florida: TLC Genealogy, 1998).

68. *A Digest of All Reported Decisions of the Courts of Ohio from the Earliest Period to Date* (Cincinnati: W.H Anderson Co., 1952).

Directories

City directories and rural directories are useful in identifying an individual's residence. City directories are especially useful in locating people in large cities. They can be used along with and as a substitute for census schedules and other genealogical sources. They may be used for studying migration patterns of rural and urban people. City and rural directories are alphabetically arranged by surname and are published chronologically by years. Directories begin in the early nineteenth century and continue to the present time. The volume and quality of directories after the 1860s improves dramatically.

In addition to the person's name (usually the head of the family), an address and occupation are shown (business and residence addresses are shown for individuals). Occasionally the wife's given name is shown and if she is a widow. Often the deceased husband's given name is shown for widows. Clues to when a person died or moved from the area may be found, and sometimes even a date of death may be given. Civic information includes names and addresses of churches, schools, business firms, and others. The preface to city and rural directories may provide a great deal of local information, including a brief history of the locality.

City and rural directories are available at public and university libraries; local historical societies; State Library of Ohio; Ohio Historical Society; Ohio Genealogical Society, Mansfield, Ohio; Library of Congress, Washington DC; Allen County Public Library, Fort Wayne, Indiana; Family History Library, Salt Lake City; and many other libraries.

County and rural directories are available for many areas of Ohio and show name of person, residence (usually road or township), and other information. Researchers will also find locations of cemeteries, churches, children's homes, schools, funeral homes, and other businesses.

"Blue Books," such as *The Cleveland Blue Book*, list names of prominent residents, their address, and sometimes names of clubs they belong to and college degrees received. Club membership rosters may be included. A list of maiden names of females may also be included in "Blue Books."

Research Publications of Connecticut has made thousands of city and local directories available on microfiche and microfilm in a collection titled *City Directories of the United States*, which may be found in larger research libraries throughout America.

Representative titles of interest for this subject are:

City Directories: Southern Midwest, 1882-1898 (selected Ohio cities and years). CD-ROM (Ancestry.com).

Ohio Museums Association. *Ohio Cultural Directory*. Columbus: Ohio: Museums Association, 1998.

Identifies historical societies, church archives, museums, genealogical societies, cemeteries, and similar organizations.

Ohio Physician and Dentist Directory, 1905 (www.ancestry.com).

Reilly, W.W. & Co. *W.W. Reilly & Co.'s Ohio State Business Directory for 1853-54*. Cincinnati: Morgan & Overend, 1853.

List of post offices in Ohio, 1853-54, and lists of businesses (such as newspapers); arranged by county.

Williams & Company, comp. *Ohio State Directory*. Cincinnati: Williams & Co., 1868-82.

Divorce Records

Jurisdiction for granting divorce in early Ohio was conferred by statute upon the State Supreme Court and the Court of Common Pleas in each respective county. Divorces may be found in Supreme Court records, Chancery records, Common Pleas records, District Court records, and elsewhere. Records of the dissolution of marriages are maintained by the Court of Common Pleas in each county. Contact the appropriate clerk of Court of Common Pleas in the county where the divorce was granted.

The State Supreme Court had jurisdiction over divorces during early statehood, but petitions were filed in the county court. Divorce records prior to 1851 may be found in the State Supreme Court, County Supreme Court, County Chancery Court, or the County Common Pleas Court. Divorce appeals may have been made to the state legislature. Divorce records after 1913 are available in a division of the County Court of Common Pleas known as the Domestic Relations Court.

A record of a divorce granted prior to 7 September 1949 may be recorded in the office of the County Clerk of Courts of the county where the divorce was granted. Divorce abstracts from 7 September 1949 to the present are recorded at the Ohio Department of Health (Vital Statistics Office) in Columbus (an abstract is not a divorce decree). Certified copies of divorce records after 1949 are not available from the Ohio Department of Health. Certified copies of earlier divorce records may be available from the Court of Common Pleas where the divorce was granted. The address of the Ohio Department of Health is:

Ohio Department of Health
Vital Statistics
P.O. Box 15098
Columbus, OH 43215-0098

Early Ohio divorce records are discussed by David G. Null in a useful article in the *National Genealogical Society Quarterly*, which includes a list of persons granted legislative divorce in Ohio between 1795 and 1852.[69] Mary L. Bowman compiled many abstracts and extracts of Ohio legislative acts and resolutions in *Abstracts and Extracts of the Legislative Acts and Resolutions of the State of Ohio, 1803-1821*, and continued for the period 1821-1831.[70]

A major guide to early Ohio divorce records is Carol Willsey Bell's *Ohio Divorces: The Early Years*.[71] An early discussion of divorce laws in Ohio is Henry Folsom Page's *A View of the Law Relative to the Subject of Divorce in Ohio, Indiana, and Michigan*.[72]

---

69. David G. Null, "Ohio Divorces, 1803-1852," *National Genealogical Society Quarterly* 69 (March 1981): 109-14.

70. Mary L. Bowman, *Abstracts and Extracts of the Legislative Acts and Resolutions of the State of Ohio, 1803-1821* (Mansfield, Ohio: Ohio Genealogical Society, 1994. Continued with volumes 20 to 29, 1821-1831 (OGS, 1996).). This work is useful for locating laws relating to marriage and divorce, inheritance, and related topics.

71. Carol Willsey Bell, *Ohio Divorces: The Early Years* (Boardman, Ohio: Bell Books, 1994). See especially the introduction to this book for a discussion of divorce records in Ohio. Indexed.

72. Henry Folsom Page, *A View of the Law Relative to the Subject of Divorce in Ohio, Indiana, and Michigan* (Columbus: J.H. Riley & Co., 1850). Discusses the early divorce laws of Ohio, Indiana, and Michigan.

Ethnic Records

Many ethnic records are housed at the Ohio Historical Society, as well as university and public libraries and historical societies in the state and the Ohio Network of American History Research Centers. African American heritage is traceable in Ohio through various resources. An African American Archives, Cleveland Jewish Archives, and Irish American Archives are maintained at the Western Reserve Historical Society in Cleveland (along with similar archives for other ethnic groups).

Serious researchers in this field should study David A. Gerber's scholarly work *Black Ohio and the Color Line, 1860-1915.*[73] Sara Fuller's *The Ohio Black History Guide* is a useful bibliography of both published and unpublished works for this subject.[74] A representative title from the ranks of published source records in this field is Joan Turpin's *Register of Black, Mulatto, and Poor Persons in Four Ohio Counties, 1791-1861.*[75] Paul E. Nitchman's *Blacks in Ohio, 1880,* arranged by counties, identifies African Americans in the Ohio 1880 U.S. census.[76] A general guidebook is *African American Genealogical*

---

73. David A. Gerber, *Black Ohio and the Color Line, 1860-1915* (Urbana, Ill.: University of Illinois Press, 1976).

74. Sara Fuller, et al., eds., *The Ohio Black History Guide* (Columbus: Ohio Historical Society, 1975). This is a guide to printed materials, dissertations and theses, manuscripts, government records, and audiovisual materials for Ohio African Americans.

75. Joan Turpin, *Register of Black, Mulatto, and Poor Persons in Four Ohio Counties, 1791-1861* (Bowie, Md.: Heritage Books, 1985).

76. Paul E. Nitchman, *Blacks in Ohio, 1880,* 10 vols. (Decorah, Iowa: Anundsen Publishing, 1985-87; 3 volumes published by Ohio Genealogical Society, Mansfield, 1997). This is a useful reference for African American research in Ohio. See also "Blacks in Ohio in 1870 Who Were Born in Ohio," *The Report* 41 (Spring 2001): 4-10, and other issues of *The Report* (now *Ohio Genealogical Society Quarterly*).

Sourcebook, edited by Paula K. Byers.[77]

Other African American titles of interest to Ohio researchers include *African American Genealogy: A Bibliography and Guide to Sources* and *Bibliography of Sources for Black Family History in the Allen County Public Library Genealogy Department*, by Curt Bryan Witcher; *Black Genealogy*, by Charles L. Blockson; *Blacks Immigrating to Ohio, 1861-1863, Special Enumeration*, by the Auditor of State, Ohio Historical Society (microfilm); *The Blacks of Pickaway County, Ohio in the Nineteenth Century*, by James Buchanan; *Guernsey County's Black Pioneers, Patriots, and Persons*, by Wayne L. Snider; and *History of Black People in Dayton and Montgomery County, 1802-1887*, by Charles Mosley Austin. The Ohio Historical Society maintains an online digital collection of historical documents, titled The African American Experience in Ohio, 1850-1920 (http://dbs.ohiohistory.org/africanam).

Native American tribes in Ohio included, among others, Delaware, Miami (the dominant group for much of Ohio), Ottawa, Seneca, Shawnee, Tuscarora, and Wyandot. It is estimated that the Native American population in Ohio did not exceed 45,000 people. By 1817 the Native American population had decreased drastically.

Bibliographies and other published resources for other ethnic groups in Ohio are also available. See the "Ethnic Sources" bibliography later in this volume.

Ohio African American Genealogy Web site is available online: (www.rootsweb.com/~ohafram/index.html).

---

77. Paula K. Byers, ed., *African American Genealogical Sourcebook* (Detroit: Gale Research, 1995).

Family and Home Sources

The first place to begin your family history research is with personal knowledge about you and your family, and then work backwards through the generations. Contact family members, such as parents and grand-parents, to determine what family history information they may have.

Family and home sources may include family Bibles, certificates (such as birth, marriage, and death), diaries, photographs, letters and postcards, church records, compiled genealogies, newspaper clippings, obituaries, funeral notices, scrapbooks, military records, naturalization papers, school records, legal papers, baby books, and other similar records. Be aware that Ohio family records, such as family Bibles, scrapbooks, and photograph albums, may be kept with older family members. Records may have been taken to another state, such as when a couple retires to Arizona, California, Florida, or some other locality.

Record your information on pedigree charts and family group records—blank forms are readily available on the Internet and at stores that sell genealogical supplies. Many people use genealogy software programs, which also print charts and forms, and many people keep their records in three-ring binders or in file folders. As you interview older family members, such as parents and grandparents, you might consider tape recording and then transcribing this oral history experience. In addition to asking specific questions about their life, be sure to ask "open-ended" questions, such as, "Tell me what it was like to experience the Great Depression when you lived in Cincinnati."

In summary, be aware of family traditions, but use them cautiously—work from known family information to the unknown, search family records and interview relatives, work on one or two generations at a time, be aware of possible spelling variations when doing research (especially surname variations), use a good note-keeping system, and cite your sources accurately and completely. You should share your family history information, copies of photographs, and oral history transcriptions with other family members, and perhaps even with local libraries and historical societies. You may wish to place your compiled genealogy on your own Web page (but do not place names of living people on the Internet without their permission). Be sure to include notes and source references.

Libraries housing Ohio family history and local history sources may be interested in having a copy of your compiled genealogy, especially if it includes a title page, documentation is included with notes and sources, and it is indexed. In addition to your local public library, local genealogical society, and LDS Family History Center, you might consider donating a copy of your compiled genealogy to one or more of the following libraries (this is a selected list; addresses are listed near the end of this volume):

> Allen County Public Library, Fort Wayne, Indiana
> Brigham Young University, Harold B. Lee Library, Provo, Utah
> Cleveland Public Library, Cleveland, Ohio
> DAR Library, Washington, DC
> Family History Library, Salt Lake City, Utah
> Newberry Library, Chicago, Illinois
> New England Historic Genealogical Society, Boston, MA
> Ohio Genealogical Society, Mansfield, Ohio
> Ohio Historical Society, Columbus, Ohio
> Public Library of Cincinnati and Hamilton County, History and
>   Genealogy Department, Cincinnati, Ohio
> St. Louis County Library, St. Louis, Missouri
> State Library of Ohio, Columbus, Ohio
> Toledo-Lucas County Public Library, Toledo, Ohio
> Western Reserve Historical Society, Cleveland, Ohio

Genealogical Collections

A substantial number of genealogical records for Ohio have been compiled by the Daughters of the American Revolution Genealogical Records Committees, popularly known as GRC books. DAR members throughout Ohio (and other states) have transcribed many vital records, church records, family Bibles, gravestones, military records, wills, and similar genealogical resources. DAR typescripts are housed at the DAR Library in Washington, DC, State Library of Ohio, Western Reserve Historical Society Library, and other libraries throughout the state. Many DAR records are on microfilm at the Family History Library, Salt Lake City, and the Ohio Historical Society, Columbus. DAR transcriptions need to be used cautiously, however, since they are known to contain some typing and transcribing errors.

A useful reference is *Master Index, Ohio Society Daughters of the American Revolution, Genealogical and Historical Records*, a listing of many DAR records found in various libraries, including records at the State Library of Ohio, Ohio Historical Society, Western Reserve Historical Society Library, and (incompletely) the Family History Library, Salt Lake City.[78] References to Bible records, cemetery records, church records, probate records, family records, and others, are identified in this work.

Other valuable Ohio genealogical collections have been compiled by various individuals and organizations. Such manuscript collections contain family Bibles, compiled genealogies, family group records,

---

78. Carol Willsey Bell, et al., eds., *Master Index, Ohio Society Daughters of the American Revolution, Genealogical and Historical Records*, vol. 1 (Westlake, Ohio: Ohio Society Daughters of the American Revolution, 1985). Although this reference is not an every-name index to all Ohio DAR records, it is a useful resource for locating DAR compilations. It indexes many personal names and locality records.

pedigree charts, abstracted public records, account books, diaries and journals, correspondence, church records, newspaper clippings, and others. Genealogical collections of this type, like those of the DAR, may be found at the Ohio Historical Society, Western Reserve Historical Society Library, county and local historical societies, and public and other libraries in Ohio, university archives, and amid the microfilm collection of the Family History Library. One example is the *Henry R. Baldwin Genealogical Records Collection*, available at the Public Library of Youngstown and Mahoning County, with copies at the Allen County Public Library, major libraries in Ohio, and the Family History Library.[79] Ancestor charts of some OGS members have been compiled, published, and indexed in a monumental and valuable genealogical reference work, *Ancestor Charts*.[80]

Records of other patriotic and lineage societies may also prove helpful, especially records that have been published or indexed. One notable example is *Our Ancestors' Families*, which contains over one thousand pages of indexed ancestor charts; it was published by the Ohio Society, Colonial Dames XVII Century.[81] The Ohio Society, Sons of the American Revolution's (SAR) published *Centennial Register, 1889 to 1989* indexes names of SAR members and their patriot ancestors and gives a brief history of SAR chapters in the state.[82]

---

79. Henry R. Baldwin, *Henry R. Baldwin Genealogical Records Collection*, 75 vols. (Youngstown, Ohio: Public Library of Youngstown and Mahoning County, 1963). Contains transcriptions of vital, cemetery, military, church, court, probate, obituaries, and other genealogical data for western Pennsylvania and eastern Ohio counties. It is separately indexed in bound volumes, *Index to the Henry R. Baldwin Genealogical Records*, 8 vols. (Youngstown, Ohio: Public Library of Youngstown and Mahoning County, 1961).

80. Ohio Genealogical Society, *Ancestor Charts of Members of the Ohio Genealogical Society* (Mansfield, Ohio: The Society, 1987).

81. Ohio Society, Colonial Dames XVII Century, *Our Ancestors' Families* (The Society, 1988).

82. Ohio Society, Sons of the American Revolution, *Centennial Register, 1889 to 1989* (Dayton, Ohio: The Society, 1988).

A significant reference source for locating manuscript collections, in Ohio and in other states as well, is the Library of Congress multivolume indexed work *National Union Catalog of Manuscript Collections* (also known as NUCMC), available at large research libraries and it is on the Internet.[83] NUCMC is available online at:

(http://lcweb.loc.gov/coll/nucmc/nucmc.html).

Many genealogical materials, such as compiled family accounts, typescript gravestone inscriptions, copies of family Bibles, newspaper clippings, correspondence, and biographies are kept in vertical files in local public libraries and are usually not identified in NUCMC. However, the OCLC and RLIN computer databases, available at major libraries throughout the country, identify references to many manuscript collections, as well as to newspapers and numerous published Ohio and national sources. Descriptions of many genealogical collections and online library catalogs are also found on the Internet.

---

83. Library of Congress, *National Union Catalog of Manuscript Collections* (Washington, DC, 1962-). Known as NUCMC, it is well indexed in *Index to Personal Names*, 2 vols. (Alexandria, Va.: Chadwyck-Healey, 1988). This is the major reference source for locating historical and genealogical manuscript collections in America. See also OCLC and RLIN computer databases for references to manuscript collections.

Handbooks, Manuals, and Bibliographies

One of the major guidebooks describing Ohio genealogical sources is Carol Bell's *Ohio Genealogical Guide*.[84] Although partially dated, this splendid reference work includes Ohio maps, historical background, addresses, and descriptions and examples of records of interest to genealogists. The Family and Church History Department in Salt Lake City has produced *Ohio Research Outline*, available on the Internet at (www.familysearch.org) under "Research Helps." Another helpful source is Mary Harter's Ohio chapter in *Genealogical Research: Methods and Sources*, which describes basic materials and gives historic background for Ohio research.[85] Ruth Douthit's *Ohio Resources for Genealogists* contains many bibliographies of Ohio sources and is a valuable reference source, although it is partially outdated.[86] A brief overview of sources may be gleaned from Betty L. McCay's *Sources for Genealogical Searching in Ohio*[87] and from John W. Heisey's *Ohio Genealogical Research Guide*.[88] *The Ohio Connection Formula for Finding Elusive Ancestors*, by Ann Fenley, is a basic guidebook for beginners and includes tips for searching ancestors in the Buckeye

84. Carol Willsey Bell, *Ohio Genealogical Guide*, 6th ed. (Youngstown, Ohio: Bell Books, 1995).

85. Mary (McCollom) Harter, "Ohio," in American Society of Genealogists, *Genealogical Research: Methods and Sources*, vol. 2, rev. ed., Kenn Stryker-Rodda, ed. (Washington, DC: The Society, 1983), pp. 22-28. This short chapter is now partially outdated but contains a lot of useful background information.

86. Ruth Long Douthit, *Ohio Resources for Genealogists with Some References for Genealogical Searching in Ohio*, rev. ed. (Detroit: Detroit Society for Genealogical Research, 1972). This work is now partially out of date.

87. Betty L. McCay, *Sources for Genealogical Searching in Ohio* (Indianapolis: The author, 1973).

88. John W. Heisey, *Ohio Genealogical Research Guide* (Indianapolis, Ind.: Heritage House, 1987).

State.[89] Of more recent interest are Carol L. Maki's Ohio article in the revised *Ancestry's Red Book*,[90] Diane Gagel's fine Ohio article in *The Genealogical Helper*,[91] and more recently George K. Schweitzer's *Ohio Genealogical Research*, a summary of many Ohio sources.[92] Another reference source is Kip Sperry's "Finding Your Ohio Ancestors," in *Everton's Genealogical Helper*.[93]

Genealogical bibliographies useful for Ohio research may also be gleaned from several works of national scope. *Genealogical and Local History Books in Print*, compiled by Netti Schreiner-Yantis, lists many Ohio titles available for sale—covering cemetery records, newspapers, church records, local histories, atlases, family histories, and many other sources.[94] For details concerning the current 5th edition, see the next reference title: *Genealogical & Local History Books in Print: Family History Volume*, 5th edition, compiled by Marian Hoffman, lists hundreds of family histories, family newsletters, and related titles in print, along with the cost of each item and a listing of vendors where the

---

89. Ann Fenley, *The Ohio Connection Formula for Finding Elusive Ancestors* (Dayton, Ohio: Ohio Connection, 1985).

90. Carol L. Maki, "Ohio," in *Ancestry's Red Book: American State, County & Town Sources*, ed. Alice Eichholz, rev.ed. (Salt Lake City: Ancestry, 1992), pp. 572-88. Useful genealogical information regarding Ohio counties is also listed in *The Handybook for Genealogists*, 10th ed. (Draper, Utah: Everton Publishers, 2002).

91. Diane VanSkiver Gagel, "Researching in Ohio," *The Genealogical Helper* 45 (January-February 1991): 10-16. Also essential for Ohio researchers is Diane Van Skiver Gagel, *Ohio Courthouse Records*, Ohio Genealogical Society Research Guide No. 1 (Mansfield, Ohio: The Society, 1997), which describes Ohio courthouse records.

92. George K. Schweitzer, *Ohio Genealogical Research* (Knoxville, Tenn.: The author, 1994).

93. Kip Sperry, "Finding Your Ohio Ancestors," *Everton's Genealogical Helper* 52 (March-April 1998): 10-15. See also Kip Sperry, "Ohio Research on the Internet," online, 18 April 2000 (www.ancestry.com).

94. Netti Schreiner-Yantis, comp., *Genealogical and Local History Books in Print*, 4th ed., 4 vols. (Springfield, Va.: Genealogical Books in Print, 1985-90). See also the 5th edition cited in the next footnote.

titles may be purchased.[95] P. William Filby's *American and British Genealogy and Heraldry* includes a list of Ohio publications and is a standard reference source for genealogists and librarians.[96] Other national genealogical bibliographies are also helpful.

On the state level, two bibliographies are particularly useful. Marilyn Adams' *Ohio Local and Family History Sources in Print* identifies many published Ohio genealogical titles.[97] *Ohio Genealogy and Local History Sources Index*, by Stuart Harter, is an even more recent publication.[98] Arranged by counties, this latter title identifies several thousand sources of genealogy and local history for the state, including books, periodical articles, and newspaper articles, among other items. A location code is given, showing the library that houses the source. Harter's work is a useful guidebook for Ohio genealogists, historians, and reference librarians.

Some of the bibliographies listed here are now at least partially out of date since online library catalogs are available on the Internet. A valuable source for identifying Ohio publications is the *2003 Ohio Genealogical Society Chapter Directory & Publications List*, which identifies genealogical titles available from OGS chapters. Refer also to the bibliographies near the end of this volume for more Ohio resources.

---

95. Marian Hoffman, comp., *Genealogical & Local History Books in Print: Family History Volume*, 5th ed., 4 vols. (Baltimore: Genealogical Publishing Co., 1996).

96. P. William Filby, comp., *American and British Genealogy and Heraldry*, 3rd ed. (Boston: New England Historic Genealogical Society, 1983); *1982-1985 Supplement* (Boston: New England Historic Genealogical Society, 1987). Though dated, this work is a comprehensive bibliography of American and British genealogical titles.

97. Marilyn Adams, comp., *Ohio Local and Family History Sources in Print* (Clarkston, Ga.: Heritage Research, 1984). This source may be useful as a collection development tool for librarians, although it is now partially out of date.

98. Stuart Harter, *Ohio Genealogy and Local History Sources Index* (Fort Wayne, Ind.: The compiler, 1986). The listings for the holdings of the Family History Library in Salt Lake City are incomplete in this work, but it is still a valuable reference source.

Institutional Records and Lodges

Various public institutions—such as jails, penitentiaries, and county children's homes—have kept records of genealogical value.[99] These include inmate records, journals, applications, admission books, case records, and registers, among other categories. Many of these records are housed at the Ohio Historical Society and in county courthouses, Ohio Network of American History Research Centers, and some are on microfilm at the Family History Library. Occasionally, institutional records are published in the *Ohio Genealogical Society Quarterly* (formerly *The Report*) and in other Ohio genealogical and historical periodicals.

Other institutional records, such as records of asylums, may also be useful to Ohio researchers, including those of such fraternal organizations as the Masons.[100] A history of Ohio Freemasonry and the Masons in the state was written by Allen E. Roberts, *Frontier Cornerstone: The Story of Freemasonry in Ohio, 1790-1980.*[101] A partial list of inmates at the Ohio State Penitentiary in Columbus are available on the Internet:

(www.genealogy.org/~smoore/marion/badguys.htm).

---

99. Carol Willsey Bell, *Little-Used Sources for the U.S. Family Historian*, World Conference on Records, lecture no. 307 (Salt Lake City: Genealogical Society, 1980), describes many Ohio sources of interest to genealogists. See also Carol Bell, "Little-Used Ohio Sources," *Genealogical Journal* 10 (March 1981): 13-24.

100. William B. Saxbe, Jr., "Masonic Records as Genealogical Sources," *The Report* 23 (Winter 1983): 195-96. Articles discussing similar organizations are frequently published in *The Report* (quarterly of the Ohio Genealogical Society, Mansfield, Ohio), now *Ohio Genealogical Society Quarterly*.

101. Allen E. Roberts, *Frontier Cornerstone: The Story of Freemasonry in Ohio, 1790-1980* (N.p., Grand Lodge of Free and Accepted Masons of Ohio, 1980). Includes a list of lodges and officers.

Internet Resources

The Internet is an international network of computers; it is also a valuable resource for Ohio genealogists. The Internet may be used to transfer documents via electronic mail (e-mail), search online library catalogs, search for compiled genealogies, search for printed and transcribed genealogical records, locate digitized records and indexes, submit online genealogical queries, locate names of other researchers with a shared pedigree interest, and for many other similar uses.

One of the major sites for Ohio genealogists, and one of the first places to begin Internet research, is the Ohio GenWeb project:

(www.scioto.org/OHGenWeb)

(www.rootsweb.com/~ohgenweb)

A valuable reference source, although partially dated, is Barbara Brattin's *Ohio Online: The Harvest of Ohio's Best Web Sites.*[102] See also Kip Sperry's "Ohio Research on the Internet," (www.ancestry.com), 18 April 2000, online. A major online directory and listing of Ohio genealogical Web sites is *Cyndi's List of Genealogy Sites on the Internet: Ohio* (www.cyndislist.com/oh.htm).

---

102. Barbara Brattin, *Ohio Online: The Harvest of Ohio's Best Web Sites* (Wilmington, Ohio: Orange Frazer Press, 1998).

Internet Addresses

Libraries and Library Catalogs

Academic Library Association of Ohio (www.alaoweb.org)

Bowling Green State University, Center for Archival Collections,
Jerome Library, Bowling Green, Ohio:
(www.bgsu.edu/colleges/library/cac/cac.html)

Center for Research Libraries (CRL)
(These materials are also included in OhioLINK)

CIC Virtual Catalog (www.lib.ohio-state.edu)
(Big Ten libraries, plus the University of Chicago library—
13 major research libraries)

Cincinnati Historical Society Library:
(www.cincymuseum.org/research/cincinnati_library.asp)

Cleveland Public Library (www.cpl.org)

Columbus Metropolitan Library, Columbus, Ohio:
(www.cml.lib.oh.us)
(www.columbuslibrary.org)

Cuyahoga County Public Library, Fairview Park Regional Library:
(http://clio1.cuyahoga.lib.oh.us/home/locations/FPR.html)

Find an Ohio Public Library (www.oplin.lib.oh.us/products/fal)

German-American Collection, University of Cincinnati:
(www.archives.uc.edu/german)

Mennonite Historical Library, Bluffton, Ohio:
(http://bcarchives.mennonite.net)

National Archives—Great Lakes Region (Chicago):
(www.archives.gov/facilities/il/chicago.html)

Oberlin College Library, Oberlin, Ohio (www.oberlin.edu/~library)

Ohio Genealogical Society, Mansfield, Ohio (www.ogs.org)

Ohioana Library Association (www.oplin.lib.oh.us/index.cfm?ID=773)

Ohio Historical Society, Columbus, Ohio (www.ohiohistory.org)
(www.ohiohistory.org/index.html)

Ohio Historical Society, Archives/Library, Columbus, Ohio:
(www.ohiohistory.org/resource/archlib)

Ohio Historical Society Resources, Columbus, Ohio:
(www.ohiohistory.org/resource/index.html)

Ohio Libraries and Genealogical Societies:
(http://home.att.net/~dottsr/ohio.html#OLIB)

Ohio Libraries and More (www.alaoweb.org/membership/local.html)

Ohio Library Council (www.olc.org)

OhioLINK: Ohio Library and Information Network:
Combined catalog of over 50 Ohio university and college libraries,
including the State Library of Ohio (www.ohiolink.edu)

OhioLINK Central Catalog (http://olc1.ohiolink.edu/search)

OHIONET (www.ohionet.org)

OHIONET, Reference Databases and Services:
(www.ohionet.org/OtherServices/ReferenceServices.asp)

Ohio Network of American History Research Centers:
(www.ohiohistory.org/textonly/resource/lgr/networkl.html)
(http://homepages.rootsweb.com/~maggieoh/ohionet.html)

Ohio Public Libraries (www.publiclibraries.com/ohio.htm)

Ohio State University, William O. Thompson Memorial Library,
Columbus, Ohio (www.lib.ohio-state.edu)

Ohio University Archives, Athens, Ohio (www.library.ohiou.edu)

OPAL, Ohio Private Academic Libraries Catalog:
(http://cat.ohionet.org/search)

OPLIN, Genealogical Libraries with Extensive Ohio Collections
(www.oplin.lib.oh.us/index.cfm?ID=3-56-319)

OPLIN, Ohio Public Library Information Network:
(www.oplin.lib.oh.us)

OPLIN, Ohio Public Library Information Network/Genealogy:
   (www.oplin.lib.oh.us/index.cfm?ID=561)
OPLIN, Ohio Public Library Information Network/History:
   (www.oplin.lib.oh.us/index.cfm?id=11)
OSCAR, Ohio State University Libraries online catalog:
   (http://library.ohio-state.edu/search)
Public Library of Cincinnati and Hamilton County, Cincinnati, Ohio:
   (www.cincinnatilibrary.org)
Society of Ohio Archivists: Links to Web Sites of Interest:
   (www.ohiojunction.net/soa/links.html)
Southeastern Ohio Regional Libraries (www.seorf.ohiou.edu/~xx018)
Stark County District Library, Genealogy Division, Canton, OH:
   (www.stark.lib.oh.us/genservs.html)
State Library of Ohio, Columbus, Ohio   (http://winslo.state.oh.us)
   (http://winslo.state.oh.us/govinfo/index.html)
   (http://winslo.state.oh.us/govinfo/stgvtop.html)
State Library of Ohio/Genealogy Services:
   (http://winslo.state.oh.us/services/genealogy/index.html)
Toledo-Lucas County Public Library (www.toledolibrary.org)
University of Akron Library, Akron, Ohio (www.uakron.edu/library)
University of Cincinnati Library, Cincinnati, Ohio:
   (www.libraries.uc.edu)
Western Reserve Historical Society, Cleveland, Ohio (www.wrhs.org)
WorldCat/OCLC FirstSearch (OCLC Online Union Catalog):
   A combined catalog of holdings of thousands of libraries.
   (www.oclc.org/home)   (http://firstsearch.oclc.org)
Wright State University, Dunbar Library, Dayton (www.wright.edu)
WWW Library Directory, Ohio:
   (www.webpan.com/msauers/libdir/usa/oh.html)
Youngstown Historical Center of Industry & Labor, Youngstown, Ohio:
   (www.ohiohistory.org/youngst/arch_lib.html)

Research Sources and Indexes

Along the Ohio Trail (www.auditor.state.oh.us)

Ancestors Resource Guide—Ohio:
(www.pbs.org/kbyu/ancestors/resourceguide/ohio.shtml)

Ancestry.com—Ohio census records and indexes; birth, marriage, and death records; biography and history; community and message boards; military records; reference and finding aids; and others:
(www.ancestry.com)

Biographical Encyclopaedia of Ohio of the Nineteenth Century:
(www.ancestry.com)
(www.hti.umich.edu/cgi/b/bib/bibperm?q1=ahu5132)

BLM Land Patents/OH GenWeb:
(www.rootsweb.com/~usgenweb/oh/oh_blm.htm)

BLM Land Records (www.ancestry.com)

Bureau of Land Management (www.glorecords.blm.gov)

Census Links (Ohio) (http://censuslinks.com)

Census Online, Ohio (www.census-online.com/links/OH)

Civil War Documents Searchable Database (Ohio):
(www.ohiohistory.org/resource/database/civilwar.html)

Civil War, Ohio in the (www.ohiocivilwar.com)

Civil War Rosters, Ohio:
(www.geocities.com/Area51/Lair/3680/cw/cw-oh.html)

Cleveland Necrology File (www.cpl.org)

Cyndi's List of Genealogy Sites on the Internet, Ohio:
(www.cyndislist.com/oh.htm)

Discover Ohio Genealogy WebRing:
(www.accessgenealogy.com/rings/oh)

Footpaths Across Ohio, County Information Page:
(http://homepages.rootsweb.com/~maggieoh/mohcoun1.html)

GeneaLinks, Ohio Genealogy (www.genealinks.com/states/oh.htm)

Genealogy Helplist Ohio (http://helplist.org/usa/oh.shtml)

Genealogy Mailing Lists for Ohio:
    (http://members.aol.com/gfsjohnf/gen_mail_states-oh.html)
Genealogy: Ohio (Everton Publishers):
    (www.everton.com/reference/usa/oh.php)
Genealogy Resources on the Internet, Ohio Resources:
    (http://www-personal.umich.edu/~cgaunt/ohio.html)
HeritageQuest Online (ProQuest)—Genealogy and Local History Online
    (www.heritagequestonline.com)
History of the Western Reserve:
    (http://homepages.rootsweb.com/~maggieoh/western.html)
Maggie's World of Courthouse Dust & Genealogy Fever:
    (http://homepages.rootsweb.com/~maggieoh/mindex.html)
Miami Valley Genealogical Index (Computerized Heritage Assoc.):
    (www.pcdl.lib.oh.us/miami/index.htm)
    (www.ogs.org/pubdb.htm)
The Official Ohio Lands Book (www.auditor.state.oh.us)
Ohio Cemeteries (OPLIN):
    (www.oplin.lib.oh.us/index.cfm?ID=3-56-2287)
Ohio Census, 1790-1890 (1820-1930 at Ancestry.com):
    (www.ancestry.com/search/rectype/inddbs/3567a.htm)
Ohio Clickable County Map:
    (www.rootsweb.com/~ohgenweb)
    (www.scioto.org/OHGenWeb)
Ohio County Courthouse Project:
    (http://homepages.rootsweb.com/~maggieoh/Courthouses/
    county_courthouses.html)
Ohio Death Certificate Index, 1913-37:
    (www.ohiohistory.org/dindex)
Ohio Deaths, 1958-69; 1970-88; 1989-91; 1992; 1993-98:
    (www.ancestry.com)

Ohio Department of Health, Columbus, Ohio:
   (www.odh.state.oh.us)
Ohio Early Land Ownership Records:
   (www.ancestry.com/search/rectype/inddbs/4642.htm)
Ohio Family History Databases:
   (www.familyhistory.com/state.asp?state=OH)
Ohio GenExchange:
   (www.genexchange.org/state.cfm?state=oh)
   (http://www.genexchange.org/genlinks2.cfm?state=oh)
Ohio GenWeb Project:
   (www.scioto.org/OHGenWeb)
   (www.rootsweb.com/~ohgenweb)
Ohio Genealogy (www.genealinks.com/states/oh.htm)
Ohio Genealogy Forum (http://genforum.genealogy.com/oh)
Ohio Genealogy (GeneaSearch):
   (http://geneasearch.com/states/ohio.htm)
Ohio History Network (www.scioto.org/OhioHistory/index.html)
Ohio Interactive Genealogy:
   (http://victorian.fortunecity.com/literary/463/igen/oh.html)
Ohio Mailing Lists (http://lists.rootsweb.com/index/usa/OH)
Ohio Maps (http://fermi.jhuapl.edu/states/oh_0.html)
Ohio Marriages, 1803-1900:
   (www.ancestry.com/search/rectype/inddbs/5194a.htm)
Ohio Memory: An Online Scrapbook of Ohio History:
   (www.ohiomemory.org)
Ohio Military Men, 1917-18:
   (www.ancestry.com/search/rectype/inddbs/4520.htm)
Ohio Municipalities (www.oplin.lib.oh.us/products/munici)
Ohio Newspaper Index (list of newspapers at OHS)
   (www.ohiohistory.org/resource/database/news.html)
Ohio Obituary Links (www.obitlinkspage.com/obit/oh.htm)
Ohio Outline (www.ancestry.com)

Ohio Public Library Information Network (OPLIN) Genealogy Section:
(www.oplin.lib.oh.us/index.cfm?ID=561)
Ohio Query Surname Index:
(www.rootsweb.com/~ohfrankl/Free/queries.htm)
Ohio Records on the USGenWeb Project:
(www.rootsweb.com/~usgenweb/oh/ohfiles.htm)
Ohio Research Outline ("Research Helps")
(www.familysearch.org)
Ohio River Valley Families (http://orvf.com)
(http://orvf.com/maillist.htm)
Ohio River Valley Families Genealogical Database:
(http://orvf.com/genweb/orvf/orvf.html)
Ohio River Valley Families Virtual Cemetery:
(www.findagrave.com/cgi-
bin/fg.cgi?page=mr&MRid=46528272&)
Ohio Resources (www.ohiohistory.org/textonly/links/ohiores.html)
Ohio, "The Buckeye State":
(www.lineages.com/usa/state.asp?StateCode=OH)
Ohio's County Almanac (www.oplin.lib.oh.us/products/OCA)
Ohio's Guide to Genealogy:
(http://usgenealogyguide.com/ohio)
OPLIN Genealogy Gleanings (online columns):
(www.oplin.lib.oh.us/index.cfm?id=561-945)
Random Acts of Genealogical Kindness, Ohio:
(www.raogk.com/ohio2.htm)
Revolutionary War Pensioners Living in the State of Ohio, 1818-19:
(http://php.indiana.edu/~jetorres/ohiorev.html)
Roots-L Databases and Files—Ohio Surnames:
(www.rootsweb.com/roots-l/USA/oh.html)
RootsWeb's Guide to Tracing Family Trees:
(www.rootsweb.com/~rwguide)

Rutherford B. Hayes Presidential Center (Online Obituary Index):
(www.rbhayes.org)
(http://index.rbhayes.org)
Scioto Valley Genealogy (Scioto.org):
(www.scioto.org)
State Archives (Ohio Historical Society):
(www.ohiohistory.org/resource/statearc/index.html)
Vital Records Agencies in Ohio:
(www.vitalchek.com/region_overview.asp?region_id=44)
Vital Records Information, Ohio Links:
(www.vitalrec.com/ohlinks.html)
(www.vitalrec.com/oh.html)
Vital Records Information, Ohio:
(www.vitalrec.com/oh.html)
War of 1812, Roster of Ohio Soldiers:
(www.ohiohistory.org/resource/database/rosters.html)
Welcome to Ohio Genealogy:
(www.geocities.com/ohgenealogy/Index.html)

Other Ohio Web Sites

Abbott's *History of the State of Ohio* (1875):
  (www.rootsweb.com/~usgenweb/oh/abbot.htm)
African American Experience in Ohio, 1850-1920:
  (http://dbs.ohiohistory.org/africanam)
African Americans in Southeastern Ohio:
  (www.seorf.ohiou.edu/~xx057)
Discover Ohio: Genealogical Resources for Ohio (OPLIN)
  (www.oplin.lib.oh.us/index.cfm?id=3-56)
Evolution of Ohio (www.oplin.lib.oh.us/products/build)
Ohio African American Genealogy:
  (www.rootsweb.com/~ohafram/index.html)
Ohio Association of Historical Societies and Museums:
  (www.ohiohistory.org/resource/oahsm/index.html)
Ohio Chapter of the Palatines to America (www.oh-palam.org)
Ohio Civil War Stories (http://ohiocivilwar.com/stori)
Ohio Family Reunions (www.rootsweb.com/~ohreunio/index.html)
Ohio Government Telephone Directories:
  (www.state.oh.us/ohio/index-sd.htm)
Ohio's Historic Canals:
  (http://my.ohio.voyager.net/C8/D7/lstevens/canal)
Ohio Historical Records Advisory Board:
  (www.ohiojunction.net/ohrab)
Ohio legislature (www.legislature.state.oh.us)
OHIONET   (www.ohionet.org)
Ohio Rail Related Websites:
  (www.centralohiontrak.org/ohiosites.htm)
Ohio Tourism (www.ohiotourism.com)
Palatines to America (www.palam.org)
Society of Ohio Archivists (www.ohiojunction.net/soa)
State of Ohio (www.state.oh.us)
State of Ohio Information (www.uscounties.com/Ohio)
Theological Consortium of Greater Columbus:
  (www.tcgc.capital.edu)

Land and Property Records

Land was Ohio's most coveted commodity during the nineteenth century—the formative years of the state's development. The history of Ohio's land divisions and surveys is more complex than that of most other states because of the various types of land grants and surveys that were common. See Introduction to Ohio Land History on the Internet (http://users.rcn.com/deeds/ohio.htm).

After the Northwest Ordinance of 1787 was passed, the new territory of Ohio was parceled out by Congress in many different (but major) divisions—the Seven Ranges, Ohio Company's Purchase, Symmes Purchase, Connecticut Western Reserve, Fire Lands (Erie and Huron counties), Virginia Military District, United States Military District, Refugee Tract, and Congress Lands. Ohio used the new rectangular (federal) survey system for much of the state, with the notable exception of the Virginia Military District, which surveyed and divided the land into tracts six miles square, known as townships. Each township was divided into thirty-six one mile square sections. Section 16 was reserved for the use of public schools. The Virginia Military District was surveyed by the metes and bounds survey system used in the colonial states.

An illustrated study of Ohio land records is George W. Knepper's *The Official Ohio Lands Book*, but also valuable is Christopher Elias Sherman's *Original Ohio Land Subdivisions*.[103] The small paperback booklet *Ohio Lands: A Short History* offers an indispensable overview of the original land subdivisions and federal land grants in Ohio; it

---

103. George W. Knepper, *The Official Ohio Lands Book* (Columbus: Auditor of State, 2002). Paperback and online (www.auditor.state.oh.us). Includes many valuable Ohio maps. Also valuable for a discussion of Ohio lands is Christopher Elias Sherman, *Original Ohio Land Subdivisions* (1925; reprint, Columbus, 1982).

includes a section giving the origins of Ohio's county names.[104]

A related and useful booklet, especially for those beginning their Ohio research, is *Along the Ohio Trail: A Short History of Ohio Lands.*[105] Every serious Ohio genealogist should own a copy of George W. Knepper's *The Official Ohio Lands Book* (paperback booklet) and *Along the Ohio Trail* (paperback booklet).

A brief description of Ohio land grants and surveys is given in *Atlas of the State of Ohio.*[106] Also, Meredith Colket's article in the

104. Thomas Aquinas Burke, *Ohio Lands: A Short History*, 9th ed. (Columbus: Auditor of State, 1997). This useful booklet, formerly titled *Ohio Land Grants*, includes valuable maps and illustrations of interest to Ohio genealogists. Also helpful is Thomas Aquinas Burke, "Digging Into Ohio's Early Land Records," *Ohio Historical Society's Preview* 4 (Spring 1995):11-13; Ulysses S. Brandt, "Land Grants in Ohio," in *Ohio History Sketches*, Francis B. Pearson and J.D. Harbor, eds. (Columbus: Fred J. Heer, 1903); Edward N. McConnell, "The Genealogical Value of Ohio County Land Records," *Genealogy* 31 (August 1977): 1-5; and John F. Vallentine, "Legal Description of Land in Ohio," *The Genealogical Helper* 32 (November-December 1978): 5-7. See also the superb treatise by Malcolm J. Rohrbough, *The Land Office Business: The Settlement and Administration of American Public Lands, 1789-1837* (New York: Oxford University Press, 1968) which describes the public domain, organization of the General Land Office, military bounty lands, and related topics. Rohrbough includes valuable maps showing land districts and offices in the Old Northwest and elsewhere. Two additional useful references are James C. Barsi, *The Basic Researcher's Guide to Homesteads and Other Federal Land Records* (Fort McKavett, Texas: Nuthatch Grove Press, 1994), and Benjamin Hibbard, *A History of the Public Land Policies* (Madison, Wisc., 1965).
An Internet site of interest to Ohio genealogists is "Introduction to Ohio Land History" (www.ultranet.com/~deeds/ohio.htm). See also, E. Wade Hone, *Land & Property Research in the United States* (Salt Lake City: Ancestry, 1997) and Thomas A. Burke (http://freepages.history.rootsweb.com/~maggie/ohio-lands/ohlands.html).
105. Tanya West Dean and W. David Speas, *Along the Ohio Trail: A Short History of Ohio Lands* (Columbus: Auditor of State, 2001). Paperback. Available from the Auditor of State in Columbus. See (www.auditor.state.oh.us). The Auditor of State also has a related and useful interactive compact disc, *Along the Ohio Trail: A Short History of Ohio Lands* (CD-ROM), available from the Auditor of State, Columbus, Ohio.
106. Walling, *Atlas of the State of Ohio*, pp. 2-3. See also William D. Pattison, *Beginnings of the American Rectangular Land Survey System, 1784-1800* (Columbus: Ohio Historical Society, 1957) and *The Public Domain: Its History with Statistics* (Washington, DC: Government Printing Office, 1880).

National Genealogical Society Quarterly puts the subject of the Old Northwest and federal lands into historical perspective.[107] William E. Peters, in his *Ohio Lands and their History*, gives a detailed and illustrated overview of Ohio lands, tracts, grants, and early settlements; it is an essential reference for a study of Ohio lands and migration in the Buckeye State.[108]

Deeds and other land records may help identify family members and their residences, and they often help determine relationships or trace family migrations. As an example, a deed recorded in Franklin County, Ohio, executed by John Eaton (grantor) and Paul Deerdorf (grantee), shows John Eaton's previous place of residence: "This Indenture made this Nineteenth day of August 1807 between John Eaton and Elizabeth his wife of the Town of Halifax in the State of North Carolina of the one part, and Paul Deerdorf of Franklin County in the State of Ohio of the other part....."[109]

Although origin and relationships are not always directly stated in a single land document, they may sometimes be ascertained by the meticulous extracting and correlating of all land records executed by a particular family. Within Ohio, land records are kept at the Recorder of Deeds Office in each respective county courthouse. Land records may also be found at regional network centers, the Ohio Historical Society, and other repositories in the state. Local records commonly contain the transfers of property between individuals. Most Ohio deeds are indexed by the *grantee* (buyer) and the *grantor* (seller); most of these indexes have been microfilmed. The Family History Library in Salt Lake City has a significant microfilm collection of Ohio deeds, mortgages,

---

107. Meredith B. Colket, Jr., "Genealogical Research in the Old Northwest," *National Genealogical Society Quarterly* 65 (March 1977): 25-34.

108. William Edward Peters, *Ohio Lands and their History*, 3rd ed. (1930; Reprint, New York: Arno Press, 1979). This work includes maps of the state showing land divisions. It is especially useful for Ohio migration studies.

109. Original deed, Franklin County, Ohio, D:96-97. FHL microfilm no. 285,067.

surveys, field notes, tract books, and related indexes to land records—
see the Family History Library Catalog under the headings "Ohio—
Land and property" and "Ohio, County—Land and property" under the
county of interest.

The majority of the early Ohio land records formerly housed at the
Auditor of State's Land Office in Columbus have been transferred to the
Ohio Historical Society in Columbus. These include copies of early
federal land grants (public domain records), Virginia Military District
(VMD) land records (land entry and survey books), WPA plat books of
Ohio counties in the VMD, card index files to VMD records, tract and
entry books, original land survey field notes, deeds issued by the state of
Ohio, records of real property owned by Ohio, card indexes to federal
land records, and other sources. This collection does not include records
for Western Reserve (northeastern Ohio) counties. An article describing
the records formerly at the State Land Office has been published in *The
Report*.[110] The only land records the Office of the Auditor of State has
retained are the actual deeds for state-owned land.

A typical land record series at the Ohio Historical Society shows
name of land office, date the land was sold, purchaser's full name,
residence (in Ohio or elsewhere), description of tract purchased (section,
township, and range), number of acres, price per acre, and total amount
of money (information varies, depending on the records).[111] Land

---

110. Stephen M. Heer, "A Description of Genealogical Records Located in the
Land Office of the Auditor of State and Suggestions Regarding Their Use," *The Report*
13 (Spring 1973): 8-12. It is wise to search the State Auditor's land files now at the
Ohio Historical Society, particularly if patents cannot be found on the Bureau of Land
Management (BLM) Internet site or on the BLM compact discs (CD-ROMs). See also,
Amy Johnson Crow, "The Virginia Military District: A Study in Contradictions," *NGS
Newsmagazine* 28 (July/August 2002): 208-209, 246, and Daphne S. Gentry, comp.,
Virginia Land Office Inventory, 3rd ed., revised by John S. Salmon (Richmond, Va.:
Archives and Records Division, Virginia State Library, 1981).

111. Ohio Historical Society, State Archives, Auditor of State, Account of Lands,
Record of Land Sales, BV 3030, Series 4340 (original land records at Ohio Historical
Society, Columbus, Ohio), is an example of early Ohio land records.

records are especially valuable as a resource for tracing migration, and sometimes give a person's previous place of residence in another state.

Land patents, survey plats, land entry case files, and federal land tract books for the public lands portion of the state of Ohio, as with other states whose original titles trace to the federal government, are available from the Eastern States Office, Bureau of Land Management (BLM), 7450 Boston Boulevard, Springfield, VA 22153. Remote access (by FAX or mail) of pre-1908 land patents for Ohio is available from the BLM.

A compact disc (data only, not document images) for Ohio is available from the Superintendent of Documents in Pittsburgh, PA, entitled *General Land Office, Automated Records Project: Ohio* (CD-ROM). The BLM compact discs are also available at federal depository libraries, such as university libraries. The Ohio CD contains information from about 98,000 pre-1908 patents and also includes general instructions, a map showing townships and ranges, samples of historically significant patents, general information, and image ordering forms. It is invaluable for early Ohio research. The BLM Federal Land Patent Records Site on the Internet, which includes Ohio, is located at (www.glorecords.blm.gov) (Search Federal Land Patents Databases). Ohio lands purchased on credit (credit entries) are not included in the BLM database. The card files of the Bureau of Land Management's Eastern States Office in Alexandria, Virginia, have been microfilmed. The BLM CD-ROM *Definitions for Ohio Land Records* are online: (www.geocities.com/~jdanielson/ohdef.htm).

An extensive card file, patents, and miscellaneous land records are also available at the BLM.[112] The original land entry files, final

---

112. Public domain states include all except the original thirteen states, Hawaii, Kentucky, Maine, Tennessee, Texas, Vermont, and West Virginia. Researchers seeking patents issued in Ohio or any of the public-lands states east of the Mississippi River (including all of Louisiana) should contact the Bureau of Land Management, Eastern States Office, 7450 Boston Blvd., Springfield, VA 22153.

certificates, and other related records—which offer more personal data on the individuals who took out land—are housed at the National Archives and Records Administration and are available, by correspondence or in person, from the National Archives.[113] The legal description of the land (range, township, and section) is needed to search federal land records that are not indexed. Federal land records (formerly housed at the Suitland Reference Branch in Suitland, Maryland) are now located at the National Archives, Washington, DC 20408. Information from the BLM Web site will lead the researcher to original land records housed at the National Archives in Washington, DC. Microfilm copies of tract books at the BLM, which guide the researcher to the patent volumes and case files, are also on microfilm at the Family History Library, Salt Lake City.

Bounty land warrant applications and other land records stemming from Virginia's grants within Ohio should be obtained from the Library of Virginia (formerly the Virginia State Library and Archives), 800 East Broad Street, Richmond, VA 23219 (www.lva.lib.va.us). Land Office Military Certificates for the Virginia Military District in Ohio are available online from the Library of Virginia's Web site. Many of these land records have been microfilmed. For example, *Ohio Land Office, Records Relating to Virginia Military Lands, 1787-1851.*

Several genealogists have published compendiums, indexes, and miscellaneous reference works that are indispensable to Ohio's land research. Carol Bell's *Ohio Lands: Steubenville Land Office, 1800-1820* contains records of federal sales from that land office and shows the names and residences of proprietors, dates of acquisition, certificate numbers, and location of lands.[114] However, many other early Ohio land

---

113. When ordering land case files from the National Archives, the request should be addressed to the attention of Textual Reference Branch-Land (NNRI), National Archives and Records Administration, Washington, DC 20408.

114. Carol Willsey Bell, comp., *Ohio Lands: Steubenville Land Office, 1800-1820* (Youngstown, Ohio: The author, 1983).

office records have not yet been published.

Other standard Ohio references that assist in tracing migrations of early settlers are *Early Ohio Settlers*, compiled by Ellen T. and David A. Berry in three volumes;[115] *First Ownership of Ohio Lands*, by Albion Morris Dyer;[116] and Mayburt Riegel's *Early Ohioans' Residences from the Land Grant Records*.[117] Also of interest is William T. Hutchinson's *The Bounty Lands of the American Revolution in Ohio*, which contains useful bibliographies and historical background on the subject.[118]

Similar guides exist for Ohio's federally dispensed lands. Genealogists researching federal land sales should consult Clifford Neal Smith's valuable published *Federal Land Series*, which has meticulous every-name indexes, historical background describing federal land records, and valuable Ohio maps; these volumes may be found in many large libraries.[119] The *American State Papers* (Public Lands Series), readily indexed in *Grassroots of America*, may also prove helpful in locating early Ohio settlers and sometimes provide personal details not

---

115. Ellen T. and David A. Berry, comps., *Early Ohio Settlers: Purchasers of Land in Southeastern Ohio, 1800-1840* (Baltimore: Genealogical Publishing Co., 1984), *Early Ohio Settlers: Purchasers of Land in Southwestern Ohio, 1800-1840* (Baltimore: Genealogical Publishing Co., 1986), and *Early Ohio Settlers: Purchasers of Land in East and East Central Ohio, 1800-1840* (Baltimore: Genealogical Publishing Co., 1989).

116. Albion Morris Dyer, *First Ownership of Ohio Lands* (1911; reprint, Baltimore: Genealogical Publishing Co., 1982). Online (www.ancestry.com).

117. Mayburt Stephenson Riegel, comp., *Early Ohioans' Residences from the Land Grant Records* (Mansfield, Ohio: Ohio Genealogical Society, 1976).

118. William Thomas Hutchinson, *The Bounty Lands of the American Revolution in Ohio* (Ph.D. diss., University of Chicago, 1927; New York: Arno Press, 1979).

119. Clifford Neal Smith, *Federal Land Series*, 4 vols. (Chicago: American Library Association, 1972-86). These volumes identify many land grants in the Virginia Military District of Ohio.

to be found elsewhere.[120]

For a monumental and detailed history of the rectangular survey system, consult C. Albert White's *A History of the Rectangular Survey System*.[121] This work includes maps and illustrations. A useful history of Ohio lands was written by William E. Peters, *Ohio Lands and their Subdivision*.[122] A verbatim copy of the entry book and records of John Cleves Symmes was compiled by Chris McHenry in his *Symmes Purchase Records*.[123] Early Chillicothe land records, an important early Ohio land office, 1800-1829, have been compiled by Marie Taylor Clark, *Ohio Lands: Chillicothe Land Office*.[124] Early Virginia military surveys in Ohio have been abstracted by Alma Aicholtz Smith, *The Virginia Military Surveys of Clermont and Hamilton Counties, Ohio, 1787-1849*.[125] Another useful source is the Governor's Deeds Card Index, 1833-1994 (microfilmed). For an introduction to land sales in Ohio, early land divisions, Land Ordinance of 1785, and related topics, consult Denise Kay Mahan Moore's *Land Sales of Ohio*.[126]

---

120. United States Congress, *American State Papers: Documents Legislative and Executive of the Congress of the United States* (Washington, DC: Gales & Seaton, 1832-61), 7 vols., Public Lands Series. Phillip W. McMullin, ed., *Grassroots of America: A Computerized Index to the American State Papers* (Salt Lake City: Gendex, 1972), indexes the volumes of land grants and claims and vol. 24 of *American State Papers* claims, but does not index the entire series.

121. C. Albert White, *A History of the Rectangular Survey System* (Washington, DC: U.S. Department of the Interior, Bureau of Land Management, 1983).

122. William E. Peters, *Ohio Lands and their Subdivision*, 2nd ed. (Athens, Ohio: W.E. Peters 1918).

123. Chris McHenry, comp., *Symmes Purchase Records* (Lawrenceburg, Ind.: The author, 1979). Transcript of land records kept by John Cleves Symmes, 1787-1800.

124. Marie Taylor Clark, comp., *Ohio Lands: Chillicothe Land Office* (Chillicothe, Ohio: The author,1984). See also *Ohio Lands: South of the Indian Boundary Line* (Chillicothe, Ohio: The author, 1984).

125. Alma Aicholtz Smith, *The Virginia Military Surveys of Clermont and Hamilton Counties, Ohio, 1787-1849* (Cincinnati: Alma A. Smith, 1985).

126. Denise Kay Mahan Moore, *Land Sales of Ohio* (Gautier, Miss.: The author, 1997).

Some Ohio land records may be found on compact discs (CD-ROMs). Representative examples are:

- *Bureau of Land Management Land Patent Records: Selected States* (Ohio). CD-ROM (Ancestry.com).

- General Land Office. *Automated Records Project: Ohio.* CD-ROM

- *Land Records: Ohio (and Other States), 1790-1907* (selected Ohio counties). CD-ROM (Family Tree Maker).

Two representative collections microfilmed at the State Auditor's Office in Columbus and available at the Family History Library include (see Family History Library Catalog, "Ohio—Land and property"):

Ohio. Auditor of State. *Tract Books and Index for U.S. Lands in Ohio.* Microfilm.

Ohio. Surveyor General. *Field Books to U.S. Lands in Ohio.* Microfilm.

Local Histories and Biographies

Regional, county, city, and other local histories are available for most Ohio localities, and some counties have more than one history or biography. In addition to historical background on the locality, most contain biographical sketches—especially of prominent citizens; lists of early settlers and township officers; military rosters; and accounts of military activities, church history with names of ministers for each denomination, and school history. Previous residence and dates of arrival are often given for early settlers. Some local histories include a map of the locality and other genealogical aids. Similarly, county and local atlases provide historical background, and many include biographical sketches. Many county histories and atlases have been reprinted with every-name indexes, although most are only partially indexed.

For assistance in locating Ohio local histories, consult online library catalogs on the Internet (described elsewhere in this volume) and P. William Filby's *A Bibliography of American County Histories.*[127] Research Publications in New Haven, Connecticut, has microfilmed many Ohio county histories, atlases, and biographies (as well as similar titles for other states). These microfilms are available at major libraries. See Research Publications, *Reel Index to the Microform Collection of County and Regional Histories of the "Old Northwest," Series II: Ohio*, a guide to Ohio county and regional histories and atlases on microfilm; many of these titles are now out of print.[128]

---

127. P. William Filby, comp., *A Bibliography of American County Histories* (Baltimore: Genealogical Publishing Co., 1985).

128. Research Publications, *Reel Index to the Microform Collection of County and Regional Histories of the "Old Northwest," Series II: Ohio* (New Haven, Conn.: Research Publications, 1975). Sources are arranged by author or title. Research Publications has microfilmed many county and regional histories and atlases for other states as well.

Biographical works, sometimes known as *mug books*, are available for most Ohio counties and contain biographical sketches of prominent pioneers and early settlers. Similar to biographies that appear in county and local histories, these are compiled sources; the genealogical information in them needs to be verified through research into original records. Nevertheless, biographies provide much genealogical and biographical information useful as research clues—dates and places of births and marriages; parents' names and their spouses, residences, names of children, and other family details; occupation; education; military service information; civic, social, political, and religious affiliation; and family migration. Sometimes portraits and sketches of family homes and farms are included. Mug books may provide valuable clues for further research. The *Ohio Biographies Project* is online at (http://homepages.rootsweb.com/~usbios/Ohio/mnpg.html).

Two representative titles are *The Biographical Encyclopedia of Ohio of the Nineteenth Century* and *Biographical History of Northeastern Ohio*.[129] Similar material may be found in such works as *Memorial to the Pioneer Women of the Western Reserve*, which is a valuable source for this area but is certainly not error free;[130] Harriet Taylor Upton's *History of the Western Reserve*, which has extensive biographical sketches and many portraits;[131] and *History of Ohio*, which

---

129. *The Biographical Encyclopedia of Ohio of the Nineteenth Century* (Cincinnati: Galaxy Publishing Co., 1876) (www.ancestry.com) and *Biographical History of Northeastern Ohio* (Chicago: Lewis Publishing Co., 1893). See the bibliography at the end of this volume for more biographical, genealogical, and other titles.

130. Gertrude van Rensselaer Wickham, ed., *Memorial to the Pioneer Women of the Western Reserve* (1896; reprint 5 vols. in 2, Evansville, Ind.: Whipporwill Publications, 1982). This biographical work includes an index to early Western Reserve pioneers.

131. Harriet Taylor Upton, *History of the Western Reserve*, 3 vols. (Chicago: Lewis Publishing Co., 1910). This work is known to contain some biographical and genealogical errors; information should be verified by research into other sources.

highlights prominent Ohio citizens.[132] A splendid example of a comprehensive history of an American city is *The Encyclopedia of Cleveland History*, which includes many biographical sketches of prominent Cleveland, Ohio, citizens.[133]

The Ohio County History Surname Index, sometimes known as the Ohio Surname Index, is a valuable statewide card file, although it is not a complete personal name index to all Ohio local histories. Housed at the Ohio Historical Society, it indexes some 450,000 names in Ohio county histories, atlases, biographical records, some newspapers and periodicals, and other sources. This personal name finding aid should be searched when researching early Ohio pedigrees in order to determine if a biographical sketch is available for an ancestor. Cards show a person's name, full bibliographic data, and page numbers where the sketch appears. Entries are alphabetical by surname. Researchers are cautioned, however, that the sources this index covers are basically those issued between about 1880 and 1915, not current publications. In addition, not every Ohio local history is indexed here nor are all counties represented. This file was compiled by DAR members during the period 1928-36. It has been microfilmed and is available at the Family History Library and other libraries. Copies of microfilms are available to libraries through interlibrary loan from the Interlibrary Loan Department at the Ohio Historical Society in Columbus.

Don H. Tolzmann's *Ohio Valley German Biographical Index* is an index to sketches found in selected German-American histories and biographical directories.[134] Some Ohio local histories are available on CD-ROM. See *County and Family Histories: Ohio, 1780-1970*.

132. Galbreath, *History of Ohio*. Separately indexed by Robertalee Lent.

133. David D. Van Tassel and John J. Grabowski, eds., *The Encyclopedia of Cleveland History*, 2 vols., 2nd ed. (Bloomington, Ind.: Indiana University Press, 1996). Online (http://ech.cwru.edu).

134. Don Heinrich Tolzmann, *Ohio Valley German Biographical Index* (Bowie, Md.: Heritage Books, 1992). Focus is on the Ohio Valley with emphasis on the tri-state region of Ohio, Indiana, and Kentucky.

Maps, Atlases, and Gazetteers

Identifying place-names (localities) where ancestors lived is one of the first steps in family history research. Maps, atlases, gazetteers, reference guides, and other resources are available to help researchers learn more about Ohio place-names. Computer programs are also available, such as AniMap (county boundary historical atlas).

One of the most useful Ohio locality finding aids is Julie Minot Overton's *Ohio Towns and Townships to 1900: A Location Guide.*[135] This monumental work is an alphabetical listing of hundreds of pre-1900 Ohio towns and township names, showing in which county they are located, year organized, and other information. Another valuable reference is John S. Gallagher and Alan H. Patera's *The Post Offices of Ohio.*[136] This reference guide shows the name of the post office, date established, the date if discontinued, where the mail should be sent.

Ohio Web sites for geographical studies include the following:

Ohio Locations:
> (http://homepages.rootsweb.com/~maggieoh/Towns)

---

135. Julie Minot Overton, *Ohio Towns and Townships to 1900: A Location Guide*, edited by Kay Ballantyne Hudson and Sunda Anderson Peters (Mansfield, Ohio: Ohio Genealogical Society, 2000). This reference source identifies pre-1900 towns and townships in Ohio. For additions see Kay Ballantyne Hudson, comp., "Ohio Towns and Townships to 1900, Addendum I," *The Report* 41 (Summer 2001): 87-90. See also "100 Largest Townships in Ohio According to the 2000 Census," *OGS Genealogy News* 34 (January/February 2003): 20. Also consult Carol Mehr Schiffman, "Geographic Tools: Maps, Atlases, and Gazetteers," in Kory L. Meyerink, ed., *Printed Sources: A Guide to Published Genealogical Records* (Salt Lake City: Ancestry, 1998), pp. 95-144.

136. John S. Gallagher and Alan H. Patera, *The Post Offices of Ohio* (Burtonsville, Md.: The Depot, 1979).

Ohio State Gazetteer and Business Directory for 1860-61:
(www.hti.umich.edu/cgi/b/bib/bibperm?q1=aja2907)

1895 U.S. Atlas for Ohio:
(www.livgenmi.com/1895oh)

Sanborn Fire Insurance Maps, 1867-1970, Ohio (valuable in showing streets, buildings, businesses, and other useful locality details):
(http://oplin.lib.oh.us/products/SanbornMaps/index.cfm).

Marriage Records

The recording of civil marriages in Ohio generally began at the date of each county's formation, while the recording of civil births and deaths began in 1867, although the recording of births and deaths in some Ohio counties may be found as early as the 1856-57 time period (see the "Vital Records" section later in this volume). Contact the Probate Court in the county where the marriage occurred. These records include marriage records, marriage returns, marriage consents of minors by parents, and ministers' license records.

Marriage records give the names of the bride and groom, date of event, county in which the marriage occurred and sometimes the specific place of the ceremony, the officiating party, and other information may be shown in later records, such as age and residence of the bride and groom. Because marriage records began at such an early date in Ohio and are complete for most periods, they are considered one of the state's most valuable genealogical resources. Names of brides and grooms are indexed on a county basis by a general index to marriage.

Both transcribed and microfilmed versions of the actual marriage records are available in a variety of repositories. Early Ohio marriage records are available from the Probate Court where the marriage occurred. Marriage records since 7 September 1949 for some counties are available at the Ohio Historical Society in Columbus. The Ohio Department of Health (Vital Statistics Office) in Columbus has marriage abstracts for Ohio counties from 7 September 1949 to the present (an abstract is not a marriage license, but rather shows the basic information found in the original marriage license). Marriage licenses are not available from the Ohio Department of Health in Columbus (contact the Probate Court in the county for a copy of a marriage license). The address of the Ohio Department of Health is:

Ohio Department of Health
Vital Statistics
P.O. Box 15098
Columbus, OH 43215-0098

Jean Nathan served as chairperson of a monumental reference work compiled by the Ohio Genealogical Society, *Ohio Marriages Recorded in County Courts through 1820: An Index.*[137] Names of brides and grooms are alphabetically arranged by surname, with date married, name of county, book or volume number, and page number. This work identifies all known court-recorded marriages in Ohio before 1821.

Transcriptions of early marriages for Ohio counties have been compiled by members of the National Society Daughters of the American Revolution (DAR) and are available at the National Society Library in Washington, DC, as well as the State Library of Ohio in Columbus. Microfilm copies of both the transcriptions and the original marriage records are available at the Family History Library, Ohio Historical Society, and other major libraries in Ohio. Ohio marriage records have also been published by some individuals and organizations. A useful reference source for early marriage records is *Ohio Marriages Extracted from the Old Northwest Genealogical Quarterly.*[138] Civil marriages, excluding church marriages, are maintained by the Probate Court at the county courthouse or at the appropriate regional network center in Ohio.

Significant research aids exist to help genealogists locate vital

---

137. Ohio Genealogical Society, comp., *Ohio Marriages Recorded in County Courts through 1820: An Index,* Jean Nathan, chairman (Mansfield, Ohio: Ohio Genealogical Society, 1996). Updated by OGS, *Ohio Marriages, 1821-1830.*

138. Marjorie Smith, ed., *Ohio Marriages Extracted from the Old Northwest Genealogical Quarterly* (Baltimore: Genealogical Publishing Co., 1980). Marriages are arranged alphabetically. *The "Old Northwest" Genealogical Quarterly,* published from 1898 to 1912 in fifteen volumes, is a valuable reference source for Ohio genealogists.

records within the state. Principal among these is the International Genealogical Index (IGI), a computer index to over 750 million names of deceased individuals.[139] The most recent version of the IGI is available on the Internet (www.familysearch.org). An older version of the IGI is available on compact disc (CD-ROM) at LDS Family History Centers, and at other libraries in Ohio and elsewhere. The IGI, which should be searched for all early Ohio pedigrees, indexes numerous pre-1895 Ohio marriage records on a statewide basis, as well as birth, church (baptisms/christenings and marriages), and several other types of records. The IGI serves as a statewide index to early Ohio marriages and other records as well.

Ohio marriages taken from several different sources and selected counties are available on Ancestry's Web site for the years 1803-1900: (http://www.ancestry.com/search/rectype/inddbs/5194a.htm)

Many early Ohio marriage records are available on compact disc (CD-ROM). Three representative examples are:

- *Marriage Index: Ohio, 1789-1850*, CD-ROM (Family Tree Maker)
- *Marriage Index: Ohio, 1851-1900*, CD-ROM (Family Tree Maker)
- *Ohio Vital Records: Marriages* (Selected Counties and Years), CD-ROM (Ancestry.com)

---

139. John L. Hart, "750 Million-Name IGI Upgraded," *LDS Church News* (9 November 2002), p. 3.

Migration and Immigration Records

Individuals and families migrated to Ohio for a variety of reasons. Among these include Ohio's rich land and the opportunity to farm, land grants, economic reasons, employment, family, follow a religious leader, as a reward for military service, political, weather, and for other reasons as well. Maps showing population migration routes are available on some Internet sites and in some historical texts.

A useful Internet site that may provide additional clues for tracing migration to Ohio is *Pioneer Migration Routes through Ohio*: (http://homepages.rootsweb.com/~maggieoh/pioneer.html).

Tracing the migration of individuals and families to Ohio, and within the state, depends on the time period, place of settlement, religion, ethnic origin, or perhaps other factors. Early immigrants to Ohio came from the New England states, Eastern (Middle-Atlantic) states, several of the Southern states—Pennsylvania, Virginia, New York, Maryland, New Jersey, Connecticut, Massachusetts, Vermont, Kentucky, Indiana, and other states. Later, immigrants arrived (or returned) from Michigan, Indiana, Illinois, Iowa, and several other Midwestern states (sometimes known as "reverse migration"). Foreign countries also provided immigrants to Ohio and included Germany, Ireland, England, France, Wales, Canada, Scotland, Switzerland, and also other countries.

The following sources may assist in tracing ancestors who migrated to Ohio or within the state (a listing of published migration sources, to Ohio and migration sources within the state, appears in the bibliography section later in this volume):

- Bible records (births, marriages, and deaths)
- Biographical works and biographical encyclopedias

- Business records
- Cemetery and sexton records
- Census population schedules (especially after 1850)
- Church histories—histories of individual churches
- Church records: baptisms, christenings, confirmations, marriages, membership records, removals, lists of church members, burials, and other similar church records
- Computer databases (Internet and compact discs)
- Correctional institution records and jail records
- Court records: dockets, minutes, orders, case files
- Directories—city and rural directories
- Divorce records
- Family and home sources, correspondence, family record books
- Fraternal organization records
- Funeral home records
- Genealogies and compiled family histories
- Gravestone and tombstone inscriptions
- Indexes, such as Ohio County History Surname Index
- International Genealogical Index (IGI)
- Internet and genealogical computer databases
- Land and property records, deeds, land grants, mortgages
- Local histories, such as town and county histories
- Manuscript collections and unpublished records
- Military records, especially pension and service records
- Military regimental and unit histories (especially Civil War)
- Mortality schedules, 1850, 1860, 1870, 1880 (incomplete)
- Naturalization and citizenship records
- Newspapers, obituaries, marriage notices, biographies
- Passport applications, 1795 to ca. 1925
- Patriotic and lineage society applications and papers
- Periodicals, genealogical and historical articles

- Photographs
- Probate records, wills, administrations, case files
- School records
- Scrapbooks
- Township records
- Vital records (civil births, marriages, and deaths)

Military Records

Military-related records may often be very valuable for gene-alogists—depending on the war, the involvement of the ancestor, and the organizations that created these records. Many soldiers from Ohio served in the military, creating a variety of service, pension, unit histories, and associated records. The major repository of federal military records for the United States is the National Archives and Records Administration in Washington, DC. Microfilm copies of many of these records are available at National Archives regional archives, Family History Library, and at other libraries with genealogical holdings. Most of these records date from the 1780s to the early twentieth century.

Generally speaking, pension records are usually more genealogically valuable than service or other military records. Sometimes pension files contain marriage certificates or related testimony, indicating the date and place of the pensioner's marriage (or marriages) and identifying the officiating party. At other times, pages from family Bibles were submitted to prove relationships. An essential reference work describing federal military records is the *Guide to Genealogical Research in the National Archives.*[140] The DAR Library in Washington DC also has a large collection of copies of Revolutionary War records and related indexes, typescripts of genealogical records, and published sources which are national in scope.

One of the most valuable Ohio statewide military research aids is

---

140. *Guide to Genealogical Research in the National Archives*, 3rd. ed., edited by Anne Bruner Eales and Robert M. Kvasnicka (Washington, DC: National Archives and Records Administration, 2000). See also Christina K. Schaefer, *The Center: A Guide to Genealogical Research in the National Capital Area* (Baltimore: Genealogical Publishing Co., 1996) which describes genealogical repositories and their holdings in the Washington, DC, area. Schaefer's book (revised from *Lest We Forget*) is a nice companion to the more comprehensive National Archives guide.

the Graves Registration Card File, housed at the Ohio Historical Society, also known as Grave Registrations of Soldiers Buried in Ohio. It identifies most soldiers buried in Ohio through 1967. Names of some Ohio soldiers buried outside the state are also included in this card file. In addition to the soldier's name, contents of each card may include address, date and place of death, cause of death, date of burial, date and place of birth (sometimes a foreign country), name of cemetery and location of grave, next of kin, and service record (war served in, company, rank, and so forth). Cards are alphabetically arranged by surname and have been microfilmed; they are available on microfilm at the Family History Library and at other libraries as well.

Often overlooked by genealogists are various military records kept in county courthouses (for Ohio, see especially records in the Recorder's Office), regional network centers in the state, veteran's services offices, Ohio Historical Society, Western Reserve Historical Society, and other repositories in the state. On the county level, these often include soldiers' discharge records, burial records, enlistments, pay records, correspondence, and others. On the state level, the Governor's Office of Veterans Affairs in Columbus maintains some military records for servicemen, as well as a card file for every person known to have served Ohio in the military. This office will answer limited mail inquiries regarding military records in their possession, mostly for World War I or later. Records at the Ohio Historical Society include military rosters, muster in and muster out rolls, printed histories, manuscript collections, the 1890 Special Union Veterans Census (or their widow), and many others. Consult the Ohio Historical Society Web site for more details.

Extensive microfilming has been done by the Genealogical Society of Utah in the military records created by Ohioans at the federal, state, and county levels. Principal among these are the following collections: Graves Registration Card File; Index to Compiled Service Records of Volunteer Union Soldiers Who Served in Organizations from Ohio,

1861-1865; Official Roster of the Soldiers of the State of Ohio in the War of the Rebellion (original muster-in and muster-out rolls); World War I draft records; and a variety of other pension and service record collections. The *Register of Federal United States Military Records* provides a catalog of military records and indexes available at the Family History Library, along with microfilm numbers, illustrations, and brief descriptions of the records.[141]

A variety of secondary publications relating to Ohio military records exist for genealogical study. *Annotated Bibliography of Ohio Patriots: Revolutionary War and War of 1812*, by W. Louis Phillips, catalogs principally published works, although a few unpublished sources are cited as well.[142] Full bibliographic data is offered in each entry, followed by a description of contents, making this a valuable reference for locating early Ohio military records. Inez Waldenmaier's *Revolutionary War Pensioners Living in Ohio before 1834* gives name, age, residence in Ohio, and unit.[143] An older publication, *The Military History of Ohio*, includes rosters of soldiers arranged by counties.[144] The twelve-volume *Official Roster of the Soldiers of the State of Ohio in the War of the Rebellion, 1861-1866* is an important source for locating Ohioans who served in the Civil War, as well as the War with Mexico,

141. Marilyn Deputy, et al., comps., *Register of Federal United States Military Records*, 3 vols. (Bowie, Md.: Heritage Books, 1986). Many additional military records on microfilm have been acquired by the Family History Library since this register was published—refer to the Family History Library Catalog (www.familysearch.org). A typescript fourth volume is available at the Family History Library in Salt Lake City.

142. W. Louis Phillips, *Annotated Bibliography of Ohio Patriots: Revolutionary War and War of 1812* (Bowie, Md.: Heritage Books, 1985). Many of the sources cited in this annotated bibliography are not limited to Ohio but are national in scope.

143. Inez Waldenmaier, *Revolutionary War Pensioners Living in Ohio before 1834* (Tulsa, Okla.: The author, 1983). See also Daughters of the American Revolution of Ohio, *The Official Roster of the Soldiers of the American Revolution Buried in the State of Ohio* (Columbus, Ohio, 1929).

144. A. Parsons Stevens, *The Military History of Ohio* (New York: H.H. Hardesty, 1885-87). This work includes historical background, portraits, and lists of deceased soldiers.

1846-48.[145] Contents of these volumes include name, rank, age, date entered service, period of service, and remarks (date died, place died, whether killed or captured, date mustered out, service information, transfer to another military company, etc.).

Two official state publications, *The Official Roster of the Soldiers of the American Revolution Buried in the State of Ohio* and *Roster of Ohio Soldiers in the War of 1812*, should be consulted for the wars they cover.[146] Additionally, regimental and unit histories are available in major research libraries to help genealogists reconstruct the military activities of their ancestors; these are comparatively abundant for Ohio. Major military collections of published unit histories and similar sources are available at the Library of Congress, Ohio Historical Society, Family History Library in Salt Lake City, Western Reserve Historical Society Library in Cleveland, Ohio, and other major libraries with genealogical collections. The Ohio Genealogical Society in Mansfield, Ohio, has published military indexes and rosters of soldiers for various wars.

Mary L. Bowman's *Some Ohio Civil War Manuscripts: A Finding Tool* describes many Ohio Civil War manuscript collections housed in seventeen repositories, most notably the Ohio Historical Society.[147] This is a valuable reference tool for Civil War research. Some of the

---

145. *Official Roster of the Soldiers of the State of Ohio in the War of the Rebellion, 1861-1866*, 12 vols. (Akron and Norwalk, Ohio [publisher varied], 1886-95). Also available on microfiche at the Family History Library, Salt Lake City, Utah. Separate index by Jana Sloan Broglin, *Rosters of the Soldiers of Ohio in the War with Mexico* (OGS).

146. Adjutant General of Ohio, *The Official Roster of the Soldiers of the American Revolution Buried in the State of Ohio* (1929-59, reprint 2 vols. in 1; Mineral Ridge, Ohio: Trumbull County Chapter of the Ohio Genealogical Society, 1973), and Adjutant General of Ohio, *Roster of Ohio Soldiers in the War of 1812* (1916; reprinted, Baltimore: Genealogical Publishing Co., 1968), online at the Ohio Historical Society's Web site. See also Ohio Society, United States Daughters of 1812, *Index to the Grave Records of Servicemen of the War of 1812, State of Ohio*, edited by Phyllis Brown Miller (Huber Heights, Ohio: The Society, 1988).

147. Mary L. Bowman, comp., *Some Ohio Civil War Manuscripts: A Finding Tool* (Mansfield, Ohio: Ohio Genealogical Society, 1997).

collections are described in great detail, and there is a name and subject index. The Ohio Genealogical Society publishes Civil War articles in their quarterly, *Ohio Civil War Genealogy Journal.* This journal includes Civil War rosters, biographies, compiled genealogies, and similar material.

A selected list of useful Internet sites regarding the subject of Ohio military records includes the following:

Civil War Documents (Ohio Historical Society):
 (www.ohiohistory.org/resource/database/civilwar.html)
Civil War Rosters: Ohio:
 (www.geocities.com/Area51/Lair/3680/cw/cw-oh.html)
Ohio Genealogy Military Resource Center:
 (www.accessgenealogy.com/military/ohio)
Ohio in the Civil War:
 (www.ohiocivilwar.com)
Ohio Military Genealogy (OPLIN):
 (www.oplin.lib.oh.us/index.cfm?ID=3-56-1691)
Ohio Military Men, 1917-18:
 (www.ancestry.com/search/rectype/inddbs/4520.htm)
Ohio Military Records:
 (www.rootsweb.com/~usgenweb/oh/military/military.htm)
Ohio Society, War of 1812:
 (www.udata.com/users/hsbaker/ohio1812.htm)
Revolutionary War Pensioners Living in Ohio, 1818-19:
 (http://php.indiana.edu/~jetorres/ohiorev.html)
War of 1812, Roster of Ohio Soldiers (Ohio Historical Society):
 (www.ohiohistory.org/resource/database/rosters.html)

Naturalization Records

Ohio's naturalization records contain important information for locating immigrants, such as date of arrival in the United States. Later records show port of arrival and other valuable genealogical information. The declaration of intention and the petition for naturalization provide much of the information of interest to genealogists, although other naturalization records do exist, such as depositions and naturalization stubs. Before 1851, the Court of Common Pleas had jurisdiction over the naturalization process in the state.

Naturalization records dating after 1851 are available in the Probate Court in each county to 1906; federal District Court; regional network centers in Ohio; and the National Archives and Records Administration—Great Lakes Region, Chicago, Illinois; as well as in other repositories.[148] A useful but dated guide to naturalization records, with a section outlining Ohio's records, is James and Lila Neagle's *Locating Your Immigrant Ancestor.*[149] Also helpful is John J. Newman's *American Naturalization Records, 1790-1990: What They Are and How*

---

148. For a descriptive article, consult Peter Bunce, "National Archives—Chicago Branch," *National Genealogical Society Newsletter* 12 (July-August 1986): 85-87, which summarizes the holdings of this regional archives. Naturalization indexes are also available in this archives, along with other valuable genealogical and historical records. The holdings of other National Archives branches are described in various issues of the *National Genealogical Society Newsletter* (now *NGS Newsmagazine*), Loretto Dennis Szucs and Sandra Hargreaves Luebking, *The Archives: A Guide to the National Archives Field Branches* (Salt Lake City: Ancestry Publishing, 1988), and *Prologue: The Journal of the National Archives.* In addition to the National Archives Web site (www.archives.gov), also useful is National Archives and Records Administration, *Guide to Records in the National Archives—Great Lakes Region,* comp. by Glenn Longacre and Nancy Malan (Chicago: National Archives and Records Administration, 1996). Numerous naturalization and related immigration records and indexes are on microfilm at the Family History Library.

149. James C. and Lila Lee Neagles, *Locating Your Immigrant Ancestor: A Guide to Naturalization Records,* rev. ed. (Logan, Utah: Everton Publishers, 1986).

to Use Them, an illustrated guidebook useful to all American genealogists working with naturalization records.[150]

The largest collection of federal and local naturalization records
and immigration records in the United States is available on microfilm at
the Family History Library in Salt Lake City. Ohio records include those
from the United States District Court naturalization records and indexes
(northern and southern districts), county Probate Court naturalization
records and indexes, Court of Common Pleas records, Board of
Elections records, and records from other local courts.

Passport applications created by the United States Immigration and
Naturalization Service are another valuable source for locating Ohioans
and other Americans. Typically they show the name of the person, birth
date and birthplace, county of residence in Ohio (or elsewhere),
occupation, physical description of applicant, and sometimes other data
(more information is included in later records). Passport applications
and related indexes are available at the National Archives in
Washington, DC; they are on microfilm at the Family History Library in
Salt Lake City from 1795 to about 1925. Passport indexes may serve as
useful genealogical finding aids for those individuals who may have
traveled to Europe or other foreign countries.

---

150. John J. Newman, *American Naturalization Records, 1790-1990: What They
Are and How to Use Them* (Bountiful, Utah: Heritage Quest, 1998).

Newspapers

Newspapers often provide valuable genealogical information, including death notices and obituaries, marriage announcements, probate matters, local news items, divorce notices, biographical sketches, accounts of church activities, and other local events and activities. Sometimes birth notices are published as well. Vital record information was frequently published in newspapers after the Civil War period.

English and foreign language newspapers are available for an early period in Ohio. They were frequently published soon after a town was established and chronicle the local events in that locality.

The earliest newspaper in the Northwest Territory was published at Cincinnati in 1793, *The Centinel of the Northwestern Territory*, a decade before Ohio was admitted as a state. Soon, thereafter, other newspapers were published in the state: *Freeman's Journal* (1796-1799); *The Scioto Gazette* [Chillicothe, 1800]; *Chillicothe Supporter; Chillicothe Fredonian; The Western Spy and Hamilton Gazette*, often cited as *Western Spy* [Cincinnati, 1799]; *Cincinnati Liberty Hall; Zanesville Muskingum Messenger; Zanesville Express and Republican Standard; St. Clairsville Ohio Federalist; American Friend and Marietta Gazette; Chillicothe Independent Republican; Chillicothe Ohio Herald; Marietta Western Spectator;* and *The Ohio Gazette and Virginia Herald* [Marietta, Ohio, 1801], to name a few.[151]

Although several of Ohio's newspapers have been published continuously for over fifty years, most newspapers frequently changed names throughout their years of publication and many were published

---

151. Andrew R.L. Cayton, *The Frontier Republic: Ideology and Politics in the Ohio Country, 1780-1825* (Kent, Ohio: Kent State University Press, 1986), pp. 180-81; and Karen Mauer Green, *Pioneer Ohio Newspapers, 1793-1810: Genealogical and Historical Abstracts* (Galveston: Frontier Press, 1986), preface.

for only a short period of time.

The Ohio Historical Society in Columbus houses the largest collection of newspapers in the state, although many newspapers are also found at the Library of Congress, Washington, DC; Western Reserve Historical Society Library, Cleveland; public and academic libraries; local historical societies; local newspaper offices in the state, and other newspaper archives. Microfilm copies of newspapers are available through interlibrary loan from the Ohio Historical Society and other libraries. An online listing of Ohio newspapers is available, Ohio Newspaper Index (www.ohiohistory.org/resource/database/news.html). Newspapers on microfilm are frequently available for sale from historical societies or from other similar agencies.

Various finding aids exist which help locate both original and microfilm copies of newspapers. Of special interest is Stephen Gutgesell's *Guide to Ohio Newspapers, 1793-1973*, a union list of newspapers available in Ohio libraries.[152] Gutgesell's guide is a major reference source for identifying newspapers in the state. Researchers should also use the Internet to assist in locating newspaper holdings of libraries.

Newspaper holdings of some libraries are identified in regional guides. An example is Marilyn Levinson, ed., *Guide to Newspaper Holdings at the Center for Archival Collections*, 2nd edition.[153] Levinson's guide identifies northwest Ohio newspapers housed at Bowling Green State University, Bowling Green, Ohio. This center has

---

152. Stephen Gutgesell, ed., *Guide to Ohio Newspapers, 1793-1973* (Columbus: Ohio Historical Society, 1976). This important reference source describes the newspaper holdings of the OHS and other libraries in Ohio, although it is partially outdated. Also valuable is Gary Arnold's "Newspapers and Newspaper Indexes Available at Ohio Historical Society Archives-Library," *The Report* 26 (Spring 1986): 33. See the OHS Web site for an up-to-date listing of Ohio newspapers.

153. Marilyn Levinson, ed., *Guide to Newspaper Holdings at the Center for Archival Collections*, 2nd ed. (Bowling Green, Ohio: Center for Archival Collections, Bowling Green State University, 1987).

been collecting and microfilming newspapers in nineteen northwest Ohio counties. A comprehensive historical overview of Ohio's newspapers is Osman Hooper's *History of Ohio Journalism, 1793-1933*.[154] Hooper details the history of journalism in each Ohio county. *Gale Directory of Publications and Broadcast Media* identifies names and addresses of current newspapers in Ohio and elsewhere.[155]

Karen M. Green's *Pioneer Ohio Newspapers* consists of genealogical and historical abstracts from some of the earliest papers published in the state.[156] These abstracts chronicle the development of the Ohio country from frontier settlement to statehood. *Annals of Cleveland* are abstracts from nineteenth-century Cleveland, Ohio, newspapers that are available on microfiche or paper copies at many large libraries, including the Ohio Genealogical Society Library, Ohio Historical Society Library, and the Family History Library in Salt Lake City. These abstracts are indexed.[157] The *Cleveland Necrology File* is online (www.cpl.org).

Public libraries and historical societies in Ohio have valuable indexes to newspapers published in their respective localities, such as card indexes and newspaper abstracts. The Ohio Historical Society in Columbus houses the state's largest collection of newspapers and indexes to Ohio newspapers (www.ohiohistory.org). Newspaper clippings and abstracts are often available for Ohio researchers. An example is *Tri-State Obituaries: Indiana, Ohio, Michigan, 1964-1977,*

154. Osman Castle Hooper, *History of Ohio Journalism, 1793-1933* (Columbus: Spahr & Glenn Co., 1933).

155. *Gale Directory of Publications and Broadcast Media*, 136th ed., 2 vols. (Detroit: Gale Group, 2002). See volume 2 for a list of current Ohio newspapers. See also *Ohio News Media Directory* (Mount Dora, Fl.: News Media Directories).

156. Karen Mauer Green, *Pioneer Ohio Newspapers, 1793-1810: Genealogical and Historical Abstracts* (Galveston, Tex.: Frontier Press, 1986), and *Pioneer Ohio Newspapers, 1802-1818: Genealogical and Historical .Abstracts* (1988). Most of the abstracts pertain to southern Ohio counties; these volumes are indexed.

157. *Annals of Cleveland* (Cleveland: Bloch & Co., n.d.). Microfiche. Online (http://web.ulib.csuohio.edu/SpecColl/annals).

where obituaries are alphabetically arranged by surname.[158]

Newspaper genealogy columns usually include articles on resources and repositories, news of recent publications, local genealogical news, how to do research (methodology), and queries. A fine example of an Ohio genealogical newspaper column is Joy Wade Moulton's "Find Your Ancestors," published in *The Columbus Dispatch*, Columbus, Ohio, which began in February 1975, but has now been discontinued. Newspapers in several large and small Ohio cities are being scanned. Newspaper images are appearing more frequently on the Internet and some Web sites include Ohio newspapers and indexes. See, for example:

- Ancestry Historical Newspapers:
  (www.ancestry.com)
- Historical Newspapers Online:
  (http://historynews.chadwyck.com/home/home.cgi?source=config2.cfg)
- Internet Public Library:
  (www.ipl.org/div/news)
- News and Newspapers Online:
  (http://library.uncg.edu/news)
- Newspaper Archive.com, Heritage Microfilm:
  (www.newspaperarchive.com)
- Newspaper Links:
  (www.newspaperlinks.com/home.cfm)
- Newspapers.com:
  (www.newspapers.com)

---

158. *Tri-State Obituaries: Indiana, Ohio, Michigan, 1964-1977*, 6 vols. (Fort Wayne, Ind.: Allen County Public Library, 1975-78). Indexed. Typescript.

- Ohio Newspaper Index (Ohio Historical Society):
  (www.ohiohistory.org/resource/database/news.html)
- Ohio Newspapers:
  (www.n-net.com/oh.htm)
- Online Newspapers:
  (www.maxpages.com/genhome/Online_Newspapers)
- Ohio Obituary Links:
  (www.obitlinkspage.com/obit/oh.htm)
- onlinenewspapers.com:
  (http://www.onlinenewspapers.com)

Patriotic and Lineage Societies

First Families of Ohio (FFO) was founded in 1964 by the Ohio Genealogical Society to identify and honor Ohio's earliest pioneers. OGS members may submit an application for membership in this lineage society if they qualify and wish to do so. Contact OGS for a list of requirements to join FFO. One of the major ancestral finding aids for the state is *First Families of Ohio Roster, 1964-2000,* which is alphabetically arranged by surname of the ancestor and cross-indexed by name of OGS member.[159] Genealogical information is also shown in this resource. *OGS Lineage Societies* online (www.ogs.org/lineage.htm).

The Ohio Genealogical Society also publishes "Society of Civil War Families of Ohio" rosters in the *Ohio Genealogical Society Quarterly* (formerly *The Report*)—see, for example, Summer 2002, 42:57-59 and other issues of *The Report* (now *Ohio Genealogical Society Quarterly*).This society is open to OGS members who descend from a person who served in the Civil War and either served in an Ohio unit or lived or died in Ohio. A monumental genealogical reference source for Ohio was compiled by the Ohio Society, Colonial Dames XVII Century, *Our Ancestors' Families.*[160] This indexed work has 1,034 pages and contains members' family group records. Some documentation is included. Another useful work (though incomplete) is *Society of Mayflower Descendants in the State of Ohio* (Cincinnati, 1931)—this resource includes lists of *Mayflower* descendants in Ohio.

---

159. Ohio Genealogical Society, *First Families of Ohio Roster, 1964-2000,* edited by Sunda Anderson Peters and Kay Ballantyne Hudson (Mansfield, Ohio: Ohio Genealogical Society, 2001). See also Amy Johnson Crow, "First Families of Ohio Roster, 2001-2002," *The Report* 42 (Summer 2002): 64-71, Jocelyn Fox Wilms, "The Society of Civil War Families of Ohio," *The Report* 42 (Summer 2002): 57-59 and other issues of *The Report* (now *Ohio Genealogical Society Quarterly*).

160. Ohio Society, Colonial Dames XVII Century, *Our Ancestors' Families* (n.p., 1987).

Periodicals

The state's premier genealogical periodical, *Ohio Genealogical Society Quarterly* (formerly *The Report*), is published quarterly by the Ohio Genealogical Society (OGS) in Mansfield, Ohio.[161] Published in this periodical are transcriptions of many Ohio source records, vital records, family Bible records, compiled genealogies, biographies, ancestor charts, names of Ohioans who resided in other states, research methodology, book notices, and advertisements. OGS also publishes *OGS Genealogy News* (formerly *The Ohio Genealogical Society Newsletter*), containing OGS chapter activities, a calendar of events, publication notices, information on seminars and workshops, research helps, computer news, recent OGS library acquisitions, queries, advertisements, and other news items of interest to Ohio genealogists. These publications include annual surname indexes. *Ohio Civil War Genealogy Journal,* published by the Ohio Genealogical Society, includes Civil War-related articles for the state.

Other periodicals, with similar material, have been and are being published throughout the state. *Ohio Records and Pioneer Families* (ORPF), a valuable companion to *The Report*, was begun in 1960 as a private publication but is now published quarterly by the Ohio Genealogical Society and is available by subscription only. Some back

---

161. The Ohio Genealogical Society is the largest state genealogical organization in America. In addition to its quarterly periodical, *Ohio Genealogical Society Quarterly* (formerly *The Report*) and *OGS Genealogy News*, the society publishes a directory of its chapters. Students of Ohio genealogy may also be interested in the lecture tapes of the 1986 National Genealogical Society Conference, held in Columbus and locally hosted by OGS. Numerous lectures on the program focused upon Ohio resources and research problems. NGS conference tapes for 1986 are available from Triad, P.O. Box 120, Toulon, IL 61483. Lecturers at NGS and other similar national conferences have also discussed genealogical research in Ohio and the Northwest Territory. Contact Repeat Performance, 2911 Crabapple Lane, Hobart, IN 46342, for a catalog. OGS publishes the syllabi of its annual convention and makes them available for sale.

issues are available from OGS. This periodical includes source material for many Ohio counties, information on pioneer families, Ohio vital records (births, marriages, and deaths), gravestone inscriptions, military records, deed abstracts, biographies, newspaper abstracts, register of physicians, prison records, lists of Ohioans in other states, tax lists, mortality schedules (1850-80), court records, family Bible records, queries, and much more. Each volume has an annual surname index, and there are published cumulative indexes, 1985-94 and 1960-84.

Gateway to the West: Ohio, privately published from 1968 to 1978 and reprinted in two volumes, is also a significant source for Ohio research. *The Firelands Pioneer*, begun in 1858 and published by the Firelands Historical Society in Norwalk, Ohio, is invaluable for north central Ohio counties (but it has publishing gaps). *The "Old Northwest" Genealogical Quarterly*, published from 1898 to 1912, is an important source not to be bypassed. Even though selected abstracts from this periodical have been published in book form, there remain many significant articles that have not been reprinted. County and local genealogical organizations, especially OGS chapters and local historical societies, publish a wealth of information in their newsletters and periodicals and as separate publications.

Other genealogical periodicals published outside the state occasionally include valuable source materials and compiled genealogies of Ohio families, principally *The American Genealogist, The Detroit Society for Genealogical Research Magazine,* and the *National Genealogical Society Quarterly*, among others. Many of the articles in the major periodicals and newsletters that publish Ohio articles are conveniently indexed in Carol Bell's *Ohio Genealogical Periodical Index: A County Guide*, which is expanded further by *Periodical Source*

Index (PERSI).[162] The Ohio locality section in PERSI is arranged by record type (biography, census, history, military, etc.) and thereunder alphabetically by counties, Adams through Wyandot. Surnames are arranged alphabetically under Family Records. PERSI is available on compact disc (CD-ROM) from Ancestry.com, and on the Internet for Ancestry.com subscribers (www.ancestry.com).

Ohio History, published by the Ohio Historical Society, contains articles and reviews on the political, social, economic, and cultural history of Ohio and the Midwest that especially interest Ohio genealogists. This scholarly historical journal is available online at the OHS Web site and it is indexed (www.ohiohistory.org). *Ohio Queries* may also contain genealogical information of interest to researchers.[163] Genealogical Publishing Company in Baltimore, Maryland, has published a trio of useful collections drawn from genealogical periodicals of Ohio. Marriages and cemetery records from *The "Old Northwest" Genealogical Quarterly* have been consolidated into two series.[164]

Genealogical Publishing Company's third series, *Ohio Source Records*, is composed of articles reprinted from *The Ohio Genealogical Quarterly*, a publication begun in 1937 by the Columbus Genealogical Society and discontinued in 1944.[165] This significant reference work

---

162. Carol Willsey Bell, *Ohio Genealogical Periodical Index: A County Guide*, 6th ed. (Youngstown, Ohio: Bell Books, 1987). Bell's index has largely been replaced by *Periodical Source Index* (PERSI), published by Allen County Public Library Foundation, P.O. Box 2270, Fort Wayne, IN 46801-2270. PERSI consists of a retrospective index, 1847-1985, and annual indexes since 1985.

163. *Ohio Queries*, Pioneer Publication, P.O. Box 130, Elk, WA 99009.

164. Smith, *Ohio Marriages and Ohio Cemetery Records Extracted from The "Old Northwest" Genealogical Quarterly.*

165. *Ohio Source Records from the Ohio Genealogical Quarterly* (Baltimore: Genealogical Publishing Co., 1986). This title is a significant contribution to Ohio genealogy. It includes a detailed every-name index, although the 1810 Ohio tax list is not indexed here (pp. 101-159). Reprinted from the *Ohio Genealogical Quarterly*, with added notes and index.

includes articles that focus primarily on Franklin County and other central Ohio counties. It includes marriages, will abstracts, Ohio local history, newspaper abstracts, tax lists, gravestone inscriptions, Bible records, and some compiled genealogies.

The Ohio Genealogical Society Periodicals Index: Topical by Location, 1960-2000, published by the Ohio Genealogical Society and compiled by Susan Dunlap Lee, is a subject index to genealogical periodicals published by OGS.[166] It is arranged by localities and surnames, such as family names and names of pensioners. The preface includes a brief history of OGS periodical publications. The volume concludes with an every-name index to this valuable reference book.

Periodicals published by the Ohio Genealogical Society include many methodology ("how-to") articles, family genealogies, Civil War articles, family Bible records, local Ohio records, ancestor charts, and much more. *The Ohio Genealogical Society Periodicals Index: Topical by Location, 1960-2000,* is the first place to search for this type of published material.

---

166. Ohio Genealogical Society, *The Ohio Genealogical Society Periodicals Index: Topical by Location, 1960-2000*, compiled by Susan Dunlap Lee (Mansfield, Ohio: The Society, 2002). Consult also Susan Dunlap Lee, *Ohio Records & Pioneer Families Ten Year Surname Index, 1985-1994* and 1960-1984 (Mansfield, Ohio: The Society).

Probate Records

Ohio's county level Probate Court, created in 1852, took the responsibility of probate matters from the Common Pleas Court. Here the genealogist will find records relating to the estates of deceased individuals, wills, administrations, and guardianships of minors and other dependants. All such probate records are valuable for determining names of family members, relationships, residences, dates of deaths, and other genealogical information; most records date from the origin each county was created.

Although some genealogists are prone to look only for a will copied in a will book, it is always advisable to locate the estate file (sometimes known as the probate packet or case file), carefully studying all documents created by or for the deceased ancestor. Probate files include not only original wills, but also other original probate documents, settlement papers, inventories, receipts, correspondence, newspaper clippings, and other similar records. Auxiliary probate documents may be useful in learning more about an ancestor and in providing background information for writing a family history. Equally important is the possibility that relationships that cannot be gleaned from a will may be stated or implied in these probate papers, and such documents normally exist whether or not a will was ever drafted. Guardianship records likewise may identify names of minors, and other family members and may be included with probate documents.

Wills and related probate records, guardianship records, and probate indexes may be found in the Probate Court office or record room within each county courthouse, or in the appropriate Ohio Network of American History Research Centers (consult the map at the end of this volume). Many probate records are on microfilm at the Ohio Historical Society and the Family History Library in Salt Lake City,

Utah—these records include will record books, administrations, inventories, dockets, probate journals, and indexes to probate records. For most Ohio counties, probate estate files (probate packets) have not been microfilmed but are generally available for researchers to use in local repositories, such as the county courthouse or a courthouse annex.

Two indispensable guides exist for using Probate Court records in the state. Carol Willsey Bell's overview of research in probate records is found in an article in *The Report*.[167] Carol Willsey Bell's *Ohio Wills and Estates to 1850: An Index* is a splendid compilation that should be available in major research libraries with a genealogical collection.[168] This probate index is one of the major pre-1850 genealogical research aids for the state and may assist in locating ancestors who died in Ohio or who left a probate record there. A valuable Ohio township and county outline map is included at the beginning of this volume. Many OGS volunteers assisted Carol Bell in indexing probate records in Ohio's eighty-eight counties.

---

167. Carol Willsey Bell, "What to Look for When Searching in the Courthouse: Probate Court," *The Report* 13 (Winter 1973): 170-74. Carol Bell has written several other useful articles in *The Report* describing Ohio genealogical sources.

168. Carol Willsey Bell, *Ohio Wills and Estates to 1850: An Index* (Youngstown, Ohio: Bell Books, 1981). This volume is the culmination of a ten-year project to provide a comprehensive index to Ohio probate records. A summary of genealogical sources used for each county is included. In addition, this work is useful in identifying which counties had courthouse fires (and the year of the courthouse fire) and which records were destroyed. *Ohio Wills and Estates to 1850: An Index* is a significant reference source for Ohio genealogists, historians, and reference librarians.

School Records

School records and enumeration returns of school-age children are available for some Ohio localities; some records begin during the early nineteenth century. Records show names of children in school, mostly from age six to twenty-one years of age, name of township and school district, age, sex, and sometimes name of parent or names of both parents. School records before 1850 are particularly useful since they may show names of children listed with their parent(s); if so, they can serve as a substitute for the lack of pre-1850 census data. Records have not been kept uniformly. Some school census records are also available. Records of less value genealogically, but important historically, include school board minutes, financial records, and attendance lists.

School records of genealogical value may be found at local public libraries, college and university libraries, historical societies, and some are on microfilm at the Family History Library. Original school records are usually not indexed; however, some early records have been published. Records of colleges and universities are also valuable, such as published school histories, yearbooks, directories, biographies, and records of alumni associations and members.

A major reference source for school records is *The Ohio Municipal, Township, and School Board Roster*.[169] An early illustrated history of schools in Ohio, school records, and school statistics is *Historical Sketches of Public Schools in Cities, Villages, and Townships of the State of Ohio*.[170]

---

169. *The Ohio Municipal, Township, and School Board Roster* (Columbus: Ohio Secretary of State, 1994-95).

170. Ohio, State Centennial Educational Committee, *Historical Sketches of Public Schools in Cities, Villages, and Townships of the State of Ohio* (n.p., 1876).

Tax Records

Often known as tax duplicates, or Auditor's duplicate of tax assessments (tax inventory books), Ohio tax records begin as early as 1800. Used as a substitute census, they may help determine place of residence and dates of migration into and out of a specific locale. Used more expertly, they often provide clues to relationships, ages, and origins.

In general, tax records include resident and nonresident owners, delinquent tax properties, and personal property listings, inheritance tax duplicates, tax lists, incorporated companies, and others. Early records are usually arranged by township and then by first letter of the surname, making them relatively easy to search. Many early Ohio tax records have been microfilmed.

Original pre-1850 (mostly pre-1838) tax records are available at county courthouses in the County Auditor's Office, the Ohio Historical Society Library, regional network centers, and various other libraries in the state. The Ohio Historical Society houses the Auditor of State's tax duplicates, 1800-1838.

Some tax records for early years have been abstracted (more or less completely) and published with indexes. Esther W. Powell's *Early Ohio Tax Records* is a transcription of many original tax lists found at the Ohio Historical Society and covers the years 1800 to 1840.[171] Powell's work is a valuable reference for locating names of early Ohio residents.

A large collection of Ohio tax records is also available on

---

171. Esther Weygandt Powell, comp., *Early Ohio Tax Records* (1971; reprint, Baltimore: Genealogical Publishing Co., 1985). This important Ohio reference source was reprinted with *The Index to Early Ohio Tax Records*, which is a surname index only. Unfortunately, this work does not contain a complete personal name index. See also the indexes to Ohio tax duplicates compiled by Gerald McKinney Petty for 1810, 1812, 1825, and 1835.

microfilm at the Family History Library. City and county directories may also be useful in locating residents in a particular locality. Another useful reference and personal name finding aid is *The 1812 Census of Ohio: A Statewide Index of Taxpayers,* which shows a person's name and residence.[172] Gerald M. Petty compiled indexes to Ohio tax duplicates for the years 1810, 1812, 1825, and 1835.[173]

---

172. *The 1812 Census of Ohio: A Statewide Index of Taxpayers* (Miami Beach, Florida: T.L.C. Genealogy, 1992).

173. Gerald McKinney Petty (Columbus: Petty's Press, 1973,1976,1981,1987). See also "An Act Levying a Tax on Land," *Laws of Ohio,* vol. 8, pp. 315-42, 19 Feb. 1810.

Township Records

Genealogists sometimes overlook township records in their Ohio research. These records may prove valuable, especially with difficult pre-1850 Ohio pedigree problems. A variety of records are found therein—minutes of meetings, lists of early township residents; names of trustees and officers; descriptions of property; and sometimes cemetery records, records of deaths, clues to relationships, ages, previous place of residence, and other information.

As with many New England town records, the researcher may find *warnings out* recorded in some Ohio township records.[174] The author of this book has solved several difficult early Ohio pedigree problems by using township records.[175] Several articles in *The Report* have noted the merits of using township records in Ohio research.[176] Township records may be found in the custody of township trustees, Ohio regional network centers, public and other local libraries, historical societies, and some are on microfilm at the Family History Library in Salt Lake City, Utah.

---

174. Warnings out is a situation that may be unfamiliar to some researchers. A custom from colonial New England, "warnings out" occurred when indigent persons or families arriving in a region, had no means of support, and promised to become an economic burden upon the community. Suspected individuals or families would be brought to the attention of the town or township authorities; if the community's concern appeared justified, the governing body would rule that the unwelcome family had to move out of its jurisdiction by a specified date or face the penalties prescribed by law. Thus they were "warned out" of the Ohio township. A useful reference is Josiah Henry Benton, *Warning Out in New England, 1656-1817* (1911; reprint. Freeport, N.Y.: Books for Libraries Press, 1970).

175. See, for example, Kip Sperry, "The Morse Family of the Western Reserve in Ohio," *The American Genealogist* 60 (Oct 1984): 205-12. Ohio sources for genealogists are described in Kip Sperry, "Finding Tools for Ohio Research," *Genealogical Journal* 1 (December 1972): 122-25; and "Genealogical Research in Ohio," *National Genealogical Society Quarterly* 75 (June 1987): 81-104.

176. Diane V. Gagel, "Township Records," *The Report* 25 (Summer 1985): 83, is an example.

Vital Records

Vital record information (births, marriages, and deaths) may be found in civil government records (often known as vital statistics or civil vital records), church records, military records (service and pension files), Daughters of the American Revolution (DAR) transcriptions, family Bibles, home sources, and elsewhere. Most Ohio vital records begin at various times during the nineteenth century. Birth and death records, divorce records, and marriage records are described in greater detail in separate sections earlier in this book. Be sure to contact the county where the event occurred for the full record.

Recording of civil birth records in Ohio began in the counties in 1867, but births in some counties were recorded earlier during the period 1856-57. Prior to 20 December 1908, births are available from the Probate Court of the county where the birth occurred. The Ohio Department of Health (Vital Statistics Office) in Columbus has birth records of people born in Ohio since 20 December 1908 to the present, records for deaths that occurred in Ohio from 1 January 1945 to the present, and marriage abstracts since 7 September 1949 to the present. Births after 20 December 1908 are also recorded with the Local Registrar of Vital Statistics or County Health Department where the birth occurred. Most government offices respond to mail requests for vital records.

Recording of civil death records in Ohio began in the counties in 1867, but a few were recorded earlier during the period 1856-57. Deaths prior to 20 December 1908 are recorded in the Probate Court of the county where the death occurred. Death records from 20 December 1908 through December 1944 are available at the Ohio Historical Society in Columbus and the Local Registrar in each county. See especially the Ohio Historical Society database, Ohio Death Certificate

Index, 1913-37 (www.ohiohistory.org/dindex). Death records from 1 January 1945 to the present are available from the Ohio Department of Health (Vital Statistics Office) in Columbus for people who died in Ohio.

Ohio death indexes and death records for recent years are on microfilm at the Family History Library in Salt Lake City. See the Family History Library Catalog under the heading "Ohio—Vital records" and "Ohio—Vital records—Indexes." Two example collections are:

Ohio. Department of Health. *Death Index, 1908-1944*. Microfilm

Ohio. Department of Health. *Certificates of Death, 1908-1944*. Microfilm.

Although recording of early marriages in the Buckeye State began with the origin of each county, the Ohio Department of Health in Columbus has Ohio marriage records and divorce records since 7 September 1949. They do not issue certified copies of these records, however. To obtain a certified copy of a marriage record, researchers should write to the Probate Court of the county where the marriage license was issued, or the Court of Common Pleas where the divorce was granted. The address of the Ohio Department of Health is:

Ohio Department of Health
Vital Statistics
P.O. Box 15098
Columbus, OH 43215-0098

The Department's telephone number is (614) 466-2531. Interested parties may write them a letter, or vital record application forms are available upon request or in Tom Kemp's vital record handbook. See *Vital Records Information, Ohio*, on the Internet (www.vitalrec.com/oh.html).

Consult also (www.odh.state.oh.us/Birth/vitalrec.htm) and Ohio Department of Health (www.odh.state.oh.us).

Sometimes vital record data may be difficult to locate—records have been destroyed, information may be missing in the records, or data may be difficult to read because of the handwriting, an ink spot, part of the record has been damaged or destroyed, or for other reasons. Substitute records for missing or incomplete Ohio civil vital records (births, marriages, and deaths) may include some of the sources on the list at the end of this section. Information in these records varies, and the reliability of the records vary since some are compiled sources while others are original records. Original records are always the best source to use for genealogical and historical research.

Many early Ohio vital records are available on compact disc (CD-ROM). Example records include:

Early Ohio Settlers, 1700s-1900s, CD-ROM (Family Tree Maker)
    Indexes some 165,000 individuals from vital and other records.

Ohio Vital Records #1, 1790s-1870s, CD-ROM (Family Tree Maker)

Ohio Vital Records #2, 1750s-1880s, CD-ROM (Family Tree Maker)

The records listed in the next section may be available in county courthouses, regional network centers in Ohio, genealogical and historical societies, public and university libraries, county archives, and so forth. Many of the sources described in this list are housed at the Ohio Historical Society, State Library of Ohio; many are on microfilm at the Family History Library in Salt Lake City, Utah, and they may be found at other libraries or archives housing Ohio records.

A vital records register (list of call numbers) is available at the Family History Library, which gives Family History Library microfilm and microfiche numbers.[177]

---

177. U.S./Canada Staff, *Register of Vital Records at the FHL & Other Repositories: U.S./Canada* (Salt Lake City: Family History Library, 2001). Thomas Jay Kemp's *International Vital Records Handbook*, 4th ed. (Baltimore: Genealogical Publishing Co., 2000) includes vital record application forms that may be useful in obtaining copies of civil vital records.

Substitutes for Missing or Incomplete Civil Vital Records Information in Ohio

Ancestor Card File (Ohio Genealogical Society card file)

Ancestral Charts (Ohio Genealogical Society)

Ancestral File (FamilySearch™) (www.familysearch.org)

Bibles (family Bibles and family records found in family and home sources, genealogical libraries, historical societies, etc.)

Bible records (Ohio Genealogical Society)

Biographies (biographical sketches, compiled biographies)

Biographical encyclopedias

Bounty land applications (federal land records)

Bureau of Land Management records (www.glorecords.blm.gov)

Business records (employment and social/commercial records)

Canadian Border Crossings, 1895-1924

Cemetery records, burial records, gravestones

Census records (federal population census schedules): 1850, 1860, 1870, 1880, 1900, 1910, 1920, 1930 (microfilm and Internet)

Century home records (biographical sketches of home owners maintained at some local historical societies)

Church histories (histories of individual congregations)

Church newspaper notices (births, marriages, deaths) and biographical sketches in newspapers

Church records (baptisms or christenings, marriages, and deaths or burials; membership records; and other church records)

Computer databases (Internet and compact discs). For example:

County and Family Histories: Ohio, 1780-1970

Early Ohio Settlers, 1700s-1900s

Marriage Index: Ohio, 1789-1850

Coroner's records, coroner's docket

Correspondence, family letters, manuscript genealogies

Court records (civil cases, divorce, Chancery, name changes, others)

Daughters of the American Revolution (DAR) transcriptions—family Bible records, vital records, genealogies, cemetery records, probate abstracts, newspaper clippings, and other records

Delayed and corrected registration of births

Diaries and journals (autobiographies)

Directories: city directories for large cities, and rural directories

Divorce records and divorce case files (see especially, Carol Bell, *Ohio Divorces: The Early Years*)

Drivers licenses

Employment records

Family Group Records Collection (Family History Library)

Family records and home sources, personal papers, scrap books, baby books, and similar family records described in this volume

First Families of Ohio (FFO) rosters (Ohio Genealogical Society)

Fraternal society records (association, lodge, membership records)

Funeral home records and mortuary records

Genealogies (compiled family histories)

Grave Registrations of Soldiers Buried in Ohio (Ohio Historical Society)

Gravestones (tombstone inscriptions)

Guardianship records

Hospital records

Immigration records (passenger arrival lists)

Institutional records (correctional, prison, or jail records)

Insurance records

International Genealogical Index—IGI. FamilySearch™, on the Internet (www.familysearch.org) and an older version on compact disc

Internet sites containing vital records, Ohio genealogical indexes, compiled genealogies, and other genealogical sources

Land records (bounty land records, homestead records and other federal
    land records, state and local land records)
Local histories (especially biographical sketches in county histories)
Manuscript collections (genealogical collections, pedigree charts, family
    group records, correspondence, journals, account books, others)
Marriage banns or intentions to marry
Marriage certificates
Marriage consents of minors by parents
Marriage license applications
Marriage returns and marriage registers
Medical certificates
Military Index—Vietnam and Korean conflicts (FamilySearch™)
Military records (service records, compiled service records, pension
    applications and records, military draft registrations, and others)
Military rosters, unit histories, regimental histories, published military
    pension lists, descriptive rolls, muster-in rolls, and others
Ministers' license records of marriages
Minority records, ethnic archives, histories, ethnic newspapers
Mortality schedules (lists of deaths): 1850, Ohio counties H- W;
    1860 (all Ohio counties); 1870 (incomplete); 1880 (counties
    Adams through Geauga, Ohio)
Mortuary files
Naturalization and citizenship records: applications, petitions, oaths,
    declaration of intention for citizenship, naturalization journals,
    certificate of arrival, final papers
Newspapers (birth, marriage, death, and divorce notices; obituaries;
    biographies; local history sketches; pioneer sketches)
Ohio Death Certificate Index, 1913-37 (www.ohiohistory.org/dindex)
Ohio Historical Society Surname Index (card index on microfilm)
Ohio Marriages, 1803-1900 (www.ancestry.com)
Ohio Veteran's Home death records

Passport applications (available at the National Archives and on microfilm at FHL; indexed), 1795 to ca. 1925

Patriotic and lineage society records (application papers and published biographies); hereditary society records

Pedigree Resource File (PRF), index at (www.familysearch.org)—genealogical data on compact discs (CD-ROM); many submissions include notes and sources

Periodicals and journal articles (genealogical and historical serials)
See *Periodical Source Index* (PERSI) and *Genealogical Periodical Annual Index* (GPAI) for periodical indexes.

Police records

Prisoner of war records (such as the Civil War, and other wars)

Probate records (wills, letters of administration, distribution and settlement of estates, probate estate files)

Railroad retirement records

Revolutionary War Pension/Bounty Land Warrant Application Files

School records (school and college records)

Sextons' records

Social Security Death Index
(www.familysearch.org) (www.ancestry.com) other Internet sites

Social Security Administration records

Society of Civil War Families of Ohio application files

Soldiers' home records

Veterans' records and grave reports, records of veterans' organizations

Vital records (state, county, and city or town vital records)

World War I Draft Registration Cards, 1917-1918

Conclusion

Many original records, compiled sources, and indexes are available for Ohio genealogists, both in Ohio and in other states. Many Ohio records are available on the Internet and on compact discs (CD-ROM). County and local sources, such as indexes to land, probate, court, tax, and other local records, are also valuable research finding aids. Some of the major personal name finding aids for genealogical research in Ohio are listed below:

Accelerated Indexing Systems (AIS) census indexes:
   microfiche and the Internet (www.ancestry.com)
Alphabetical Index to Official Roster of the Soldiers of the State of Ohio in the War of the Rebellion (WPA)
Ancestor Card File (Ohio Genealogical Society card file)
Ancestral Charts (Ohio Genealogical Society)
Ancestral File (database in FamilySearch™ and on the Internet):
   (www.familysearch.org)
Bible records (Ohio Genealogical Society)
Census indexes—statewide census indexes for the years
   1820, 1830, 1840, 1850, 1860, 1870, 1880, 1900, 1910, 1920
   (published, compact disc, microfiche, and Internet)
Census indexes on the Internet and compact disc (CD-ROM)
Census indexes for individual counties and cities
Census Soundex indexes, 1880, 1900, 1910, and 1920 indexes
1880 Ohio Census Index (FHL 1880 census and national index on CD-ROM, published book index, and Automated Archives CD-ROM). 1880 census online (www.familysearch.org).
Directories—city directories and rural directories
Early Ohio Settlers, 1700s-1900s, CD-ROM (Family Tree Maker)
Early Ohio Tax Records (Esther Weygandt Powell)

First Families of Ohio Roster, 1964-2000
Gateway to the West, 2 vols. (Ruth Bowers and Anita Short)
Genealogical Periodical Annual Index (GPAI)
General Land Office (BLM)—Ohio compact disc (federal land records)
    and on the Internet (www.glorecords.blm.gov)
Grave Registrations of Soldiers Buried in Ohio (OHS)
Index to Compiled Service Records of Volunteer Union Soldiers
    Who Served in Organizations from the State of Ohio
Index to Ohio death certificates (1908-44, microfilmed)
International Genealogical Index (IGI), database in FamilySearch™
    available on the Internet (www.familysearch.org)
Marriage Index: Selected Counties of Ohio, 1789-1850 (compact disc)
Mortality schedule indexes, 1850, 1860, 1870, 1880
Ohio Cemetery Records
Ohio County History Surname Index—Ohio Surname Index
    (card index at OHS and on microfilm)
Ohio Death Certificate Index, 1913-37 (www.ohiohistory.org/dindex)
Ohio Genealogical Periodical Index: A County Guide (Carol Willsey
    Bell)
*Ohio Marriages Extracted from the Old Northwest Genealogical
    Quarterly* (Marjorie Smith)
Ohio Marriages Recorded in County Courts through 1820: An Index
Ohio Source Records from the Ohio Genealogical Quarterly
Ohio Wills and Estates to 1850: An Index (Carol Willsey Bell)
Periodical Source Index (Allen County Public Library) available on
    compact disc (CD-ROM), printed volumes, microfiche, and the
    Internet (www.ancestry.com)
Public Library of Cincinnati and Hamilton County, Cincinnati, Ohio:
    Family Surname (genealogy file) online using CINCH
    (www.plch.lib.oh.us)
Tax record indexes

As has been shown in this book, many resources are available that will help genealogists locate their ancestors in Ohio, extend pedigrees, and write family histories and compiled genealogies. In addition to the traditional sources more commonly used by genealogists (i.e., census population schedules, vital records, church records, land and military records, city directories, local histories, probate records, and so forth), many other records, either published, on microfilm or microfiche, compact disc (CD-ROM), or computer databases and the Internet, are readily available for genealogical and family history research in this state. Sources cited in the footnotes and bibliographies at the end of this volume will guide the researcher to many of these titles and Web sites.

Genealogists are strongly encouraged to do original research, thoroughly document their findings, and share their research with others through publishing and by other means.[178] In this way, Ohio genealogical scholarship will continue to progress. The abundant genealogical records of the Buckeye State await discovery, critical evaluation, publication, creation of more personal name indexes and genealogical finding aids, and placing digitized records and indexes on the Internet. [179]

---

178. A valuable genealogical style guide is Henry B. Hoff, ed., *Genealogical Writing in the 21st Century: A Guide to Register Style and More* (Boston: New England Historic Genealogical Society, 2002). Other style guides are also available.

179. Several valuable references are Elizabeth Shown Mills, ed., *Professional Genealogy: A Manual for Researchers, Writers, Editors, Lecturers, and Librarians* (Baltimore: Genealogical Publishing Co., 2001); Elizabeth Shown Mills, *Evidence! Citation and Analysis for the Family Historian* (Baltimore: Genealogical Publishing Co.,1997); Eugene A. Stratton, "The Validity of Genealogical Evidence," *National Genealogical Society Quarterly* 72 (December 1984): 273-87; and various issues of *Association of Professional Genealogists Quarterly* (Association of Professional Genealogists, P.O. Box 350998, Westminster, CO 80035-0998 (www.apgen.org). The Board for Certification of Genealogists publishes "skill building" articles online from the BCG educational newsletter, *OnBoard* (www.bcgcertification.org). *Cyndi's List of Genealogy Sites on the Internet* identifies many online genealogy resources of interest to Ohio genealogists and others (www.cyndislist.com).

OHIO COUNTIES

COUNTY	YEAR EST.	COUNTY SEAT	REGIONAL CENTER
Adams	1797	West Union	UC
Allen	1820	Lima	BGSU
Ashland	1846	Ashland	UA
Ashtabula	1808	Jefferson	WRHS
Athens	1805	Athens	OU
Auglaize	1848	Wapakoneta	WSU
Belmont	1801	St. Clairsville	OU
Brown	1818	Georgetown	UC
Butler	1803	Hamilton	UC
Carroll	1833	Carrollton	Y
Champaign	1805	Urbana	WSU
Clark	1818	Springfield	WSU
Clermont	1800	Batavia	UC
Clinton	1810	Wilmington	UC
Columbiana	1803	Lisbon	Y
Coshocton	1810	Coshocton	UA
Crawford	1820	Bucyrus	BGSU
Cuyahoga	1808	Cleveland	WRHS
Darke	1809	Greenville	WSU
Defiance	1845	Defiance	BGSU
Delaware	1808	Delaware	OHS
Erie	1838	Sandusky	BGSU
Fairfield	1800	Lancaster	OHS
Fayette	1810	Washington C.H.	OHS

COUNTY	YEAR EST.	COUNTY SEAT	REGIONAL CENTER
Franklin	1803	Columbus	OHS
Fulton	1850	Wauseon	BGSU
Gallia	1803	Gallipolis	OU
Geauga	1806	Chardon	WRHS
Greene	1803	Xenia	WSU
Guernsey	1810	Cambridge	OU
Hamilton	1790	Cincinnati	UC
Hancock	1820	Findlay	BGSU
Hardin	1820	Kenton	BGSU
Harrison	1813	Cadiz	Y
Henry	1820	Napoleon	BGSU
Highland	1805	Hillsboro	UC
Hocking	1818	Logan	OU
Holmes	1824	Millersburg	UA
Huron	1809	Norwalk	BGSU
Jackson	1816	Jackson	OU
Jefferson	1797	Steubenville	Y
Knox	1808	Mt. Vernon	OHS
Lake	1840	Painesville	WRHS
Lawrence	1815	Ironton	OU
Licking	1808	Newark	OHS
Logan	1818	Bellefontaine	WSU
Lorain	1822	Elyria	WRHS
Lucas	1835	Toledo	BGSU
Madison	1810	London	OHS
Mahoning	1846	Youngstown	Y
Marion	1820	Marion	OHS

COUNTY	YEAR EST.	COUNTY SEAT	REGIONAL CENTER
Medina	1812	Medina	WRHS
Meigs	1819	Pomeroy	OU
Mercer	1820	Celina	WSU
Miami	1807	Troy	WSU
Monroe	1813	Woodsfield	OU
Montgomery	1803	Dayton	WSU
Morgan	1817	McConnelsville	OU
Morrow	1848	Mt. Gilead	OHS
Muskingum	1804	Zanesville	OU
Noble	1851	Caldwell	OU
Ottawa	1840	Port Clinton	BGSU
Paulding	1820	Paulding	BGSU
Perry	1818	New Lexington	OU
Pickaway	1810	Circleville	OHS
Pike	1815	Waverly	OU
Portage	1808	Ravenna	UA
Preble	1808	Eaton	WSU
Putnam	1820	Ottawa	BGSU
Richland	1808	Mansfield	UA
Ross	1798	Chillicothe	OU
Sandusky	1820	Fremont	BGSU
Scioto	1803	Portsmouth	OU
Seneca	1820	Tiffin	BGSU
Shelby	1819	Sidney	WSU
Stark	1808	Canton	UA
Summit	1840	Akron	UA

COUNTY	YEAR EST.	COUNTY SEAT	REGIONAL CENTER
Trumbull	1800	Warren	Y
Tuscarawas	1808	New Philadelphia	UA
Union	1820	Marysville	OHS
Van Wert	1820	Van Wert	BGSU
Vinton	1850	McArthur	OU
Warren	1803	Lebanon	UC
Washington	1788	Marietta	OU
Wayne	1808	Wooster	UA
Williams	1820	Bryan	BGSU
Wood	1820	Bowling Green	BGSU
Wyandot	1845	Upper Sandusky	BGSU

Ohio Regional Network Centers
Abbreviations Used

BGSU	Bowling Green State University, Bowling Green
OHS	Ohio Historical Society, Columbus
OU	Ohio University, Athens
UA	University of Akron, Akron
UC	University of Cincinnati, Cincinnati
WRHS	Western Reserve Historical Society, Cleveland
WSU	Wright State University, Dayton
Y	Youngstown Historical Center, Youngstown

Notes:

The date for each county in the above chart is the date it was established, which may differ from the year actually organized. Some useful references are:

Auditor of State's Web page (www.auditor.state.oh.us).

Burke, Thomas Aquinas. *Ohio Lands: A Short History*, 9th ed. Columbus: Ohio Auditor of State, 1997. (http://freepages.history.rootsweb.com/~maggie/ ohio-lands/ohlands.html)

Dean, Tanya West and W. David Speas. *Along the Ohio Trail: A Short History of Ohio Lands*. Edited by George W. Knepper. Columbus: Auditor of State, 2001. (www.auditor.state.oh.us)

Knepper, George W. *The Official Ohio Lands Book*. Columbus: Auditor of State, 2002. (www.auditor.state.oh.us)

Parent county (or counties) are listed in Alice Eichholz, ed., *Ancestry's Red Book: American State, County & Town Sources*, rev. ed. (Salt Lake City: Ancestry, 1992), and *The Handybook for Genealogists*, 10th ed. (Draper, Utah: Everton Publishers, 2002). Both of these works are valuable reference sources for American genealogists. See also *Ohio Vital Record Data* on the Ohio GenWeb Internet site which shows name of county, year formed, name of parent county (or counties), and county seat (www.scioto.org/OHGenWeb/statedocs/vital.html). An alphabetical list of Ohio county courthouse addresses is available on the Ohio Historical Society's Web page:
(www.ohiohistory.org/resource/archlib/cthouse.html).

OHIO COUNTY RECORDS

County	B	M	D	Land	Prob.	Court
Adams	1888	1881	1888	1797	1849	1797
Allen	1867	1831	1867	1831	1831	1831
Ashland	1867	1846	1867	1846	1846	1846
Ashtabula	1867	1811	1867	1798	1811	1811
Athens	1867	1817	1867	1792	1800	1806
Auglaize	1867	1848	1867	1824	1848	1848
Belmont	1867	1803	1867	1800	1804	1801
Brown	1867	1818	1867	1818	1817	1818
Butler	1856	1803	1856	1803	1851	1803
Carroll	1867	1833	1867	1831	1833	1833
Champaign	1867	1805	1867	1805	1804	1805
Clark	1867	1818	1867	1818	1818	1818
Clermont	1856	1801	1856	1797	1800	1801
Clinton	1867	1810	1867	1806	1810	1810
Columbiana	1867	1803	1867	1795	1803	1803
Coshocton	1867	1811	1867	1800	1811	1811

County	B	M	D	Land	Prob.	Court
Crawford	1866	1831	1866	1816	1826	1831
Cuyahoga	1867	1810	1868	1810	1811	1823
Darke	1867	1817	1867	1817	1818	1817
Defiance	1866	1845	1866	1823	1845	1845
Delaware	1867	1835	1867	1805	1812	1818
Erie	1856	1838	1856	1837	1838	1838
Fairfield	1867	1803	1867	1801	1803	1801
Fayette	1867	1810	1868	1810	1810	1828
Franklin	1867	1803	1867	1804	1805	1803
Fulton	1867	1864	1867	1835	1853	1850
Gallia	1864	1803	1867	1803	1803	1811
Geauga	1867	1806	1867	1795	1806	1806
Greene	1869	1803	1870	1798	1803	1803
Guernsey	1867	1810	1867	1802	1812	1810
Hamilton	1846	1808	1881	1787	1791	1844
Hancock	1867	1828	1867	1820	1828	1828
Hardin	1867	1833	1867	1826	1830	1833

County	B	M	D	Land	Prob.	Court
Harrison	1867	1813	1867	1800	1813	1814
Henry	1867	1847	1867	1846	1847	1847
Highland	1867	1805	1867	1804	1809	1805
Hocking	1867	1818	1867	1818	1819	1818
Holmes	1867	1821	1867	1808	1824	1825
Huron	1867	1818	1867	1809	1815	1818
Jackson	1867	1816	1867	1816	1819	1816
Jefferson	1867	1803	1867	1795	1798	1804
Knox	1867	1808	1867	1808	1808	1808
Lake	1867	1840	1867	1840	1840	1840
Lawrence	1867	1817	1867	1816	1847	1817
Licking	1875	1808	1875	1800	1875	1809
Logan	1867	1818	1867	1810	1851	1818
Lorain	1867	1824	1867	1822	1840	1825
Lucas	1867	1835	1868	1808	1835	1835
Madison	1867	1810	1867	1810	1810	1810
Mahoning	1864	1846	1864	1795	1846	1847

County	B	M	D	Land	Prob.	Court
Marion	1867	1824	1867	1821	1825	1824
Medina	1867	1818	1867	1818	1819	1818
Meigs	1867	1819	1867	1820	1822	1819
Mercer	1867	1828	1867	1823	1824	1824
Miami	1853	1807	1867	1807	1807	1807
Monroe	1867	1866	1867	1836	1867	1818
Montgomery	1866	1803	1866	1805	1803	1803
Morgan	1867	1819	1867	1793	1818	1819
Morrow	1867	1848	1867	1848	1848	1848
Muskingum	1867	1804	1867	1800	1804	1804
Noble	1867	1851	1867	1851	1851	1851
Ottawa	1867	1840	1869	1820	1840	1840
Paulding	1867	1839	1867	1835	1842	1839
Perry	1867	1818	1867	1818	1817	1818

County	B	M	D	Land	Prob.	Court
Pickaway	1867	1810	1867	1810	1810	1810
Pike	1867	1815	1867	1799	1817	1815
Portage	1867	1808	1867	1795	1808	1809
Preble	1867	1808	1867	1805	1808	1808
Putnam	1854	1834	1867	1830	1835	1834
Richland	1856	1813	1856	1814	1813	1820
Ross	1867	1798	1867	1797	1798	1798
Sandusky	1867	1820	1867	1822	1820	1820
Scioto	1856	1804	1856	1803	1810	1809
Seneca	1867	1841	1867	1822	1828	1824
Shelby	1867	1824	1867	1819	1825	1818
Stark	1867	1809	1867	1809	1811	1809
Summit	1866	1840	1870	1840	1839	1840
Trumbull	1867	1803	1867	1795	1803	1807
Tuscarawas	1867	1808	1867	1808	1810	1808
Union	1867	1820	1867	1811	1820	1820
Van Wert	1867	1840	1867	1824	1839	1837

County	B	M	D	Land	Prob.	Court
Vinton	1867	1850	1867	1850	1852	1850
Warren	1867	1803	1867	1795	1803	1803
Washington	1867	1789	1867	1788	1788	1790
Wayne	1867	1813	1867	1813	1816	1812
Williams	1867	1824	1867	1823	1825	1824
Wood	1867	1820	1867	1817	1820	1823
Wyandot	1867	1845	1867	1826	1845	1845

Key:

B   beginning date of county civil birth records (some county civil birth and death records began as early as 1856-57)

M   beginning date of county civil marriage records

D   beginning date of county civil death records

Land   beginning date of county land records, such as deeds, etc.

Prob beginning date of county wills or other probate records

Court beginning date of county court records

References:

Family History Library Catalog (FHLC) (www.familysearch.org).

The Handybook for Genealogists. 10th ed. Draper, Utah: Everton Publishers, 2002.

Maki, Carol L. "Ohio." In *Ancestry's Red Book: American State, County & Town Sources.* Rev. ed. Edited by Alice Eichholz. Salt Lake City: Ancestry, 1992, pp. 572-88.

Ohio Vital Record Data: Ohio County Origins (Ohio GenWeb site): (www.scioto.org/OHGenWeb/statedocs/vital.html).

ADDRESSES— OHIO

Ada: Ohio Northern University, Heterick Memorial Library, 525 South Main Street, Ada, OH 45810

Ada Public School District, 320 North Main Street, Ada, OH 45810

Adams County Genealogical Society, P.O. Box 231, West Union, OH 45693

Akron: Hower House, University of Akron, 60 Fir Hill Street, Akron, OH 44325

Akron: Oral History in Ohio, 550 Copley Road, Akron, OH 44320-2324

Akron: Portage Lakes Historical Society, 95 Parisette Lane, Akron, OH 44319

Akron: Summit County Historical Society, 550 Copley Road., Akron, OH 44320-2324

Akron: University of Akron, University Libraries, 302 Buchtel Mall, Akron, OH 44325

Akron: University of Akron, Archival Services, Polsky Building, Akron, OH 44325-1702

Akron-Summit County Public Library, 1040 East Tallmadge Avenue, Akron, OH 44310

Alexandria Public Library, 10 Maple Drive Alexandria, OH 43001

Alger Public Library, P.O. Box 18, 100 West Wagner Street, Alger, OH 45812

Alliance: Mount Union College Library, 1972 Clark Avenue, Alliance, OH 44601

Alliance: Rodman Public Library, Alliance Room, 215 East Broadway Street, Alliance, OH 44601

Alliance Genealogical Society, P.O. Box 3630, Alliance, OH 44601

Alliance Historical Society, P.O. Box 2044, 1042 Parkside Drive, Alliance, OH 44601

Amelia: Grassy Run Historical/Arts Committee, P.O. Box 338, Amelia, OH 45102

Amherst Historical Society, P.O. Box 272, Amherst, OH 44001

Amherst Public Library, 221 Spring Street, Amherst, OH 44001

Andover Public Library, 142 West Main Street, P.O. Box 1210, Andover, OH 44003

Arcanum Public Library, 101 North Street, Arcanum, OH 45304

Archbold: McLaughlin Memorial Public Library, 301½ Stryker Street, Archbold, OH 43502

Ashland County Historical Society & Museum, P.O. Box 484, 4141 Center Street, Ashland, OH 44805

Ashland Public Library, 224 Claremont Avenue, Ashland, OH 44805

Ashland University Library, 401 College Avenue, Ashland, OH 44805

Ashley: Wornstaff Memorial Public Library, 302 East High, Ashley, OH 43003

Ashtabula: Harbor-Topky Memorial Library, 1633 Walnut Blvd., Ashtabula, OH 44004

Ashtabula County District Library, 335 West 44th Street, Ashtabula, OH 44004

Athens: Ohio University, Archives and Special Collections, Vernon R. Alden Library, Athens, OH 45701-2978

Athens County Historical Society & Museum, 65 North Court Street, Athens, OH 45701

Attica: Seneca East Public Library, 14 North Main Street, P.O. Box 572, Attica, OH 44807-0572

Attica Area Historical Society, P.O. Box 226, Attica, OH 44807

Auditor of State. *See* Columbus: Auditor of State

Aurora Historical Society, P.O. Box 241, 115 East Pioneer Trail, Aurora, OH 44202

Austintown Historical Society, 1181 South Raccoon Road, Austintown, OH 44515

Avon Historical Society, 2940 Stoney Ridge Road, Avon, OH 44011
Avon Lake Historical Society, 535 Avon Belden Road, Avon Lake, OH 44012
Avon Lake Public Library, 32649 Electric Blvd., Avon Lake, OH 44012-1669
Barberton Public Library, 602 West Park Avenue, Barberton, OH 44203-2458
Barnesville Hutton Memorial Library, 308 East Main Street, Barnesville, OH 43713
Batavia: Clermont County Genealogical Society, P.O. Box 394, 326 Broadway Street, Batavia, OH 45103
Batavia: Clermont County Public Library, 326 Broadway Street, Batavia, OH 45103
Bay Village Historical Society, 27715 Lake Road, Bay Village, OH 44140
Beachwood: Jewish Genealogical Society of Cleveland, 27100 Cedar Road., Beachwood, OH 44122
Beavercreek Community Library, 3618 Dayton-Xenia Road, Beavercreek, OH 45432
Bedford Historical Society, P.O. Box 46282, Bedford, OH 44146
Bedford Historical Society Library, 30 South Park Street, Bedford, OH 44146
Bellaire Public Library, 330 32nd Street, Bellaire, OH 43906
Bellbrook: Winters-Bellbrook Community Library, 57 Franklin Street, Bellbrook, OH 45305
Bellefontaine: Logan County District Library, 220 North Main Street, Bellefontaine, OH 43311-2288
Bellefontaine: Logan County Genealogical Society, P.O. Box 36, 521 East Columbus Avenue, Bellefontaine, OH 43311
Bellefontaine: Logan County Historical Society, P.O. Box 296, 521 East Columbus Avenue, Bellefontaine, OH 43311

Bellevue Public Library, 224 East Main Street, Bellevue, OH 44811

Berea: Baldwin-Wallace College, Ritter Library, 275 Eastland Road, Berea, OH 44017

Berea Area Historical Society, P.O. Box 173, 118 East Bridge Street, Berea, OH 44017

Berlin Center Historical Society, P.O. Box 175, Berlin Center, OH 44401-0112

Berlin Heights Historical Society, P.O. Box 175, Berlin Heights, OH 44814

Bettsville Public Library, 233 State Street, Bettsville, OH 44815-9999

Bexley Historical Society, 2242 East Main Street, Bexley, OH 43209

Bexley Public Library, 2411 East Main Street, Bexley OH 43209

Blanchester Area Historical Society, 313 Bland Avenue, Blanchester, OH 45107

Blanchester Public Library, 110 North Broadway, Blanchester, OH 45107-1250

Bloomville: Bliss Memorial Public Library, 20 South Marion Street, Bloomville, OH 44818-0038

Blue Rock: Brush Creek Historical Society, 8785 Dozer Ridge Road, Blue Rock, OH 43720

Bluffton College, Musselman Library, 280 West College Avenue, Bluffton, OH 45817-1196

Bluffton-Richland Public Library, 145 South Main Street, Bluffton, OH 45817-1265

Bluffton: Mennonite Historical Library, 280 West College Avenue, Bluffton, OH 45817

Bluffton: Swiss Community Historical Society, P.O. Box 5, Bluffton, OH 45817

Bowerston Public Library, 200 Main Street, P.O. Box 205, Bowerston, OH 44695-0205

Bowling Green: Wood County District Public Library, 251 North Main

Street, Bowling Green, OH 43402

Bowling Green: Wood County Historical Society, 13660 County Home Road, Bowling Green, OH 43402

Bowling Green State University, Center for Archival Collections, Jerome Library, 1001 East Wooster Street, Bowling Green, OH 43403-0175

Bradford Public Library, 138 East Main Street, Bradford, OH 45308-1108

Bratenahl Historical Society, 10119 Foster Avenue, Bratenahl, OH 44108

Bristolville: Public Library, 1855 Greenville Road N.W., P.O. Box 220, Bristolville, OH 44402-0220

Bristolville: Bristol Historical Society, 4934 State Route 45 NW, Bristolville, OH 44402

Bristolville: Girard Historical Society, 4934 State Route 45 NW, Bristolville, OH 44402

Brooklyn Historical Society, 4442 Ridge Rd., Brooklyn, OH 44144

Brookville Historical Society Library, P.O. Box 82, Brookville, OH 45309

Bryan: Williams County Genealogical Society, P.O. Box 293, Bryan, OH 43506-0293

Bryan Public Library, 107 East High Street, Bryan, OH 43506

Bucyrus Public Library, 200 East Mansfield St., Bucyrus, OH 44820

Burton: Geauga County Historical Society Library, 14653 East Park Street, Burton, OH 44021

Burton: Geauga County Historical Society, 14653 East Park Street, P.O. Box 153, Burton, OH 44021

Burton Public Library, 14588 West Park Street, P.O. Box 427, Burton OH 44021

Butler-Clearfork Valley Historical Society, Box 186, Butler, OH 44822

Cadiz: Harrison County Genealogical Chapter Library, 45507

Unionvale Road, Cadiz, OH 43907

Cadiz: Puskarich Public Library, 200 East Market Street, Cadiz, OH 43907-1185

Caldwell Public Library, 517 Spruce Street, Box 230, Caldwell OH 43724-0230

Cambridge: Guernsey County District Public Library, 800 Steubenville Avenue, Cambridge, OH 43725-2385

Cambridge: Guernsey County Law Library, Guernsey County Court House, Cambridge, OH 43725

Campbell Historical Society, 211 Struthers-Liberty Road, Campbell, OH 44405-1935

Canal Fulton Heritage Society, 103 Tuscarawas, Canal Fulton, OH 44614

Canal Fulton Public Library, 154 Market Street N.E., Canal Fulton, OH 44614

Canal Society of Ohio, 550 Copley Road, Akron, OH 44320

Canal Winchester Area Historical Society, P.O. Box 15, Canal Winchester, OH 43110

Canton: Hoover Historical Center, 1875 Easton Street NW, Canton, OH 44720

Canton: Jackson Township Historical Society, P.O. Box 34171, Canton, OH 44735

Canton: Malone College, Everett L. Cattell Library, 515 25th Street NW, Canton, OH 44709

Canton: Stark County District Library, 715 Market Avenue North, Canton, OH 44702

Canton: Stark County District Library, Genealogy Division, 715 Market Avenue North, Canton, OH 44702

Canton: Stark County Historical Society and McKinley Museum, 800 McKinley Monument Drive, Canton, OH 44708

Canton: Stark County Historical Society, P.O. Box 20070, Canton, OH

44701

Cardington-Lincoln Public Library, 128 East Main Street, P.O. Box 38, Cardington, OH 43315

Carey: Dorcas Carey Public Library, 236 East Findlay Street, Carey, OH 43316-1250

Carroll County District Library, 70 Second Street NE, Carrollton, OH 44615

Cedarville Community Library, 74 East Main St., Cedarville, OH 45314

Cedarville University Library, 251 North Main Street, Cedarville, OH 45314

Celina: Dwyer-Mercer County District Library, 303 North Main Street, Celina, OH 45822

Celina: Mercer County Historical Society, 130 West Market Street, P.O. Box 512, Celina, OH 45822

Celina: Mercer County Law Library Association, Court House, Celina, OH 45822

Centerburg Public Library, 49 East Main Street, Centerburg, OH 43011

Centerville Historical Society, 89 West Franklin Street, Centerville, OH 45459

Centerville: Washington-Centerville Public Library, 111 West Spring Valley Road, Centerville, OH 45458

Central Ohio Alliance of Historical Societies, 1742 Franklin Avenue, Columbus, OH 43205

Chagrin Falls Historical Society, 21 Walnut Street, Chagrin Falls, OH 44022

Champaign County Library, 1060 Scioto Street, Urbana, OH 43078

Chardon: Geauga County Public Library, 110 East Park Street, Chardon OH 44024

Chesterland: Geauga West Library, 13455 Chillicothe Road, Chester-land, OH 44026

Chesterville: Selover Public Library, P.O. Box 25, 31 State Road 95,

Chesterville, OH 43317-0025

Chillicothe & Ross County Public Library, 140-146 South Paint Street, P.O. Box 185, Chillicothe, OH 45601-0185

Chillicothe: Ross County Genealogical Society, P.O. Box 6352, 444 Douglas Avenue, Chillicothe, OH 45601

Chillicothe: Ross County Genealogical Society Library, 270 South Paint Street, Chillicothe, OH 45601

Chillicothe: Ross County Historical Society, 45 West 5th Street, Chillicothe, OH 45601

Cincinnati: American Jewish Archives, 3101 Clifton Avenue, Cincinnati, OH 45220

Cincinnati: Anderson Township Historical Society, P.O. Box 30174, 6550 Clough Pike, Cincinnati, OH 45244

Cincinnati: Blue Ash Historical Society, 7 Trailbridge Drive, Cincinnati, OH 45241

Cincinnati: Coleraine Historical Society, P.O. Box 39726, Cincinnati, OH 45239

Cincinnati: College Hill Historical Society, P.O. Box 24008, Cincinnati, OH 45224

Cincinnati: Delhi Historical Society, 468 Anderson Ferry Road, Cincinnati, OH 45238

Cincinnati: Eugene H. Maly Memorial Library, 6616 Beechmont Avenue, Cincinnati, OH 45230-2091

Cincinnati: Green Township Historical Association, 3973 Grave Avenue, Cincinnati, OH 45211

Cincinnati: Hebrew Union College-Jewish Institute of Religion, Klau Library, 3101 Clifton Avenue, Cincinnati, OH 45220

Cincinnati Historical Society Library, 1301 Western Avenue, Cincinnati, OH 45203

Cincinnati: Indian Hill Historical Society, 8100 Given Road, Cincinnati, OH 45243

Cincinnati Law Library Association, Court House, Cincinnati, OH 45202

Cincinnati: Lloyd Library and Museum, 917 Plum Street, Cincinnati, OH 45202

Cincinnati: Mariemont Preservation Foundation, 3919 Plainville Road, Cincinnati, OH 45227

Cincinnati: Montgomery Historical Society, 7650 Cooper Road, Cincinnati, OH 45242

Cincinnati: Price Hill Historical Society, P.O. Box 7020, 4434 Glenway Avenue, Cincinnati, OH 45205-7020

Cincinnati: Public Library of Cincinnati and Hamilton County, History and Genealogy Department 800 Vine Street, Cincinnati, OH 45202-2071

Cincinnati: University of Cincinnati, Archives Department, Carl Blegan Library, P.O. Box 210033, Cincinnati, OH 45221-0033 (Mail: Archives and Rare Books, Blegen Library, University of Cincinnati, Cincinnati OH 45221-0113)

Cincinnati: University of Cincinnati, College of Law, Robert S. Marx Law Library, Cincinnati, OH 45221-0040

Cincinnati: University of Cincinnati, Raymond Walters College Library, Cincinnati, OH 45221-0113

Cincinnati: Wyoming Historical Society, 325 Reily Road, Cincinnati, OH 45215

Cincinnati: Xavier University, McDonald Memorial Library, 3800 Victory Parkway, Cincinnati, OH 45207-5211

Circleville: Pickaway County Historical/Genealogical Society, P.O. Box 85, 304 South Court Street, Circleville, OH 43113

Circleville: Pickaway County District Public Library, 165 East Main Street, Circleville, OH 43113-1795

Cleveland: Afro-American Historical and Genealogical Society, P.O. Box 200382, Cleveland, OH 44120

Cleveland: Case Western Reserve University, Kelvin Smith Library, 11055 Euclid Avenue., Cleveland, OH 44106-7151

Cleveland: Cuyahoga Community College Library, 700 Carnegie Avenue, Cleveland, OH 44115

Cleveland: Cuyahoga County Archives, 2905 Franklin Blvd., Cleveland, OH 44113

Cleveland: Cuyahoga County Public Library, Fairview Park Regional Library, 21255 Lorain Road, Fairview Park, OH 44126-2120

Cleveland Heights-University Heights Public Library, 2345 Lee Road, Cleveland, OH 44118-3493

Cleveland Law Library Association, 1 West Lakeside Avenue FL 4, Cleveland, OH 44113-1078

Cleveland: Mayfield Township Historical Society, 606 Som Center Road, Cleveland, OH 44143

Cleveland Police Historical Society, 1300 Ontario Street, Cleveland, OH 44113

Cleveland Public Library, 325 Superior Avenue N.E., Cleveland, OH 44114-1271

Cleveland State University, University Library, 2121 Euclid Avenue, Cleveland, OH 44115-2214

Cleveland: Ukranian Museum/Archives, 1202 Kenilworth Avenue, Cleveland, OH 44113

Cleveland: Western Reserve Historical Society Library, 10825 East Boulevard, Cleveland, OH 44106-1788

Clyde Heritage League, P.O. Box 97, Clyde, OH 43410

Clyde Public Library, 222 West Buckeye Street, Clyde, OH 43410

Coldwater Public Library, 305 West Main Street, Coldwater, OH 45828-1604

Columbiana-Fairfield Township Historical Society, 410 North Main Street, Columbiana, OH 44408

Columbiana Public Library, 332 North Middle Street, Columbiana, OH

44408

Columbus: Adjutant General's Department Library, 2825 West Dublin Granville Road, Columbus, OH 43235-2712

Columbus: Auditor of State, State Land Office, 88 East Broad Street, P.O. Box 1140, Columbus, OH 43216-1140

Columbus: Capital University, Blackmore Library, 2199 East Main Street, Columbus, OH 43209

Columbus: Division of Veterans' Affairs, 30 East Broad Street, Columbus, OH 43266-0422

Columbus: Franklin County Genealogical Society, P.O. Box 44309, Columbus, OH 43204

Columbus: Franklin County Genealogical Society Library, 570 West Broad Street, P.O. Box 2406, Columbus, OH 43216

Columbus: Governor's Office of Veterans Affairs, 77 South High Street, Columbus, OH 43215

Columbus: Hilltop Historical Society, 2300 West Broad Street, Columbus, OH 43204

Columbus Jewish Historical Society, 1175 College Avenue, Columbus, OH 43209

Columbus Law Library Association, 369 High Street, 10th Floor, Columbus, OH 43215

Columbus Metropolitan Library, 96 South Grant Avenue, Columbus, OH 43215-4781

Columbus: Ohio Attorney General, Law Library, 30 East Broad Street, 17th Floor, Columbus, OH 43266-0410

Columbus: Ohio Department of Health, Vital Statistics, P.O. Box 15098, Columbus, OH 43215-0098

Columbus: Ohio Division of Travel and Tourism, P.O. Box 1001, Columbus, OH 43216-1001

Columbus: Ohio Historical Society, Archives/Library Division, 1982 Velma Avenue, Columbus, OH 43211-2497

Columbus: Ohio Humanities Council, 471 East Broad Street, Columbus, OH 43215

Columbus: Ohio Memory Project, Ohio Historical Society, 1982 Velma Avenue, Columbus, OH 43211-2497

Columbus: Ohio State University, College of Law Library, Drinko Hall, 55 West 12th Avenue, Columbus, OH 43210

Columbus: Ohio State University, William Oxley Thompson Memorial Library, 1858 Neil Avenue Mall, Columbus, OH 43210-1286

Columbus: Ohioana Library, 274 East First Avenue, Columbus, OH 43201

Columbus: Palatines to America Library, 611 East Weber Road, Columbus, OH 43211-1097

Columbus: Pontifical College Josephinum, A.T. Wehrle Memorial Library, 7625 North High Street, Columbus, OH 43235-1498

Columbus: Sons of the American Revolution, 545 East Weisheimer Road, Columbus OH 43214

Columbus State Community College Library, 550 East Spring Street, Columbus, OH 43215

Columbus: State Library of Ohio, 274 East First Avenue, Columbus, OH 43201

Columbus: Supreme Court of Ohio, Law Library, 30 East Broad Street, Columbus, OH 43215-3431

Columbus: Trinity Lutheran Seminary, Hamma Library, 2199 East Maine Street, Columbus, OH 43209-2334

Columbus: University District Organization, 2231 North High Street, Room 200, Columbus, OH 43201

Conneaut Carnegie Library, 282 State Street, Conneaut, OH 44030

Cortland: Bazetta Cortland Historical Society, P.O. Box 411, Cortland, OH 44410

Coshocton: Roscoe Village Foundation, 381 Hill Street, Coshocton, OH 43812

Coshocton Public Library, 655 Main Street, Coshocton, OH 43812

Covington: J.R. Clarke Public Library, 102 Spring Street, Covington, OH 45318

Creston Historical Society, 176 Main Street, Creston, OH 44217

Crestline Public Library, 324 North Thomas St., Crestline, OH 44827

Cridersville Historical Society, P.O. Box 2444, Cridersville, OH 45806

Cuyahoga County Public Library, Fairview Park Regional Library, 21255 Lorain Road, Fairview Park, OH 44126-2120

Cuyahoga Falls: Taylor Memorial Public Library, Cuyahoga Falls Public Library, 2015 Third St., Cuyahoga Falls, OH 44221

Cuyahoga Falls Historical Society, P.O. Box 108, Cuyahoga Falls, OH 44222

Dayton and Montgomery County Public Library, 215 East Third Street, Dayton, OH 45402

Dayton: Jewish Genealogical Society of Dayton, P.O. Box 338, Dayton, OH 45406-1364

Dayton: Miami Valley Genealogical Society, P.O. Box 1364, Dayton, OH 45401-1364

Dayton: Montgomery County Genealogical Society, P.O. Box 1584, Dayton, OH 45401-1584

Dayton: Oakwood Historical Society Library, 1947 Far Hills Avenue, Dayton, OH 45419

Dayton: Sinclair Community College Library, 444 West Third Street, Dayton, OH 45402

Dayton: United Theological Seminary Library, 1810 Harvard Blvd., Dayton, OH 45406

Dayton: University of Dayton Libraries, Roesch Library, 300 College Park, Dayton, OH 45469-1360

Dayton: Wright Memorial Public Library, 1776 Far Hills Avenue, Dayton (Oakwood), OH 45419

Dayton: Wright State University, Archives and Special Collections, Paul

Laurence Dunbar Library, 3640 Colonel Glenn Highway, Dayton, OH 45435-0001

Deerfield Historical Society, P.O. Box 34, Deerfield, OH 44411

Defiance College, Pilgrim Library, 201 College Place, Defiance, OH 43512

Defiance County Historical Society, P.O. Box 801, Defiance, OH 43512

Defiance Public Library, 320 Fort Street, Defiance, OH 43512

Delaware: Methodist Theological School in Ohio, John W. Dickhaut Library, 3081 Columbus Pike, P.O. Box 8004, Delaware, OH 43015-8004

Delaware: Ohio Wesleyan University, L.A. Beeghly Library, 43 Rowland Avenue, Delaware, OH 43015

Delaware: United Methodist Archives, Beeghly Library, 43 Rowland Avenue, Delaware, OH 43015

Delaware County District Library, 84 East Winter Street, Delaware, OH 43015

Delaware County Historical Society, P.O. Box 317, 157 East William Street, Delaware, OH 43015

Delphos Public Library, 309 West Second Street, Delphos, OH 45833

Delta Public Library, 402 Main Street, Delta, OH 43515

Dennison: Tuscarawas County Genealogical Society, 307 Center Street, Dennison, OH 44621

Deshler: Henry County Genealogical Society, P.O. Box 231, 208 North East Avenue, Deshler, OH 42516

Deshler: Patrick Henry School District Public Library, 208 North East Avenue, Deshler, OH 43516

Dover Public Library, 525 North Walnut St., Dover, OH 44622-2851

Doylestown: Chippewa-Rogues' Hollow Historical Society, P.O. Box 283, 17500 Gale House Road, Doylestown, OH 44230

Dublin Historical Society, P.O. Box 2, 6659 Coffman Road, Dublin, OH 43017

East Cleveland Public Library, 14101 Euclid Avenue, East Cleveland, OH 44112-3891

East Liverpool: Carnegie Public Library, 219 East Fourth Street, East Liverpool, OH 43920

East Palestine Memorial Public Library, 309 North Market Street, East Palestine, OH 44413

Eaton: Preble County District Library, 450 South Barron Street, Eaton, OH 45320

Elmore: Harris-Elmore Public Library, 328 Toledo Street, Box 45, Elmore, OH 43416

Elmore Historical Society, P.O. Box 154, Elmore, OH 43416

Elyria: Lorain County Community College Library, 1005 Abbe Road North, Elyria, OH 44035-1691

Elyria: Lorain County Historical Society, Gerald Hicks Memorial Library, 509 Washington Avenue, Elyria, OH 44035

Elyria: North Ridgeville Historical Society, 145 Stanford Avenue, Elyria, OH 44035

Elyria Public Library, 320 Washington Avenue, Elyria, OH 44035

Enon Community Historical Society, P.O. Box 442, 45 Indian Drive, Enon, OH 45323

Euclid Historical Society, 21129 North Street, Euclid, OH 44117

Euclid Public Library, 631 East 222nd Street, Euclid, OH, 44123-2091

Fairborn Community Library, 1 East Main Street, Fairborn, OH 45324

Fairport Public Library, 335 Vine Street, Fairport Harbor, OH 44077-5799

Fairview Park: Cuyahoga County Public Library, Fairview Park Regional Library, 21255 Lorain Road, Fairview Park, OH 44126-2120

Farmersville Historical Society, P.O. Box 198, Farmersville, OH 45325

Fayette: Normal Memorial Library, 301 North Eagle, Fayette, OH 43521

Findlay-Hancock County Public Library, 206 Broadway Street, Findlay, OH 45840

Findlay: Hancock Historical Museum Association, 422 West Sandusky Street, Findlay, OH 45840

Findlay: University of Findlay, Shafer Library, 1000 North Main Street, Findlay, OH 45840-3695

Firelands Council of Historical Societies. *See* Monroeville.

Forest-Jackson Public Library, 102 West Lima St., Forest, OH 45843

Fort Loramie Historical Association, Box 276, Fort Loramie, OH 45845

Fort Recovery Bicentennial Committee, 839 Watkins Road, Fort Recovery, OH 45846

Fort Recovery Historical Society, P.O. Box 533, One Fort Site Street, Fort Recovery, OH 45846

Fort Recovery Public Library, 113 North Wayne, Fort Recovery, OH 45846

Fostoria: Tri-County Lineage Research Society, Kaubisch Memorial Public Library, 205 Perry Street, Fostoria, OH 44830

Fostoria Area Historical Society & Museum, P.O. Box 142, Fostoria, OH 44830

Franklin County Genealogy Society, P.O. Box 44309, Columbus, OH 43204-0309

Franklin Area Historical Society, Harding Museum, 302 Park Avenue, Franklin, OH 45005

Franklin Public Library, 400 Anderson Street, Franklin, OH 45005

Fredericktown Area Historical Society, 11 East Sandusky Street, Fredericktown, OH 43019

Fremont: Birchard Public Library of Sandusky County, 423 Croghan Street, Fremont, OH 43420

Fremont: Rutherford B. Hayes Library, Spiegel Grove, 1337 Hayes Avenue, Fremont, OH 43420

Fremont: Sandusky County Historical Society, 1337 Hayes Avenue,

Fremont, OH 43420

Fremont: Sandusky County Kin Hunters, 1337 Hayes Avenue, Fremont, OH 43420

Fremont: Terra Community College Library, 2830 Napoleon Road, Fremont, OH 43420-9670

Gahanna: Virginia S. Milligan Memorial Library, 5720 Sunbury Road, Gahanna, OH 43230

Galion Historical Society, P.O. Box 125, Galion, OH 44833

Galion Public Library Association, 123 North Market Street, Galion, OH 44833-1979

Gallipolis: Dr. Samuel L. Bossard Memorial Library, 7 Spruce Street, Gallipolis, OH 45631-1220

Gallipolis: Gallia County Historical & Genealogical Society, P.O. Box 295, Gallipolis, OH 45631

Gambier: Kenyon College, Olin-Chalmers Memorial Library, Gambier, OH 43022-9623

Gambier Folklore Society, Kenyon College, Gambier, OH 43022-9624

Garfield Heights Historical Society, 5404 Turney Road, Garfield Heights, OH 44125

Garrettsville: James A. Garfield Historical Society, P.O. Box 326, Garrettsville, OH 44231

Garrettsville: Portage County District Library, 10482 South Street, Garrettsville, OH 44231

Gates Mills Historical Society, P.O. Box 191, 7580 Old Mill Road, Gates Mills, OH 44040

Geneva: Ashtabula County Genealogical Society, 860 Sherman Street, Geneva OH 44041-1227

Geneva Branch, Ashtabula County District Library, 860 Sherman Street, Geneva, OH 44041

Geneva: Harpersfield Heritage Society, 5491 Route 307, Geneva, OH 44041

Georgetown: Brown County Genealogy Society, P.O. Box 83, Georgetown, OH 45121

Georgetown: Mary P. Shelton Library, 200 West Grant Avenue, Georgetown, OH 45121-1299

Germantown: Historical Society of Germantown, 47 West Center Street, P.O. Box 144, Germantown, OH 45327

Germantown Public Library, 51 North Plum Street, Germantown, OH 45327-1357

Girard Free Public Library, 105 East Prospect Street, Girard, OH 44420-1899

Gnadenhutten Historical Society, P.O. Box 396, 352 South Cherry Street, Gnadenhutten, OH 44629

Gnadenhutten Public Library, 160 North Walnut St., P.O. Box 216, Gnadenhutten, OH 44629-0216

Goshen: Little Miami-East Fork River Historical Society, 6641 Linton Road, Goshen, OH 45122

Grafton-Midview Public Library, 983 Main Street, Grafton, OH 44044-1492

Granville: Denison University, Doane Library, Box L, Granville, OH 43023

Granville: Robbins Hunter Museum/Avery Downer House, 221 East Broadway, P.O. Box 183, Granville, OH 43023

Granville Public Library, 217 East Broadway, Granville, OH 43023-1398

Gratis: Marion Lawrence Memorial Library, 15 East Franklin Street, Gratis, OH 45330

Greenville: Carnegie Library, 520 Sycamore Street, Greenville, OH 45331-1438

Greenville: Darke County Historical Society, 205 North Broadway Street, Greenville, OH 45331

Greenville: Garst Museum, Genealogical Library, 205 North Broadway,

Greenville, OH 45331

Greenville Public Library, 520 Sycamore Street, Greenville, OH 45331-1438

Grove City: Southwest Public Libraries, Grove City Library, SPL Admin., 3359 Park Street, Grove City, OH 43123

Groveport: Motts Military Museum, 5075 South Hamilton Road, Groveport, OH 43125

Hamden: Vinton County Historical & Genealogical Society, P.O. Box 306, Hamden, OH 45634-0306

Hamilton: Butler County Historical Society, 327 North Second Street, Hamilton, OH 45011

Hamilton: Lane Public Library, 300 North Third Street, Hamilton, OH 45011

Harrison: Village Historical Society, Harrison, OH 45030

Hartville: Marlboro Township Historical Society, 6124 Edison Street, Hartville, OH 44632

Hebron Public Library, 934 West Main Street, Hebron, OH 43025

Hicksville Historical Society, P.O. Box 162, Hicksville, OH 43526

Hilliard: Northwest Franklin County Historical Society, 4162 Avery Road, P.O. Box 413, Hilliard, OH 43026

Hillsboro: Highland County District Library, 10 Willettsville Pike, Hillsboro, OH 45133

Hillsboro: Southern Ohio Genealogical Society, P.O. Box 414, Hillsboro, OH 45133

Hillsboro: Southern State Community College Library, 100 Hobart Drive, Hillsboro, OH 45133

Hinckley Historical Society, P.O. Box 471, 889 Center Road, Hinckley, OH 44233

Hiram College, Hiram College Library, P.O. Box 67, Hiram, OH 44234

Hiram Historical Society, P.O. Box 1775, Hiram, OH 44234

Holgate Community Library, 204 Railway Ave., Holgate, OH 43527

Homer Public Library, 385 South Street NW, P.O. Box 25, Homer, OH 43027

Hubbard Public Library, 436 West Liberty Street, Hubbard, OH 44425-1793

Hubbard Historical Society, 396 Hager St., Hubbard, OH 44425

Hudson Library & Historical Society, 22 Aurora Street, Hudson, OH 44236

Huron: Bowling Green State University, Firelands College Library, 901 Rye Beach Road, Huron, OH 44839-9791

Huron Public Library, 333 Williams Street, Huron, OH 44839-1640

Ironton: Briggs Lawrence County Public Library, 321 South 4th Street, Ironton, OH 45638

Ironton: Lawrence County Historical Society, P.O. Box 73, Ironton, OH 45683

Italian American War Veterans, National Headquarters, 115 South Meridian Road, Youngstown, OH 44509

Jackson City Library, 21 Broadway Street, Jackson, OH 45640-1695

Jamestown Community Library, 86 Seaman Dr., Jamestown, OH 45335

Jefferson Branch, Carnegie Public Library, 22 South Main Street, Jeffersonville, OH 43218

Jefferson: Henderson Memorial Public Library, 54 East Jefferson Street, Jefferson, OH 44047-1198

Jefferson: Lenox Historical Society, Box 58, 2520 State Route 46 South, Jefferson, OH 44047

Johnston Public Library, 1 South Main Street, Johnstown, OH 43031

Kalida: Putnam County Historical Society, P.O. Box 264, Kalida, OH 45853

Kent Free Library, 312 West Main, Kent, OH 44240-2493

Kent Historical Society, P.O. Box 663, 152 Franklin Avenue, Kent, OH 44240

Kent State University, Libraries & Media Services, Kent, OH 44242

Kenton: Hardin County Historical Museums, P.O. Box 521, North Main Street, Kenton, OH 43326-1505

Kenton: Mary Lou Johnson Hardin County District Library, 325 East Columbus Street, Kenton, OH 43326-1546

Kidron Community Historical Society, P.O. Box 234, 13153 Emerson Road, Kidron, OH 44636

Killbuck Valley Historical Society, P.O. Box 142, Killbuck, OH 44637

Kingsville Public Library, 6006 Academy Street, Kingsville, OH 44048-0057

Kinsman Free Public Library, 6420 Church Street, P.O. Box 166 Kinsman, OH 44428-9702

Kirtland Hills: Lake County Historical Society, 8610 Mentor Road, Kirtland Hills, OH 44060

Kirtland Public Library, 9267 Chillicothe Road, Kirtland, OH 44094-8500

Kirtland: Lakeland Community College Library, 7700 Clocktower Drive, Kirtland, OH 44094-5198

Lakewood Historical Society & Library, 14710 Lake Avenue, Lakewood, OH 44107

Lakewood Public Library, 15425 Detroit Avenue, Lakewood, OH 44107-3890

Lancaster: Fairfield County District Library, 219 North Broad Street, Lancaster, OH 43130-3098

Lancaster: Fairfield Heritage Association, 105 East Wheeling Street, Lancaster, OH 43130

Lancaster: Ohio University-Lancaster Library, 1570 Granville Pike, Lancaster, OH 43130

Lebanon Public Library, 101 South Broadway, Lebanon, OH 45036

Lebanon: Warren County Genealogical Resource Center, Warren County Courthouse, 300 East Silver Street, Lebanon, OH 45036

Lebanon: Warren County Historical Society, Museum & Library, 105

South Broadway, P.O. Box 223, Lebanon, OH 45036

LeRoy Heritage Association, 12941 Girdled Road, LeRoy, OH 44077

Lewisburg: Brown Memorial Library, 101 South Commerce, P.O. Box 640, Lewisburg, OH 45338

Liberty Center Public Library, 124 East Street, P.O. Box 66, Liberty Center, OH 43532

Lima: Allen County Historical Society, Elizabeth M. MacDonell Memorial Library, 620 West Market St., Lima, OH 45801

Lima Public Library, 650 West Market Street, Lima, OH 45801

Lisbon: Lepper Library, 303 East Lincoln Way, Lisbon, OH 44432

Lithopolis: Wagnalls Memorial Library, 150 East Columbus Street, P.O. Box 217, Lithopolis, OH 43136-0217

Logan County District Library, 220 North Main Street, Bellefontaine, OH 43311-2288

Logan County Genealogical Society, Box 36, Bellefontaine, OH 43311

London Public Library, 20 East First Street, London, OH 43140-1200

Lorain: Black River Historical Society, 309 Fifth Street, Lorain, OH 44052

Lorain Public Library, 351 Sixth Street, Lorain, OH 44052

Loudonville Public Library, 122 East Main Street, Loudonville, OH 44842

Louisville Area Historic Preservation Society, 523 East Main Street, Louisville, OH 44641

Louisville Public Library, 700 Lincoln Avenue, Louisville, OH 44641

Loveland: Greater Loveland Historical Society & Museum, 201 Riverside Drive, Loveland, OH 45140

Luckey Library, 228 Main Street, Luckey, OH 43443

Madison: Mackenzie Memorial Public Library, Madison Public Library, 6111 Middle Ridge Road, Madison, OH 44057

Madison Historical Society, P.O. Box 91, 6193 Selkirk Drive, Madison, OH 44057

Malta: Morgan County Historical Association, RR 1, Malta, OH 43758

Manchester: Manchester Public Library, 401 Pike Street, Manchester, OH 45144

Mansfield: Ohio Genealogical Society, 713 South Main Street, Mansfield, OH 44907-1644

Mansfield: Richland County Historical Society, 348 Oak Hill Place, Mansfield, OH 44902

Mansfield-Richland County Public Library, 43 West Third Street, Mansfield, OH 44902-1295

Mantua Historical Society, P.O. Box 220, 1188 SR 44, Mantua, OH 44255

Marietta: Campus Martius Museum Library, 601 Second Street, Marietta, OH 45750

Marietta College, Dawes Memorial Library, 215 Fifth Street, Marietta, OH 45750

Marietta: Washington County Historical Society, P.O. Box 103, 417 2nd Street, Marietta, OH 45750

Marietta: Washington County Public Library, 615 Fifth Street, Marietta, OH 45750

Marietta: Washington State Community College, Learning Resource Center, 710 Colegate Drive, Marietta, OH 45750

Marion County Historical Society, 169 East Church Street, Marion, OH 43302

Marion Public Library, 445 East Church St., Marion, OH 43302-4290

Martins Ferry Public Library, 20 James Wright Plaza., P.O. Box 130, Martins Ferry, OH 43935-0130

Marysville Public Library, 231 South Plum Street, Marysville, OH 43040-1596

Mason Historical Society, P.O. Box 82, 207 West Church Street, Mason, OH 45040

Mason Public Library, 200 Reading Road, Mason, OH 45040-1694

Massillon Heritage Foundation, 210 4thStreet NE, Massillon, OH 44646

Massillon Museum, 212 Lincoln Way East, Massillon, OH 44646

Massillon: Ohio Society of Military History, 316 Lincoln Way East, Massillon, OH 44646

Massillon Public Library, 208 Lincoln Way East, Massillon, OH 44646

Maumee Valley Historical Society, 1031 River Road, Maumee, OH 43537

McArthur: Herbert Wescoat Memorial Library, 120 North Market Street, McArthur, OH 45651-1218

McComb Public Library, 113 South Todd St., McComb, OH 45858

McConnelville: Kate Love Simpson Library, 358 East Main Street, McConnelville, OH 43765

Mechanicsburg Public Library, 60 South Main Street, Mechanicsburg, OH 43044

Medina: Granger Library & Historical Society, 1195 Granger Road, Medina, OH 44256

Medina Community Design Committee, 141 South Prospect Street, Medina, OH 44256

Medina County District Library, 210 South Broadway Street, Medina, OH 44256-2602

Medina County Historical Society, 206 North Elmwood Street, Medina, OH 44256

Mentor: Lake County Historical Society Library, 8610 King Memorial Road, Mentor, OH 44060

Mentor: Library of Henry J. Grund, 4897 Corduroy Road, Mentor Headlands, Mentor, OH 44060-1216

Mentor Public Library, 8215 Mentor Ave., Mentor, OH 44060

Metamora: Evergreen Community Library, 253 Maple Street, Metamora, OH 43540

Miamisburg Historical Society, P.O. Box 774, Miamisburg, OH 45343

Miamitown: Miami Historical Society of Whitewater Township, P.O. Box 622, Miamitown, OH 45041

Middletown Public Library, 125 South Broad Street, Middletown, OH 45044-4004

Milan-Berlin Township Public Library, East Church Street, P.O. Box 1550, Milan, OH 44846

Milan Public Library, P.O. Box 1550, Milan, OH 44846

Milford Area Historical Society, 906 Main Street, Milford, OH 45150

Millersburg: Holmes County District Public Library, 3102 Glen Drive, P.O. Box 111, Millersburg, OH 44654-1397

Minerva Area Historical Society, P.O. Box 373, 103 Murray Avenue, Minerva, OH 44657

Minerva Public Library, 677 Lynnwood Drive, Minerva, OH 44657

Minster: Fort Loramie Historical Association, 12049 Thelma Drive, Minster, OH 45865

Monroeville: Firelands Council of Historical Societies, P.O. Box 11, Monroeville, OH 44847

Monroeville Public Library, 34 Monroe Street, P.O. Box 276, Monroeville, OH 44847-9722

Montpelier: Williams County Historical Society, P.O. Box 415, 619 East Main Street, Montpelier, OH 43543

Montpelier Public Library, 216 East Main Street, Montpelier, OH 43543-1199

Morrow: Salem Township Public Library, 535 West Pike Street, Morrow, OH 45152-1093

Mount Gilead Free Public Library, 35 East High Street, Mount Gilead, OH 43338-1429

Mount Pleasant: Historical Society of Mount Pleasant, Union and Concord, State Route 150 and State Route 647, Box 35, Mount Pleasant, OH 43939

Mount Sterling Public Library, 60 West Columbus Street, Mount

Sterling, OH 43143-1236

Mount Vernon: Knox County Historical Society, P.O. Box 522, Mount Vernon, OH 43050

Mount Vernon Nazarene University, Thorne Library, 800 Martinsburg Road, Mount Vernon, OH 43050-9500

Mount Vernon: Public Library of Mount Vernon & Knox County, 201 North Mulberry St., Mount Vernon, OH 43050-2413

Mount Victory: Ridgemont Public Library, 124 East Taylor Street, P.O. Box 318, Mount Victory, OH 43340

Napoleon Public Library, 310 West Clinton Street, Napoleon, OH 43545-1597

Navarre-Bethlehem Township Historical Society, 123 High Street, Navarre, OH 44662

Nelsonville: Hocking College Library, Nelsonville, OH 45764

Nelsonville Public Library, 95 West Washington, Nelsonville, OH 45764-1177

New Albany-Plain Township Historical Society, P.O. Box 219, New Albany, OH 43054

New Bremen Historic Association, 122 North Main Street, New Bremen, OH 45869

New Carlisle Public Library, 111 East Lake Avenue, New Carlisle, OH 45344-1418

New Concord: Muskingum College Library,163 Stormont Street, New Concord, OH 43762-1199

New Lexington: Perry County District Library, 117 South Jackson Street, New Lexington, OH 43764-1382

New London Public Library, 67 South Main Street, New London, OH 44851

New Madison Public Library, 142 South Main Street, P.O. Box 32, New Madison, OH 45346-0032

New Matamoras: Matamoras Area Historical Society, P.O. Box 1846,

200 Main Street, New Matamoras, OH 45767

New Philadelphia: Ragersville Historical Society, 144 Tuscora Avenue NW, New Philadelphia, OH 44663

New Philadelphia: Tuscarawas County Public Library, 121 Fair NW, New Philadelphia, OH 44663-2600

New Straitsville Public Library, P.O. Box 8, 102 East Main Street, New Straitsville, OH 43766

Newark: Emerson R. Miller Library, 990 West Main Street, Newark, OH 43055

Newark: Licking County Genealogical Society Library, 101 West Main Street, P.O. Box 4037, Newark, OH 43055-5054

Newark: Licking County Historical Society, 101 West Main Street, Newark, OH 43055

Newark Public Library, 101 West Main Street, Newark, OH 43055

Newcomerstown Public Library, 123 North Bridge Street, Newcomerstown, OH 43832-1093

Newton Falls Public Library, 204 South Canal, Newton Falls, OH 44444-1694

Niles: McKinley Memorial Library, 40 North Main Street, Niles, OH 44446-5082

North Baltimore Public Library, 230 North Main Street, North Baltimore, OH 45872-1195

North Canton Heritage Society, 200 Charlotte Street NW, Suite 102, North Canton, OH 44720

North Canton Public Library, 185 North Main Street, North Canton, OH 44720

North Fairfield Historical Society, P.O. Box 13, North Fairfield, OH 44855

North Royalton Historical Society, 13759 Ridge Road, Cleveland, OH 44133

Northfield: Historical Society of Olde Northfield, 9390 Olde Eight

Road, P.O. Box 99, Northfield, OH 44067

Norwalk: Firelands Historical Society Library, P.O. Box 572, 4 Case Avenue, Norwalk, OH 44857

Norwalk: First Presbyterian Church Library, 21 Firelands Blvd., Norwalk, OH 44857

Norwalk Public Library, 46 West Main Street, Norwalk, OH 44857-1440

Norwood Public Library, 4325 Montgomery Road, Norwood, OH 45212

Novelty: Russell Historical Society, 8450 Kinsman Road, Novelty, OH 44072

Oak Harbor Public Library, 147 West Main Street, Oak Harbor, OH 43449-1344

Oak Hill: Welsh-American Heritage Museum, 412 East Main Street, Oak Hill, OH 45656

Oberlin College Library, 148 West College Street, Oberlin, OH 44074-1532

Oberlin Public Library, 65 South Main St., Oberlin, OH 44074-1626

Ohio Department of Health. *See* Columbus: Ohio Department of Health

Ohio Genealogical Society. *See* Mansfield: Ohio Genealogical Society

Ohio Historical Society. *See* Columbus: Ohio Historical Society

Ohio Society of Military History. *See* Massillon

Ohio State Library. *See* Columbus: State Library of Ohio

Orrville Historical Museum, P.O. Box 437, 142 Depot Street, Orrville, OH 44667

Orrville Public Library, 230 North Main Street, Orrville, OH 44667-1640

Orrville: University of Akron, Wayne College Library, 1901 Smucker Road, Orrville, OH 44667

Orwell: Grand Valley Public Library, P.O. Box 188, 71 North School Street, Orwell, OH 44076-1640

Ottawa: Putnam County District Library, 525 North Thomas Street, P.O. Box 308, Ottawa, OH 43875-0308

Oxford: Miami University, University Libraries, Oxford, OH 45056

Oxford: Smith Library of Regional History, Lane Public Library, Oxford Branch, 15 South College Ave., Oxford, OH 45056

Painesville: Morley Library, 184 Phelps Street, Painesville, OH 44077

Parma: Cuyahoga County Public Library, 2111 Snow Road, Parma, OH 44134-2792

Pataskala Public Library, 101 South Vine Street, Pataskala, OH 43062-9210

Paulding County Carnegie Public Library, 205 South Main Street, Paulding, OH 45879-1492

Pemberville Public Library, 375 East Front Street, Pemberville, OH 43450

Peninsula Library & Historical Society, 6105 Riverview Road, P.O. Box 236, Peninsula, OH 44264-0236

Pepper Pike: Ursuline College, Ralph M. Besse Library, 2550 Lander Road, Pepper Pike, OH 44124

Perry Historical Society of Lake County, P.O. Box 216, Perry, OH 44081

Perry Public Library, 3753 Main Street, Perry, OH 44081-9501

Perrysburg: Historic Perrysburg, P.O. Box 703, Perrysburg, OH 43552

Perrysburg: Way Public Library, 101 East Indiana Avenue, Perrysburg, OH 43551

Perrysville: Greentown Historical Society, 2518 State Route 39, Perrysville, OH 44864

Pickaway County Historical and Genealogical Library, P.O. Box 85, Circleville, OH 43113

Pickerington Public Library, 201 Opportunity Way, Pickerington, OH 43147-2221

Pickerington-Violet Township Historical Society, 471 North Center

Street, Pickerington, OH 43147

Piqua: Edison Community College Library, 1973 Edison Drive, Piqua, OH 45356

Piqua: Flesh Public Library, 124 West Greene Street, Piqua, OH 45356-2399

Piqua: Historical Society, 124 West Greene Street, Piqua, OH 45356

Piqua: Rossville Museum & Cultural Center, 8280 McFarland Road, P.O. Box 627, Piqua, OH 45356

Piqua: Rossville-Spring Creek Historical Society, P.O. Box 627, Piqua, OH 45356

Plain City Public Library, 305 West Main Street, Plain City, OH 43064

Pleasant Hill: Oakes-Beitman Library & Newton Museum, 12 North Main Street, 2nd Floor, Pleasant Hill, OH 45359

Plymouth Area Historical Society 7 East Main Street, Plymouth, OH 44865

Plymouth Historical Society, 315 Plymouth Springmill Road, Plymouth, OH 44865

Pomeroy: Meigs County District Public Library, 216 West Main Street, Pomeroy, OH 45769-1032

Pomeroy: Meigs County Genealogical Society, P.O. Box 346, Pomeroy, OH 45769

Pomeroy: Meigs County Pioneer & Historical Society, P.O. Box 145, Pomeroy, OH 45769

Port Clinton: Ida Rupp Public Library, 310 Madison Street, Port Clinton, OH 43452-1921

Port Clinton: Ottawa County Historical Society, P.O. Box 385, Port Clinton, OH 43452-0385

Portsmouth Public Library, 1220 Gallia Street, Portsmouth, OH 45662

Portsmouth: Shawnee State University, Clark Memorial Library, 940 Second Street, Portsmouth, OH 45662

Preble County District Library, 450 South Barron St., Eaton, OH 45320

Preble County Genealogical Society, 450 South Barron Street, Eaton, OH 45320

Put-In-Bay: Perry's Victory & International Peace Memorial, 93 Delaware Avenue, P.O. Box 549, Put-In-Bay, OH 43456

Ravenna: Portage County Historical Society & Library, 6549 North, Chestnut Street, Ravenna, OH 44266

Ravenna: Reed Memorial Library, Ravenna Public Library, 167 East Main Street, Ravenna, OH 44266-3197

Raymond-Newton Historical Society, P.O. Box 135, Raymond, OH 43067

Reynoldsburg-Truro Historical Society, P.O. Box 144, 1399 Lancaster Avenue, Reynoldsburg, OH 43068

Richfield Historical Society, 3942 Humphrey Road, Richfield, OH 44286

Richwood North Union Public Library, Four East Ottawa Street, Richwood, OH 43344-1296

Rio Grande: University of Rio Grande and Rio Grande Community College Library, Rio Grande, OH 45674

Ripley: Union Township Public Library, 27 Main Street, Ripley, OH 45167-1631

Rock Creek Public Library, Frederick A. Swan Memorial Bldg., 2988 High Street, P.O. Box 297, Rock Creek, OH 44084-9703

Rockford Carnegie Library, 162 South Main Street, P.O. Box 330, Rockford, OH 45882

Rocky River Public Library, 1600 Hampton Road, Rocky River, OH 44116-2699

Rossford Public Library, 720 Dixie Hwy, Rossford, OH 43460-1289

Sabina Public Library, 11 East Elm Street, Sabina, OH 45169-1330

Saint Clairsville Public Library, 108 West Main Street, Saint Clairsville, OH 43950-1225

Saint Martin: Chatfield College Library, 20918 State Route 251, Saint Martin, OH 45118-9705

Saint Marys: Community Public Library, 140 South Chestnut, Saint Marys, OH 45885-2316

Saint Paris Public Library, 127 East Main Street, Saint Paris, OH 43072-9702

Salem Public Library, 821 East State Street, Salem, OH 44460-2298

Sandusky: Erie County Historical Society, P.O. Box 944, 629 South Market Street, Sandusky, OH 44870

Sandusky: Follet House Museum, c/o Sandusky Library Association, 404 Wayne Street, Sandusky, OH 44870

Sandusky Library, 114 West Adams Street, Sandusky, OH 44870

Sardinia: Southern State Community College, Learning Resources Center, 12681 U.S. Route 62, Sardinia, OH 45171

Sebring RR Museum & Historical Society, 216 East Penn Avenue, Sebring, OH 44672

Shaker Heights Public Library, 16500 Van Aken Blvd., Shaker Heights, OH 44120-5318

Sharon Center: Sharon Township Heritage Society, P.O. Box 154, Sharon Center, OH 44274

Sharonville: Society of Historic Sharonville, 10900 Reading Road, Sharonville, OH 45241

Sheffield Lake: 103rd OVI Memorial Foundation, 5501 East Lake Road 7, Sheffield Lake, OH 44054

Shelby County Genealogical Society, 17755 State Route 47, Sidney, OH 45365-9242

Shelby County Historical Society, P.O. Box 376, Sidney, OH 45365-0376

Shelby: Marvin Memorial Library, 29 West Whitney, Shelby, OH 44875-1252

Shelby Museum of History, 76 Raymond Avenue, Shelby, OH 44875

Sidney: Amos Memorial Public Library, 230 East North Street, Sidney, OH 45365-2733

Sidney: Titanic Memorial Museum, P.O. Box 127, 10741 Russell Road, Sidney, OH 45365

Solon Historical Society, 33975 Bainbridge Road, Solon, OH 44139

South Euclid: Notre Dame College of Ohio, Clara Fritzsche Library, 4545 College Road, South Euclid, OH 44121

Southern Ohio Genealogical Society. *See* Hillsboro

Springboro Area Historical Society, P.O. Box 114, Springboro, OH 45066

Springfield: Clark County Genealogical Society, P.O. Box 2524, Springfield, OH 45501-2524

Springfield: Clark County Historical Society Library, P.O. Box 2157, Springfield, OH 45501

Springfield: Clark County Public Library, 201 South Fountain Avenue, P.O. Box 1080, Springfield, OH 45501-1080

Springfield,: Clark State Community College Library, 570 East Leffel Lane, Springfield, OH 45501

Springfield: Warder Public Library, 137 East High Street, Springfield, OH 45502

Springfield: Wittenberg University, Thomas Library, P.O. Box 7207, Springfield, OH 45501-7207

State Library of Ohio. *See* Columbus: State Library of Ohio

Steubenville: Jefferson County Historical Association, P.O. Box 4268, Steubenville, OH 43952-4268

Steubenville: Jefferson County Historical Society Library, 426 Franklin Avenue, Steubenville, OH 43952

Steubenville: Public Library of Steubenville & Jefferson County, 407 South Fourth Street, Steubenville, OH 43952-2942

Steubenville: Schiappa Branch Library, 4141 Mall Drive, Steubenville, OH 43952

Stony Ridge Library, 5805 Fremont Pike, Stony Ridge, OH 43463

Stow-Munroe Falls Public Library, 3512 Darrow Road, Stow, OH 44224-2097

Strongsville Historical Society, 13305 Pearl Road, Strongsville, OH 44136

Struthers Historical Society, 50 Terrace Street, Struthers, OH 44471

Sunbury: Community Library, P.O. Box 239, 44 Burrer Drive, Sunbury, OH 43074

Swanton Public Library, 305 Chestnut Street, Swanton, OH 43558

Tallmadge Historical Society Library, P.O. Box 25, Tallmadge, OH 44278

Tiffin: Heidelberg College, Beeghly Library, 310 East Market Street, Tiffin, OH 44883-2462

Tiffin: Seneca County Historical Society, 6741 South State Route 100, Tiffin, OH 44883-9713

Tiffin: Seneca County Museum Foundation, 28 Clay Street, Tiffin, OH

44883

Tiffin-Seneca Public Library, 77 Jefferson Street, Tiffin, OH 44883

Tipp City Public Library, 11 East Main Street, Tipp City, OH 45371

Tipp City: Studebaker Family National Association, 6555 South State Route 202, Tipp City, OH 45371

Tipp City: Tippecanoe Historical Society, P.O. Box 42, Tipp City, OH 45371

Toledo Area Genealogical Society, P.O. Box 352258, Toledo, OH 43635-2258

Toledo Firefighters' Museum, 918 West Sylvania Avenue, Toledo, OH 43612

Toledo Law Association Library, Lucas County Court House, Toledo, OH 43624-2672

Toledo-Lucas County Public Library, 325 North Michigan Street, Toledo, OH 43624-1628

Toledo: Owens Community College Library, P.O. Box 10,000, Toledo, OH 43699

Toledo Public Library, Local Historical and Genealogical Department, 325 Michigan Street, Toledo, OH 43624-1628

Toledo: University of Toledo, College of Law, LaValley Law Library, Toledo, OH 43606

Toledo: University of Toledo, William S. Carlson Library, 2801 West Bancroft Street, Toledo, OH 43606-3399

Trenton Historical Society, 17-A East State Street, Trenton, OH 45067

Troy Historical Society, 301 West Main Street, Troy, OH 45373

Troy: Miami County Historical and Genealogical Society, P.O. Box 305, Troy, OH 45373

Troy-Miami County Public Library, 419 West Main Street, Troy, OH 45373-3243

Twinsburg Public Library, 10050 Ravenna Road, Twinsburg, OH 44087-1796

University Heights: John Carroll University, Grasselli Library, 20700 North Park Blvd., University Heights, OH 44118

Upper Arlington Historical Society, 1901 Arlington Avenue, Upper Arlington, OH 43212

Upper Arlington Public Library, 2800 Tremont Road, Upper Arlington, OH 43221-3199

Upper Sandusky Community Library, 301 North Sandusky Avenue, Upper Sandusky, OH 43351-1139

Urbana: Champaign County Library, 1060 Scioto Street, Urbana, OH 43078

Utica Historical Society, P.O. Box 5, 45 North Main Street, Utica, OH 43080

Utica: Hervey Memorial Library, 15 North Main Street, Utica, OH 43080

Van Wert: Brumback Library, Van Wert County Public Library, 215 West Main Street, Van Wert, OH 45891-1695

Van Wert County Historical Society, P.O. Box 621, 602 North Washington Street, Van Wert, OH 45891

Vermilion: Friends of Harbour Town, 5741 Liberty Avenue, Vermilion, OH 44089

Vermilion: Great Lakes Historical Society, Clarence S. Metcalf Research Library, 480 Main Street, P.O. Box 435, Vermilion, OH 44089-0435

Vermilion: Ritter Public Library, 5680 Liberty Avenue, Vermilion, OH 44089-1196

Versailles: Worch Memorial Public Library, 161 East Main Street, Versailles, OH 45380-1519

Wadsworth: Ella M. Everhard Public Library, 132 Broad Street, Wadsworth, OH 44281-1850

Wapakoneta: Auglaize County Public District Library, 203 South Perry Street, Wapakoneta, OH 45895-1999

Warren: Trumbull County Historical Society, 303 Monroe NW, Warren, OH 44483-2283

Warren-Trumbull County Public Library, 444 Mahoning Avenue NW, Warren, OH 44483-4692

Washington Court House: Carnegie Public Library, 127 South North Street, Washington Court House, OH 43160-2283

Washington Court House: Fayette County Historical Society, 517 Columbus Avenue, Washington Court House, OH 43160

Waterville Historical Society, 625 Canal Road, Waterville, OH 43566

Wauseon: Fulton County Historical Society, 229 Monroe Street, Wauseon, OH 43567

Wauseon Public Library, 117 East Elm Street, Wauseon, OH 43567-

1444
Waverly: Garnet A. Wilson Public Library of Pike County, 207 North Market Street, Waverly, OH 45690-1189
Waverly: Pike Heritage Foundation, 110 South Market Street, P.O. Box 663, Waverly, OH 45690
Wayne Public Library, 137 East Main Street, Wayne, OH 43466
Waynesville: Mary L. Cook Public Library, 381 Old Stage Road, Waynesville, OH 45068
Wellington: Herrick Memorial Library, 101 Willard Memorial Square, Wellington, OH 44090-1342
Wellston: Ohio Valley Area Libraries, 252 West 13th Street, Wellston, OH 45692
Wellston: Sylvester Memorial Wellston Public Library, 135 East Second Street, Wellston, OH 45692
Wellsville Carnegie Public Library, 115 Ninth Street, Wellsville OH 43968-1431
Wellsville: Scots Settlement Genealogical Center, 18790 Fife Coal Road, Wellsville, OH 43968
Wellsville Historical Society, P.O. Box 13, 1003 Riverside Avenue, Wellsville, OH 43968
Western Reserve Historical Society Library, 10825 East Boulevard, Cleveland, OH 44106-1788
Westerville: Otterbein College, Courtright Memorial Library, 138 West Main Street, Westerville, OH 43081-1436
Westerville Public Library, 126 South State Street, Westerville, OH 43081-2095
West Jefferson: Hurt-Battelle Memorial Library of West Jefferson, 270 Lily Chapel Road, West Jefferson, OH 43162-1202
Westlake: Porter Public Library, 27333 Center Ridge Road, Westlake, OH 44145
West Milton: Milton-Union Public Library, 560 South Main Street, West Milton, OH 45383-1406
West Milton: Union Township Heritage Association, 47 North Miami Street, West Milton, OH 45383
West Union: Adams County Genealogical Society, P.O. Box 231, West Union, OH 45693
Westerville Historical Society, 160 West Main Street, Westerville, OH

43081

Westerville: Otterbein College, Courtright Memorial Library, 138 West Main Street, Westerville, OH 43081

Westerville Public Library, Local History Resource Center, 126 South State Street, Westerville, OH 43081-2095

Westlake Historical Society, P.O. Box 45064, Westlake, OH 44145

Weston Public Library, 13153 Main Street, P.O. Box 345, Weston, OH 43569

Wickliffe Historical Society, 900 Worden Road, Wickliffe, OH 44092

Wickliffe Public Library, 1713 Lincoln Road, Wickliffe, OH 44092-2499

Wilberforce: Central State University, Hallie Q. Brown Memorial Library, 1400 Brush Row Road, Wilberforce, OH 45384

Wilberforce: National Afro-American Museum and Cultural Center, P.O. Box 578, Wilberforce, OH 45384

Wilberforce University, Rembert E. Stokes Learning Resources Center Library, 1055 North Bickett Road, P.O. Box 1003, Wilberforce, OH 45384-1003

Willard Area Historical Society, 704 Myrtle Avenue, Willard, OH 44890

Willard Memorial Library, Six West Emerald Street, Willard, OH 44890-1498

Willoughby Historical Society, 30 Public Square, Willoughby, OH 44094

Willoughby: Little Red Schoolhouse Association, 38470 Bell Road, Willoughby, OH 44094

Willowick-Eastlake Public Library, 263 East 305th Street, Willowick, OH 44095

Wilmington: Clinton County Genealogical Society, P.O. Box 529, Wilmington, OH 45177

Wilmington: Clinton County Historical Society & Museum, 149 East Locust Street, Wilmington, OH 45177

Wilmington College, Sheppard Arthur Watson Library, Pyle Box 1227, Wilmington, OH 45177-2499

Wilmington Public Library of Clinton County, 268 North South Street, Wilmington, OH 45177-1696

Windsor Historical Society, P.O. Box 302, Windsor, OH 44099

Woodsfield: Monroe County District Library, 96 Home Avenue, Woodsfield, OH 43793

Woodsfield: Monroe County Genealogical Society, P.O. Box 641, Woodsfield, OH 43793-0641

Woodsfield: Monroe County Historical Society, 118 Home Avenue, P.O. Box 538, Woodsfield, OH 43793

Woodsfield: Monroe County Park District, 105 West Court Street, Room 2, Woodsfield, OH 43793

Wooster: College of Wooster, Andrews Library, 1140 Beall Avenue, Wooster, OH 44691-2364

Wooster: Wayne County Historical Society, 546 East Bowman Street, Wooster, OH 44691

Wooster: Wayne County Public Library, 304 North Market Street, Wooster, OH 44691-3593

Worthington: Ohio Genealogy Center, P.O. Box 245, Worthington, OH 43085

Worthington Historical Society Library, 50 West New England Avenue, Worthington, OH 43085-3536

Worthington Public Library, 820 High Street, Worthington, OH 43085-4108

Xenia Community Library, Greene County Room, 76 East Market Street, Xenia, OH 45385

Xenia: Greene County Historical Society, 74 West Church Street, Xenia, OH 45385

Xenia: Greene County Public Library, 76 East Market Street, P.O. Box 520, Xenia, OH 45385

Yellow Springs: Antioch College, Olive Kettering Library, 795 Livermore Street, Yellow Springs, OH 45387

Yellow Springs Community Library, 415 Xenia Avenue, Yellow Springs, OH 45387

Yellow Springs Historical Society, P.O. Box 501, Yellow Springs, OH 45387

Youngstown Historical Center of Industry and Labor, P.O. Box 533, 151 West Wood Street, Youngstown, OH 44501-0533

Youngstown: Public Library of Youngstown and Mahoning County, 305 Wick Avenue, Youngstown, OH 44503-1079

Youngstown State University, William F. Maag Jr. Library, One

University Plaza, Youngstown, OH 44555

Zanesville: Muskingum County Genealogical Society Library, 220 North Fifth Street, Zanesville, OH 43701-0391

Zanesville: Muskingum County Library, 220 North Fifth Street, Zanesville, OH 43701

Zoar Community Association, P.O. Box 621, 221 East Foltz, Zoar, OH 44697

References:

American Association for State and Local History. *Directory of Historical Organizations in the United States and Canada.* 15th ed. Walnut Creek, Calif.: Alta Mira Press, 2002.

American Library Directory, 2002-2003. Vol. 1. 55th ed. Medford, N.J.: Information Today, 2002.

Bentley, Elizabeth Petty. *The Genealogist's Address Book.* 4th ed. Baltimore: Genealogical Publishing Co., 1998.

Directory of Genealogical and Historical Libraries, Archives and Collections in the US and Canada. Edited by Dina C. Carson. Niwot, Colo.: Iron Gate Publishing, 2001.

Internet. See especially Google (www.google.com).

Ohio Historical Society. *A Directory of Historical Organizations in Ohio.* 6th ed. Columbus: Ohio Historical Society, 1999.

Smith, Juliana Szucs. *The Ancestry Family Historian's Address Book.* 2nd ed. Orem, Utah: Ancestry, 2003.

State Library of Ohio. *Directory of Ohio Libraries.* Columbus: State Library of Ohio, 1998.

Zacharias, Susan. "Ohio Public Libraries: Genealogical Collections." *OGS Genealogy News* 33 (May/June 2002): 90-93.

ADDRESSES—OUTSIDE OHIO

Allen County Public Library, 900 Webster Street, P.O. Box 2270, Fort Wayne, IN 46801-2270

Boston Public Library, 700 Boylston Street, Boston, MA 02117

Brigham Young University, Harold B. Lee Library, Provo, UT 84602

Bureau of Land Management, Eastern States Office, 7450 Boston Boulevard, Springfield, VA 22153-3121

California State Library. *See* Sutro Library

Clayton Library Center for Genealogical Research, 5300 Caroline, Houston, TX 77004

Dallas Public Library, Genealogy Section, 1515 Young Street, Dallas, TX 75201

Daughters of the American Revolution Library. *See* National Society Daughters of the American Revolution, DAR Library

Denver Public Library, Western History/Genealogy Department, 10 West 14th Avenue Parkway, Denver, CO 80204

Detroit Public Library, Burton Historical Collection, 5201 Woodward Avenue, Detroit, MI 48202

Family History Library, 35 North West Temple Street, Salt Lake City, UT 84150-3400

Genealogical Forum of Oregon, P.O. Box 42567, Portland, OR 97242

Heart of America Genealogical Society Library, c/o Kansas City Public Library, 311 East 12th Street, Kansas City, MO 64106

Kansas City Public Library, 311 East 12th Street, Kansas City, MO 64106

Library of Congress, Local History and Genealogy Division, 101 Independence Avenue S.E., Washington, DC 20540

The Library of Virginia, 800 East Broad St., Richmond, VA 23219-8000

Los Angeles Public Library, History and Genealogy Department, 630 West Fifth Street, Los Angeles, CA 90071

Mid-Continent Public Library, Genealogy and Local History, 317 West 24 Highway, Independence, MO 64050

National Archives and Records Administration, 700 Pennsylvania Avenue N.W., Washington, DC 20408

National Archives and Records Administration—Great Lakes Region, 7358 South Pulaski Road, Chicago, IL 60629-5898

National Genealogical Society, 4527 17th Street North, Arlington, VA 22207-2399 (see also St. Louis County Library, St. Louis, MO)

National Personnel Records Center, Military Personnel Records, 9700 Page Avenue., St. Louis, MO 63132-5100

National Society Daughters of the American Revolution, DAR Library, 1776 D Street NW, Washington, DC 20006-5303

Newberry Library, 60 West Walton Street, Chicago, IL 60610-7324

New England Historic Genealogical Society Library, 101 Newbury Street, Boston, MA 02116-3007

New York Public Library, Humanities and Social Sciences Library, Fifth Avenue and 42nd Street, New York, NY 10018-2788

Orlando Public Library, 101 East Central Blvd., Orlando, FL 32801

St. Louis County Library, 1640 South Lindbergh Blvd., St. Louis, MO 63131-3598

St. Louis Public Library, History and Genealogy Department, 1301 Olive Street, St. Louis, MO 63103

Seattle Public Library, 800 Pike Street, Seattle, WA 98101

Sutro Library, California State Library, 480 Winston Drive, San Francisco, CA 94132

Virginia State Library and Archives. *See* The Library of Virginia

Wisconsin Historical Society Library, 816 State Street, Madison, WI 53706

References:

American Association for State and Local History. *Directory of Historical Organizations in the United States and Canada.* 15th ed. Walnut Creek, Calif.: Alta Mira Press, 2002.

American Library Directory, 2002-2003. Vol. 1. 55th ed. Medford, N.J.: Information Today, 2002.

Bentley, Elizabeth Petty. *The Genealogist's Address Book.* 4th ed. Baltimore: Genealogical Publishing Co., 1998.

Internet. See especially Google (www.google.com).

Smith, Juliana Szucs. *The Ancestry Family Historian's Address Book.* 2nd ed. Orem, Utah: Ancestry, 2003.

State Library of Ohio. *Directory of Ohio Libraries.* Columbus: State Library of Ohio, 1998.

FAMILY HISTORY CENTERS IN OHIO

Family History Centers are branch libraries of the Family History Library in Salt Lake City, Utah. Copies of most of the microfilms at the main library in Salt Lake City may be loaned to Family History Centers. In addition, most Centers have their own reference collection and other resources, such as microfilms, microfiche, books, indexes, and compact discs (CD-ROMs). Actual locations of Centers (not mailing addresses) in Ohio are listed below (excluding very small meetinghouse libraries). Most centers are located in LDS meetinghouses, such as stake centers. They are open to the public. See a local telephone book under The Church of Jesus Christ of Latter-day Saints (Family History Center). Library hours vary.

Adams Ohio, 1185 Grace's Run Road, Winchester, Adams County
Akron Ohio, 106 East Howe Road, Tallmadge, Summit County
Ashtabula Ohio, 571 Seven Hills Road, Ashtabula, Ashtabula County
Athens Ohio, 7795 Lemaster Road, The Plains, Athens County
Canton Ohio, 735 Easthill Street SE, North Canton, Stark County
Centerville Ohio, 901 E. Whipp Rd., Centerville, Montgomery County
Chillicothe Ohio, 553 4th Street, Chillicothe, Ross County
Cincinnati Ohio, 5505 Bosworth Place, Cincinnati, Hamilton County
Cincinnati Ohio 5th & 7th, 695 Clough Pike, Cincinnati, Clermont
    County
Cincinnati Ohio North, Cornell & Snider Road, Cincinnati, Hamilton
    County
Cleveland Ohio, 25000 Westwood Road, Westlake, Cuyahoga County
Columbus Ohio East, 2135 Baldwin Road, Reynoldsburg, OH 43068,
    Franklin County

Columbus Ohio North, 7135 Coffman Road, Dublin, OH 43017,
   Franklin/ Delaware/ Union County
Columbus Westland/Scioto Ohio, 2400 Red Rock Blvd., Grove City,
   OH 43123, Franklin County
Dayton Ohio, 1500 Shiloh Springs Road, Dayton, Montgomery County
Dayton Ohio East, 3060 Terry Drive, Fairborn, Greene County
Fairfield/Hamilton Ohio, 4831 Pleasant Ave., Fairfield, Hamilton Co.
Findlay Ohio, 2800 Crystal Avenue, Findlay, Hancock County
Galion Ohio, 250 South Road, Galion, Crawford County
Georgetown Ohio, State Road 125, Georgetown, Brown County
Kirtland Ohio, 8854 Chillicothe Road, Kirtland, Lake County
Lima Ohio, 1195 Brower Road, Lima, Allen County
Lisbon Ohio, 7250 Market Street, Lisbon, Columbiana County
Mansfield Ohio, 1951 Middle Bellville Rd., Mansfield, Richland Co.
Marion Ohio, 1725 Marion-Edison Road, Marion, Marion County
Medina Ohio, 4411 Windfall Road, Medina, Medina County
Middletown Ohio, 4930 Central Avenue, Middletown, Butler/Warren
   County
Mount Vernon Ohio, 1010 Beech Street, Mt. Vernon, Knox County
Oxford Ohio, 6600 Contreras Road, Oxford, Butler County
Perrysburg Ohio, State Route 795, Perrysburg, Wood County
Rootstown Ohio, 2776 Hartville Road, Rootstown, Portage County
Sandusky Ohio, 4511 Galloway Road, Sandusky, Erie County
Toledo Ohio, State Route 795, Perrysburg, Wood County
Warren/Youngstown Ohio, 2205 Tibbetts Wick Road, Girard, Trumbull
   County
Wauseon Ohio, 858 South Shoop Avenue, Wauseon, Fulton County
West Chester Ohio, 7118 Dutchland Parkway, Middletown, Butler
   County
Westerville Ohio, 307 Huber Village Blvd., Westerville, OH 43081,
   Franklin Co.

Wilmington Ohio, State Route 73, Wilmington, Clinton County
Wintersville Ohio, 437 Powells Lane, Wintersville, Jefferson County
Wooster Ohio, 1388 Liahona Drive, Wooster, Wayne County
Zanesville Ohio, 3300 Kearns Drive, Zanesville, Muskingum County

References:

Family History Center Support, Family and Church History Department,
Salt Lake City, UT 84150

Family History Centers, North Central States (list available from the
Family History Library, Salt Lake City, UT 84150). Contact the
Family History Library for locations of other Family History
Centers throughout the world.

Family History Library e-mail (FHL@LDSCHURCH.ORG)

FamilySearch™ Internet Genealogy Service (www.familysearch.org)
Library / Family History Centers / Ohio

OHIO GENEALOGICAL SOCIETY CHAPTERS

Allen County, 620 West Market Street, Lima, OH 45801-4665

Alliance Genealogical Society, P.O. Box 3630, Alliance, OH 44601-7630

Ashland County, P.O. Box 681, Ashland, OH 44805-0681

Ashtabula County, Geneva Public Library, 860 Sherman Street, Geneva, OH 44041-9101

Athens County, 65 North Court St., Athens, OH 45701-2506

Auglaize County, P.O. Box 2021, Wapakoneta, OH 45895-0521

Belmont County, P.O. Box 285, Barnesville, OH 43713-0285

Brown County, P.O. Box 83, Georgetown, OH 45121-0083

Butler County, P.O. Box 2011, Middletown, OH 45044-2011

Carroll County, 24 Second St., P.O. Box 36, Carrollton, OH 44615-0036

Champaign County, P.O. Box 682, Urbana, OH 43078-0680

Clark County, P.O. Box 2524, Springfield, OH 45501-2524

Clermont County, P.O. Box 394, Batavia, OH 45103-0394

Cleveland: Greater Cleveland, P.O. Box 40254, Cleveland, OH 44140-0254

Clinton County, P.O. Box 529, Wilmington, OH 45177-0529

Colorado Chapter, P.O. Box 470189, Aurora, CO 80047-0189

Columbiana County, P.O. Box 861, Salem, OH 44460-0861

Coshocton County, P.O. Box 128, Coshocton, OH 43812-0128

Crawford County, P.O. Box 92, Galion, OH 44833-0092

Cuyahoga: East Cuyahoga, P.O. Box 24182, Lyndhurst, OH 44124-0182

Cuyahoga: Greater Cleveland, P.O. Box 40254, Cleveland, OH 44140-0254

Cuyahoga: Southwest Cuyahoga, 13305 Pearl Road, Strongsville, OH

44136-3403

Cuyahoga Valley, P.O. Box 41414, Brecksville, OH 44141-0414

Cuyahoga West, P.O. Box 26196, Fairview Park, OH 44126-0196

Darke County, P.O. Box 908, Greenville, OH 45331-0908

Defiance County, P.O. Box 7006, Defiance, OH 43512-7006

Delaware County, P.O. Box 1126, Delaware, OH 43015-8126

Erie County, P.O. Box 1301, Sandusky, OH 44871-1301

Fairfield County, P.O. Box 1470, Lancaster, OH 43130-0570

Fayette County, P.O. Box 342, Washington C.H., OH 43160-0342

Florida Chapter, P.O. Box 56433, Jacksonville, FL 32241-6433

Franklin County, P.O. Box 44309, Columbus, OH 43204-0309

Fulton County, P.O. Box 337, Swanton, OH 43558-0337

Gallia County, P.O. Box 295, Gallipolis, OH 45631-0295

Geauga County, 110 East Park Street, Chardon, OH 44024-1213

Greene County, P.O. Box 706, Xenia, OH 45385-0706

Guernsey County, P.O. Box 661, 8583 Georgetown Road, Cambridge, OH 43725-0661

Hamilton County, P.O. Box 15865, Cincinnati, OH 45215-0865

Hancock County, P.O. Box 672, Findlay, OH 45839-0672

Hardin County, P.O. Box 520, Kenton, OH 43326-0520

Harrison County, 45507 Unionvale Rd., Cadiz, OH 43907-9723

Henry County, P.O. Box 231, Deshler, OH 43516

Highland County: Southern Ohio Genealogical Society, P.O. Box 414, Hillsboro, OH 45133-0414

Hocking County, P.O. Box 115, Rockbridge, OH 43149-0115

Holmes County, P.O. Box 136, Millersburg, OH 44654-0136

Hudson Library and Historical Society, 22 Aurora Street, No. G, Hudson, OH 44236-2947

Huron County, P.O. Box 923, Norwalk, OH 44857-0923

Jackson County, P.O. Box 807, Jackson, OH 45640-0807

Jefferson County, P.O. Box 4712, Steubenville, OH 43952-8712

Knox County, P.O. Box 1098, Mt. Vernon, OH 43050-1098

Lake County, Morley Library, 184 Phelps Street, Painesville, OH 44077-3927

Lawrence County, P.O. Box 1035, Proctorville, OH 45669-1035

Licking County, 101 West Main Street, Newark, OH 43055-5054

Logan County, P.O.Box 36, Bellefontaine, OH 43311-0036

Lorain County, P.O.Box 865, Elyria, OH 44036-0865

Lucas County, 325 N. Michigan Street, Toledo, OH 43624-1614

Madison County, P.O. Box 102, London, OH 43140-0102

Mahoning County, P.O. Box 9333, Boardman, OH 44513

Marion Area, P.O. Box 844, Marion, OH 43301-0844

Medina County, P.O. Box 804, Medina, OH 44258-0804

Meigs County, P.O. Box 346, Pomeroy, OH 45769-0346

Mercer County, P.O. Box 437, Celina, OH 45822-0437

Miami County Historical and Genealogical Society, P.O. Box 305, Troy, OH 45373-0305

Monroe County, P.O. Box 641, Woodsfield, OH 43793-0641

Montgomery County, P.O. Box 1584, Dayton, OH 45401-1584

Morgan County, P.O. Box 418, McConnelsville, OH 43756-0418

Morrow County, P.O. Box 401, Mt. Gilead, OH 43338-0401

Muskingum County, P.O. Box 2427, Zanesville, OH 43702-2427

Noble County, P.O. Box 174, Caldwell, OH 43724-0174

Ottawa County, P.O. Box 193, Port Clinton, OH 43452-0193

Paulding County, 205 South Main Street, Paulding, OH 45879-1492

Perry County, P.O. Box 275, Junction City, OH 43748-0275

Pickaway County Historical Society, P.O. Box 85, Circleville, OH 43113

Pike County, P.O. Box 224, Waverly, OH 45690-0224

Portage County, P.O. Box 821, Ravenna, OH 44266-0821

Preble County, 450 S. Baron Street, Eaton, OH 45320-1705

Putnam County, P.O. Box 403, Ottawa, OH 45875-0403

Richland County, P.O. Box 3823, Mansfield, OH 44907-0823

Richland-Shelby Genealogical Society, P.O. Box 766, Shelby, OH 44875-0766

Ross County, P.O. Box 6352, Chillicothe, OH 45601-6352

Sandusky County Kin Hunters, Spiegle Grove, Fremont, OH 43420-2796

Scioto County, P.O. Box 812, Portsmouth, OH 45662-0812

Seneca County, P.O. Box 157, Tiffin, OH 44883-0157

Southern Ohio Genealogical Society, P.O. Box 414, Hillsboro, OH 45133-0414

Stark County, P.O. Box 9035, Canton, OH 44711-9035

Summit County, P.O. Box 2232, Akron, OH 44309-2232

Trumbull County, P.O. Box 309, Warren, OH 44482-0309

Tuscarawas County, P.O. Box 141, New Philadelphia, OH 44663-0141

Union County, P.O. Box 438, Marysville, OH 43040-0438

Van Wert County, P.O. Box 485, Van Wert, OH 45891-0485

Vinton County, P.O. Box 306, Hamden, OH 45634-0306

Warren County, 406 Justice Drive, Lebanon, OH 45036

Washington County, P.O. Box 2174, Marietta, OH 45750-2174

Wayne County, P.O. Box 856, Wooster, OH 44691-0856

Williams County, P.O. Box 293, Bryan, OH 43506-0293

Wood County, P.O. Box 722, Bowling Green, OH 43402-0722

Wyandot County, P.O. Box 414, Upper Sandusky, OH 43351-0414

References:

OGS Genealogy News. Mansfield, Ohio: Ohio Genealogical Society, 2003 (published six times a year by OGS). This publication provides an up-to-date listing of Ohio Genealogical Society chapters.

"Ohio Genealogical Society Chapter Addresses" on the OGS Internet home page (www.ogs.org/chap.htm).
Provides links to OGS chapter Web sites and e-mail addresses.

Ohio Genealogical Society. *2003 Ohio Genealogical Society Chapter Directory & Publications List.* Mansfield, Ohio: Ohio Genealogical Society, 2003.

Ohio Genealogical Society Quarterly (formerly *The Report*). Mansfield, Ohio: Ohio Genealogical Society, quarterly.

Internet. See especially Google (www.google.com).

Appreciation is extended to Thomas Stephen Neel, Library Director, Ohio Genealogical Society Library, Mansfield, Ohio, for providing revised and updated addresses of OGS chapters.

Bibliography

Bibliographies, Guides, and Finding Aids

Adams, Marilyn L., comp. *Ohio Local and Family History Sources in Print.* Clarkston, Georgia: Heritage Research, 1984.

_____, comp. *Southeastern Ohio Local and Family History Sources in Print.* Atlanta: Heritage Research, 1979.

Adams, Marjorie E. and Martha S. Alt, comps. *Encyclopedia of Ohio Associations: A Guide to Statewide Organizations.* Rev. ed. Columbus: OHIONET, 1988.

A comprehensive list of non-profit associations in Ohio which are statewide in scope or interest.

Beers, Henry Putney. *The French & British in the Old Northwest: A Bibliographical Guide to Archive and Manuscript Sources.* Detroit: Wayne State University Press, 1964.

Benson, Marjorie, comp. *Awesome Almanac: Ohio.* Walworth, Wisc.: B&B Publishing, 1995.

Bentley, Elizabeth Petty. *County Courthouse Book.* 2nd ed. Baltimore: Genealogical Publishing Co., 1995.

_____. *The Genealogist's Address Book.* 4th ed. Baltimore: Genealogical Publishing Co., 1998.

Biggs, Deb. *Guide to Local Government Records at the Center for Archival Collections.* Bowling Green, Ohio: Bowling Green State University, 1981.

Britton, J.D., comp. *Ohio History Resource Guide for Teachers.* Columbus: Ohio Historical Society, 1991.

See especially "Educational Resources for Ohio History Teachers."

Burke, Thomas Aquinas. *Ohio Lands: A Short History.* 9th ed. Columbus: Auditor of State, 1997.

(http://freepages.history.rootsweb.com/~maggie/ohio-lands/ohlands.html)

Carson, Dina C., ed. *Directory of Genealogical and Historical Publications in the U.S. and Canada.* Niwot, Colo.: Iron Gate Publishing, 1992.

_____, ed. *Directory of Genealogical and Historical Societies in the U.S. and Canada.* Niwot, Colo.: Iron Gate Publishing, 1992.

Central Ohio Interlibrary Network. *Union List of Genealogy Material.* Mansfield, Ohio: Central Ohio Interlibrary Network, 1975.

Christian, Donna. *Guide to Newspaper Holdings at the Center for Archival Collections.* Bowling Green, Ohio: Bowling Green State University, 1980.

City and County Directories at the Ohio Historical Society. Bowie, Md.: Heritage Books, 1985.

Clark, Donna K. *Ohio State Directory of Genealogical Records by TAD (The Ancestor Detective).* Arvada, Colo.: Ancestor Publishers, 1986.

Lists of Ohio sources and bibliographic details.

Clements, John. *Ohio Facts: A Comprehensive Look at Ohio Today, County by County.* Dallas, Texas: Clements Research II, 1988.

A chronological history of Ohio, with a county-by-county summary of local information—the people, land, economy, etc. Useful for locating telephone numbers and addresses of county offices.

Columbus Area Library and Information Council of Ohio. *CALICO Genealogical Resources.* N.p., 1981.

Curtin, Michael F. *The Ohio Politics Almanac.* Kent, Ohio: Kent State University Press, 1996.

A guide to Ohio government and politics—both historical and contemporary. Shows details on each Ohio county.

Dean, Tanya West and W. David Speas. *Along the Ohio Trail: A Short History of Ohio Lands.* Edited by George W. Knepper. Columbus: Auditor of State, 2001. See (www.auditor.state.oh.us).

Dictionary of Ohio Historic Places. Ed. By Lorrie K. Owen. 2 vols. St. Clair Shores, Mich.: Somerset Publishers, 1999.

Describes Ohio's historical buildings, libraries, houses, etc.; arranged by county.

Douthit, Ruth Long. *Ohio Resources for Genealogists, with Some References for Genealogical Searching in Ohio.* Rev. ed. Detroit: Detroit Society for Genealogical Research, 1972.

Downes, Randolph C. *Evolution of Ohio County Boundaries.* 1927. Reprint. Columbus: Ohio Historical Society, 1970.

The Encyclopedia of Ohio, 1999. 2 vols. St. Clair Shores, Mich.: Somerset Publishers, 1999.

Ohio history, chronology, dictionary of places, historic places, and other state information.

Filby, P. William, comp. *A Bibliography of American County Histories.* Baltimore: Genealogical Publishing Co., 1985.

Folck, Linda L., comp. *Local Government Records in the American History Research Center at the University of Akron.* Rev. ed. N.p., 1982.

Gagel, Diane VanSkiver. *Ohio Courthouse Records.* Ohio Genealogical Society Research Guide No. 1. Mansfield, Ohio: The Society, 1997.

A valuable description of genealogical records kept in Ohio county courthouses.

―――――. *Ohio Photographers, 1839-1900.* Nevada City, Calif.: Carl Mautz Publishing, 1998.

Genealogical Researcher's Manual: With Special References for Using the Ohio Historical Society Library. Columbus: Franklin County Chapter, Ohio Genealogical Society, 1982.

Gilkey, Elliot Howard. *The Ohio Hundred Year Book.* Columbus: Fred J. Heer, 1901.

Lists of members of the General Assembly, senators,

representatives, and biographical sketches. This work is a revised and enlarged edition of *Taylor's Ohio Statesmen and Hundred Year Book* (1892).

The Golden Census Guide for the State of Ohio. Des Moines, Iowa: Golden Census Guide, 1991.

Goulder, Grace. *This Is Ohio: Ohio's 88 Counties in Words and Pictures.* Rev. ed. Cleveland: World Publishing Co., 1965.

A brief history of Ohio's counties and regions. Illustrated.

Gray, Judy Price. *Colorado Territorial Families from Ohio.* Denver: Colorado Chapter, Ohio Genealogical Society, n.d.

————, comp. *County-by-County [Ohio] Research by Members.* Longmont, Colo.: Colorado Chapter, Ohio Genealogical Society, 1998.

Includes county, name of researcher, and surnames they are researching.

The Great 88: A Brief Guide to Each of Ohio's 88 Counties and their Beautiful Courthouses. Columbus: Ohio Department of Development, 1993.

Includes a brief history of each Ohio courthouse.

Green, Karen Mauer. *Pioneer Ohio Newspapers, 1793-1810: Genealogical and Historical Abstracts.* Galveston, Texas: Frontier Press, 1986.

————. *Pioneer Ohio Newspapers, 1802-1818: Genealogical and Historical Abstracts.* Galveston, Texas: Frontier Press, 1988.

Gutgesell, Stephen, ed.. *Guide to Ohio Newspapers, 1793-1973: A Union Bibliography of Ohio Newspapers Available in Ohio Libraries.* Columbus: Ohio Historical Society, 1976.

Hall, William K. *The Shane Manuscript Collection: A Genealogical Guide to the Kentucky and Ohio Papers.* Galveston: Frontier Press, 1990.

Harfst, Linda L., ed. *Local History and Genealogy Resources Guide to*

Southeastern Ohio. Wellston, Ohio: Ohio Valley Area Libraries, 1984.

Identifies genealogical and historical records found in libraries in Southeastern Ohio. See the work edited by Gail Zachariah listed later in this section.

Harter, Stuart. *Ohio Genealogy and Local History Sources Index.* Ft. Wayne, Ind.: CompuGen Systems, 1986.

Hehir, Donald M. *Ohio Families: A Bibliography of Books about Ohio Families.* Bowie, Md.: Heritage Books, 1993.

An alphabetical listing by surname of genealogies that have some Ohio connection.

Historical Records Survey (Ohio). *American Imprints Inventory: Check List of Ohio Imprints, 1796-1820.* 1941. Reprint. New York: Kraus Reprint Corp., 1964.

_____. *Inventory of the County Archives of Ohio.* Columbus, 1940.

_____. *Inventory of the State Archives of Ohio.* Columbus: Ohio Historical Records Survey Project, 1940.

Although dated, this inventory briefly describes records of the Secretary of State—house and senate journals, accounts, bonds, etc. Includes subject index.

Hutchinson, William Thomas. *The Bounty Lands of the American Revolution in Ohio.* 1927. Reprint. New York: Arno Press, 1979.

Kalette, Linda Elise. *The Papers of Thirteen Early Ohio Political Leaders: An Inventory of the 1976-77 Microfilm Editions.* Columbus: Ohio Historical Society, 1977.

Knepper, George W. *The Official Ohio Lands Book.* Columbus: Auditor of State, 2002. See (www.auditor.state.oh.us).

League of Women Voters of Ohio. *Know Your Ohio Government.* 4th ed. Columbus, 1978.

Describes the organization of Ohio state government—Court of Common Pleas, Court of Appeals, and other courts.

Lee, Susan Dunlap, comp. *The Ohio Genealogical Society Periodicals Index: Topical by Location, 1960-2000.* Mansfield, Ohio: Ohio Genealogical Society, 2002.
Indexes topics in periodicals published by OGS; arranged by localities.

Leggett, Nancy G. and Dorothy E. Smith, comps. *A Guide to Local Government Records and Newspapers Preserved at the Department of Archives and Special Collections, Wright State University Library.* N.p., 1987.

Levine, David, ed. *Ohio Municipal Records Manual,* comp. by George Bain, et al. Rev. ed. Columbus: Ohio Historical Society, 1986.
Written to aid city and local officials in the retention and disposition of records in the state.

Levinson, Marilyn, ed. *Guide to Newspaper Holdings at the Center for Archival Collections.* 3rd ed. Bowling Green, Ohio: Center for Archival Collections, Libraries and Learning Resources, Bowling Green State University, 1991.

Linck, Bonnie J. and Suzanne Wolfe Mettle. *Bible Records: A Survey of Bibles and Related Books for Family and Historic Information in the Archives-Library Division of the Ohio Historical Society.* Columbus: Ohio Historical Society, 1994.
An inventory of many family Bibles housed at the Ohio Historical Society, Columbus.

Masley, Betty. *Ohio Books in Print: Genealogy Resources.* Indianapolis: Betty Masley, 1994.
A listing, though dated, of Ohio books in print, along with other Ohio reference aids.

Martz, Linda. *Ohio Records Finder: How to Use Public Documents to Uncover Information.* Mansfield, Ohio: The author, 1998.

Matusoff, Karen L., comp. *Central Ohio Local Government Records at the Ohio Historical Society.* Columbus: Ohio Historical Society,

1978.

McConnell, Edward N. and Theodore S. Foster. *Local Government Records at the Ohio University Library.* Columbus, 1979.

Mettle, Suzanne Wolfe, et al., comps. *Genealogical Researcher's Manual with Special References for Using the Ohio Historical Society Library.* Columbus: Franklin County Chapter, Ohio Genealogical Society, 1981.

Meyer, Mary Keysor, ed. *Meyer's Directory of Genealogical Societies in the U.S.A. and Canada.* 10th ed. Mt. Airy, Md.: Libra Publications, 1994.

Morrison, Patricia, comp. *Southern California Library Survey of Books on Ohio.* Los Alamitos, Calif.: Southern California Chapter of the Ohio Genealogical Society, 1990.

Mullin, Patrick Joseph, comp. *Ohio Census Population Schedules in Ohio Libraries.* Columbus: Ohio Library Association, 1977.
    A union list of Ohio census population schedules, 1800-1890, in eighty-three Ohio libraries.

North Central Library Cooperative. *Ohio Genealogy and Local History: A Resource Guide to the Holdings of Twenty-three Member Libraries.* Ed. by Michael G. Snyder. Mansfield, Ohio: North Central Library Cooperative, 1984.

Northwest Library District. *Genealogical Resources Guide, Northwest Ohio Libraries.* Bowling Green, Ohio: NORWELD, 1996.
    Details genealogical holdings of libraries in northwest Ohio.

O'Bryant, Michael, ed. *The Ohio Almanac.* Wilmington, Ohio: Orange Frazer Press, 1997-98.
    An encyclopedia of Ohio facts, addresses, biographies, and many other details pertaining to the state.

The Ohio Almanac. 9th ed. Dayton, Ohio: Ohio Almanac, 1980.
    Includes a brief history of Ohio counties; illustrated.

The Ohio Almanac: An Encyclopedia of Indispensable Information

About the Buckeye Universe. Edited by Michael O'Bryant. Wilmington, Ohio: Orange Frazer Press, 1997.

Ohio. Department of Development. *Ohio's Museums and Mementos.* Columbus: Columbus Blank Book Co., 1967.

Briefly describes Ohio museums and some historical societies.

_____. *1982 Ohio County Profiles.* Columbus, 1982.

Ohio Genealogical Society. *2003 Ohio Genealogical Society Chapter Directory & Publications List.* Mansfield, Ohio: The Society, 2003.

Gives OGS chapter address and telephone number, meeting information, a list of publications, and other useful details.

_____. *Ohio Cemeteries.* Ed. Maxine Hartmann Smith. Mansfield, Ohio: The Society, 1998.

Identifies Ohio cemeteries. Arranged by counties and townships. Includes county maps. This title and the 1990 addendum were updated in 2003 as an OGS Bicentennial project (see below).

_____. *Ohio Cemeteries Addendum.* Baltimore: Gateway Press, 1990.

_____. Cemetery Committee, comp. *Ohio Cemeteries, 1803-2003.* Mansfield, Ohio: The Society, 2003.

Ohio Historical Society. *Abstract of Ohio County Records Inventory, 1803 through 1977.* Columbus: The Society, n.d.. Microfilm.

_____. *A Directory of Historical Organizations in Ohio.* 6th ed. Columbus: Ohio Historical Society, 1999.

Arranged by locality, this essential Ohio reference gives address, telephone numbers, describes major programs, and other details regarding each institution listed.

_____. *Guide to Local Government Records at the Ohio University Library.* Athens, Ohio: Ohio University Library, 1992.

_____. *A Guide to Manuscripts at the Ohio Historical Society.* Edited by Andrea D. Lentz and Sara S. Fuller. Columbus: The Society, 1972.

Describes private papers and manuscript collections housed at the Ohio Historical Society. This guide is partially outdated.

_____. Local Government Records Program. *Guide to Local Government Records at the Ohio University Library.* Rev. ed. Athens, Ohio: Ohio University Library, 1992.

A county-by-county description of county and other local records housed at the Ohio University Library, Athens.

_____. *OAHSM Lending Library Catalog and Local History Bibliography.* Columbus: Ohio Historical Society, 1997.

_____. *Ohio County Records Manual.* Rev. ed. Columbus: The Society, 1983.

Arranged by county office, a brief description and duties of each office, a description of the records of each office, and retention schedule.

_____. *Ohio Newspaper Microfilm Catalog.* Columbus: The Society, 1991. Microfiche.

_____. *Union Bibliography of Ohio Printed State Documents, 1803-1970.* Compiled by Patricia Swanson, et al. Columbus: Ohio Historical Society, 1973.

A comprehensive union list of documents published by the state of Ohio between 1803 and 1970. Arranged by agencies.

Ohio Legal Resources: An Annotated Bibliography and Guide. 3rd ed. Columbus: Ohio Regional Association of Law Libraries and Ohio Library Association, 1990.

Ohio Library Council. *Directory of Special Collections.* Columbus: The Council, 1998.

Ohio Library Foundation. *Checklist: Publications of the State of Ohio, 1803-1952.* Columbus, 1964.

Ohio Museums Association. *Ohio Cultural Directory.* Columbus: Ohio Museums Association, 1998.

Identifies historical societies, church archives, museums,

genealogical societies, cemeteries, and similar organizations.

Ohio. Secretary of State. *Annual Report of the Secretary of State to the Governor of the State of Ohio*. Columbus: Nevins & Myers, 1878.

Ohio State Library. *Checklist, Publications of the State of Ohio, 1803-1952*. Columbus: Ohio Library Foundation, 1964.

Phillips, William Louis. *Annotated Bibliography of Ohio Patriots: Revolutionary War & War of 1812*. Bowie, Md.: Heritage Books, 1985.

_____. *City and County Directories at the Ohio Historical Society*. N.p. 1985.

_____. *Jurisdictional Histories for Ohio's Eighty-Eight Counties, 1788-1985*. Bowie, Md.: Heritage Books, 1986.

_____. *Ohio City & County Directories: The Ohio Historical Society Collection*. Bowie, Md.: Heritage Books, 1986.

Pike, Kermit J., comp. *A Guide to the Manuscripts and Archives of the Western Reserve Historical Society*. Cleveland: Western Reserve Historical Society, 1972.

_____. *A Guide to Shaker Manuscripts in the Library of the Western Reserve Historical Society*. Cleveland: Western Reserve Historical Society, 1974.

An inventory of Shaker diaries, journals, sermons, and writings housed at the Western Reserve Historical Society.

_____, comp. *A Guide to Major Manuscript Collections Accessioned and Processed by the Library of the Western Reserve Historical Society Since 1970*. Cleveland: Western Reserve Historical Society, 1987.

Putnam, Melanie K. and Susan M. Schaefgen. *Ohio Legal Research Guide*. Buffalo, N.Y.: William S. Hein & Co., 1997.

Research Publications. *Reel Index to the Microform Collection of County and Regional Histories of the "Old Northwest," Series II: Ohio*. New Haven: Research Publications, 1975.

Identifies author, title, and imprint of Ohio local histories, atlases, and biographies filmed by Research Publications.

Rieger, Paul E., comp. *The Upper Ohio Valley: A Bibliography and Price Guide.* Baltimore: Gateway Press, 1983.

Rose, Albert H. *Ohio Government, State and Local.* 3rd ed. Dayton: University of Dayton Press, 1966.

Describes growth of townships from Ohio land grants, Ohio municipalities, and state government.

Smith, Clifford Neal. *Federal Land Series.* Chicago: American Library Association, 1972-86.

Smith, Dorothy and Maggie Yax. *A Guide to Manuscripts, Special Collections and Archives, Paul Laurence Dunbar Library.* Dayton Ohio: Wright State University Libraries, 1996.

Society of Ohio Archivists. *Guide to Manuscripts Collections & Institutional Records in Ohio.* Edited by David R. Larson. Columbus: Society of Ohio Archivists, 1974.

Identifies church records, genealogical collections, account books, diaries, family papers, administrative records, and many other manuscript collections in Ohio.

State Library of Ohio. *County by County in Ohio Genealogy.* By Petta Khouw and Genealogy Staff. Rev. ed. Columbus: The Library, 1992.

A listing of Ohio county sources housed at the State Library of Ohio, Columbus—atlases, census and cemetery records, DAR records, and many others. A valuable reference, but it is updated by the State Library of Ohio's online catalog.

_____. *Directory of Ohio Libraries.* Columbus: State Library of Ohio, 1998.

Stebbins, Clair C. *Ohio's Court Houses.* Columbus: Ohio State Bar Association, 1980.

Stith, Bari, comp. *A Guide to Local Government Records in the Library*

of the Western Reserve Historical Society. Cleveland: Western
   Reserve Historical Society, 1987.
Swanson, Hal. *The Ohio Township Helper.* N.p., n.d.
Thomson, Peter Gibson. *A Bibliography of the State of Ohio.* 2 vols.
   1880-90. Reprint. Ann Arbor, Mich.: University Microfilms, 1966;
   Salem, Mass.: Higginson Book Co., n.d.
   An extensive bibliography of Ohio titles—histories, periodicals,
   directories, pamphlets, and many other titles.
Thrane, Susan W. *County Courthouses of Ohio.* Bloomington, Ind.:
   Indiana University Press, 2000.
   Brief histories of Ohio's 88 county courthouses; illustrated.
United States Federal Writers Project (Ohio). *The Ohio Guide.* New
   York: Oxford University Press, 1940, 1956.
   Historical background and chronology, tours of Ohio, maps,
   descriptions of cities, and photographs.
Vicory, Jacqueline, comp. *MILO: Union List of Genealogies in the
   Libraries of Champaign, Clark, Darke, Green, Miami, Mont-
   gomery, and Preble Counties, Ohio.* Dayton, Ohio: Miami Valley
   Library Organization, 1977.
Vonada, Damaine. *Amazing Ohio.* Wilmington, Ohio: Orange Frazer
   Press, 1989.
_____. *Matters of Fact.* Wilmington, Ohio: Orange Frazer Press, 1987.
_____, ed. *The Ohio Almanac.* Wilmington, Ohio: Orange Frazer
   Press, 1992.
   A listing of Ohio libraries, religious organizations, businesses, and
   similar information on each county.
Wagher, Victor S., ed. *Guide to Local Government Records at the
   Center for Archival Collections.* 2nd ed. Bowling Green, Ohio:
   The Center, 1988.
Weaver, Clarence L. and Helen M. Mills, comps. *County and Local
   Historical Material in the Ohio State Archaeological and*

Historical Society Library. 2nd ed. Columbus, 1945.

Weaver, Polly Ann, comp. *Off the Ground and Into Your Family Tree.* Greenville, Ohio: Greenville Public Library, 1987.

Western Pennsylvania Genealogical Society. *Resources for Ohio Research in Pittsburgh, Pennsylvania.* Pittsburgh: The Society, 1978.

Western Reserve Historical Society, Genealogical Advisory Committee. *Ohio Genealogical Records.* Ed. by Mrs. Carl Main. Cleveland: The Society, 1968.

Wheeler, Robert C. *Ohio Newspapers: A Living Record.* Columbus: Ohio History Press, 1950.

Whitacre, Donald. *Ohio Firsts.* Lebanon, Ohio: Curious Facts Features, 1980.

Firsts in Ohio, by Ohioans, and for Ohioans.

Work Projects Administration. *Inventory of Federal Archives in the States, Series II, The Federal Courts, No. 34, Ohio.* Columbus: Ohio Historical Records Survey Project, 1940.

Though dated, this is an inventory of Ohio federal court records identified before 1940.

Wright, David K. *Ohio Handbook.* Emeryville, Calif.: Moon Publications, 1999.

Writers' Program (Ohio). *The Ohio Guide.* 1940. Reprint. St. Clair Shores, Mich.: Scholarly Press, 1979.

State and city history, government, chronology, tours, and other valuable Ohio information; partially outdated.

W.W. Reilly & Company. *Ohio State Business Directory for 1853-54.* Cincinnati: Morgan & Overend, 1853.

Arranged by type of business (such as plow manufacturers), county, name of person, and residence.

Wyllie, Stanley Clarke, Jr., comp. *A Guide to Genealogical Materials in the Dayton and Montgomery County Public Library.* Dayton,

Ohio, 1987.

Yon, Paul D. *Guide to Ohio County and Municipal Records for Urban Research*. Columbus: Ohio Historical Society, 1973.

Arranged by counties and municipalities. Shows government record series, dates, size of collection, and location (courthouse, etc.).

Zachariah, Gail, ed. *Local History and Genealogy Resources Guide to Southeastern Ohio*. 2 vols. Wellston, Ohio: Ohio Valley Area Libraries, 1994.

Zacharias, Susan. "Ohio Public Libraries: Genealogical Collections." *OGS Genealogy News* 33 (May/June 2002): 90-93.

Biographies and Genealogies

Anderson-Burton, Robin J., ed. *Ohio Family Farm Heritage*. Marceline, Mo.: Walsworth Press, 1985.

Biographies of many Ohio farmers; illustrated.

Bell, Carol Willsey, comp. *Abstracts from Biographies in John Struthers Stewart's History of Northeastern Ohio*. Indianapolis: Ye Olde Genealogie Shoppe, 1983.

The Biographical Annals of Ohio: A Handbook of the Government and Institutions of the State of Ohio. 3 vols. Compiled by Frank Edgar Scobey, et al. Springfield, Ohio: State Printers, 1902-1908.

List of members of the General Assembly, Ohio House of Representatives, Ohio Senate; biographies, portraits, and population statistics. See also William A. Taylor, *Hundred-Year Book* (Columbus, 1891).

The Biographical Cyclopaedia and Portrait Gallery with An Historical Sketch of the State of Ohio. 6 vols. Cincinnati: Western Biographical Publishing Co., 1883-95.

A monumental six-volume biographical encyclopedia of the state, with detailed sketches and many portraits of major Ohio citizens. Index to biographies.

Biographical Directory, General Assembly, Ohio, 1929-1930. Columbus: F.J. Heer Printing Co., 1931.

List of members of the General Assembly, residence, term of service, biographies, portraits.

The Biographical Encyclopaedia of Ohio of the Nineteenth Century. Ed. Charles Robson. Cincinnati: Galaxy Publishing Co., 1876.

Biographical sketches and portraits of many prominent Ohio citizens. Indexed. Online: (www.ancestry.com) and (www.hti.umich.edu/cgi/b/bib/bibperm?q1=ahu5132).

Biographical History of Northeastern Ohio, Embracing the Counties of Ashtabula, Geauga, and Lake. Chicago: Lewis Publishing Co., 1893.

Index compiled by Joan A. Vaughn (1998).

Biographical History of Northeastern Ohio, Embracing the Counties of Ashtabula, Trumbull and Mahoning .Chicago: Lewis Publishing Co., 1893.

Biography & Genealogy Master Index, CD-ROM (Ancestry.com).

The Book of Ohio: Illustrating the Growth of Her Resources. 2 vols. Cincinnati: Queen City Publishing Co., 1910-12.

Biographical sketches of prominent Ohioans; illustrated.

Boswell, Harry James. *American Blue Book: Attorneys of Ohio.* Minneapolis: N.p., 1924.

Bowers, Ruth and Anita Short, comps. *Gateway to the West.* 2 vols. 1967-78. Reprint. Baltimore: Genealogical Publishing Co., 1989.

Reprint of articles from *Gateway to the West* published 1967-78. Indexed.

Brennan, Joseph Fletcher, ed. *A Biographical Cyclopaedia and Portrait Gallery of Distinguished Men, with an Historical Sketch of the State of Ohio.* 6 vols. Cincinnati: John C. Yorston & Co., 1879.

Portraits and lengthy biographical sketches of prominent Ohio residents. A monumental biographical work.

————, ed. *A Biographical Cyclopaedia and Portrait Gallery of Distinguished Men: With An Historical Sketch of the State of Ohio.* 2 vols. Cincinnati: Yorston, 1879.

Brien, Lindsay Metcalfe. *Miami Valley Genealogies.* 5 vols. N.p., n.d. Typescript.

————, comp. *Miami Valley Records: Quaker Records.* N.p., 1935-.

Caccamo, James F. *Marriage Notices from the Ohio Observer Series, 1827-1855.* Apollo, Penn.: Closson Press, 1994.

Chataigne, J.H. *Photogravure Memories and B.P.O.E. Album of the*

Benevolent and Protective Order of Elks, Ohio Edition. Columbus: New Franklin Printing Co., 1903.

Citizens Historical Association. "Ohio Biographical Sketches." 13 vols. Indianapolis, 1938-51.
Sketches of Ohioans, with genealogical notes on their ancestry. Typescript at Ohio Historical Society.

Clark, Marie Taylor. *Ohio Lands: Chillicothe Land Office, 1800-1829.* Chillicothe, Ohio: The author, 1984.

———. *Ohio Lands South of the Indian Boundary Line.* Chillicothe, Ohio: The author, 1984.

Cleave, Egbert. *Cleave's Biographical Cyclopaedia of the State of Ohio, Ashtabula,Geauga, Lake, Lorain, Lucas, Mahoning, and Trumbull Counties.* Philadelphia: J.B. Lippincott & Co., 1875.
Volumes available for other Ohio major cities and counties.

Colonial Dames of America. Ohio. *Historic Counties and Court Houses of Ohio and the Prominent Men Associated with Them.* N.p., 1966.

Comley, W.J. and W. D'Eggville. *Ohio: The Future Great State.* Cincinnati: Comley Brothers Manufacturing, 1875.

Commemorative Biographical Record of the Upper Lake Region Containing Biographical Sketches of Prominent and Representative Citizens and Many of the Early Settled Families. Chicago: J.H. Beers & Co., 1905.

Commemorative Biographical Record of Northwestern Ohio, Including the Counties of Defiance, Henry, Williams, and Fulton. Chicago: J.H. Beers & Co., 1899.

County and Family Histories: Ohio, 1780-1970, CD-ROM (Family Tree Maker).

Coyle, William, ed. *Ohio Authors and their Books: Biographical Data and Selective Bibliographies for Ohio Authors, Native and Resident, 1796-1950.* Cleveland: World Publishing Co., 1962.
Brief biographical sketches and selective bibliographies of works

written by Ohio authors, 1796-1950.

Crabb, W. Darwin. *Biographical Sketches of the State Officers and of the Members of the Sixtieth General Assembly of the State of Ohio.* Columbus: Ohio State Journal Book, 1872.

Cutler, Julia Perkins. *The Founders of Ohio: Brief Sketches of the Forty-eight Pioneers.* Cincinnati: Robert Clarke & Co., 1888.

Daughters of the American Revolution. *Ohio State History of the Daughters of the American Revolution,* comp. by Annie Jopling Lester, n.d.

Downes, Randolph C. *History of Lake Shore, Ohio.* 3 vols. New York: Lewis Historical Publishing Co., 1952.

Volume 3 contains many biographical sketches.

Duff, William Alexander. *History of North Central Ohio, Embracing Richland, Ashland, Wayne, Medina, Lorain, Huron, and Knox Counties.* 3 vols. Topeka-Indianapolis.: Historical Publishing Co., 1931.

Volumes 2 and 3 contain biographical sketches of prominent residents of the Ohio counties stated in the title to this work.

Early Ohio Settlers, 1700s-1900s, CD-ROM (Family Tree Maker).

Eaton, S.J.M. *History of the Presbytery of Erie.* New York: Hurd and Houghton, 1868.

Encyclopedia of Ohio: A Volume of Encyclopedia of the United States. St. Clair Shores, Mich.: Somerset Publishers, 1982.

Famous Ohioans. Online: (www.oplin.lib.oh.us/products/PPF/ohioans).

Fess, Simeon Davidson. *Ohio: A Four-Volume Reference Library on the History of A Great State.* 5 vols. Chicago: Lewis Publishing Co., 1937.

Volumes 4 and 5 contain biographical sketches.

Galbreath, Charles Burleigh. *History of Ohio.* 5 vols. Chicago: American Historical Society, 1925.

Volumes 3-5 contain biographical sketches of prominent Ohio residents. See "Cross Index to Charles B. Galbreath's 1925, 5 Volume History of Ohio," compiled by Robertalee Lent (Post Falls, Idaho: Genealogical Reference Builders, 1969).

Gardner, Frank W. *Central Ohio Genealogical Notes and Queries.* Columbus: N.p., n.d. Indexed.

Genealogical Data Relating to Women in the Western Reserve before 1840 (1850). Cleveland: Women's Department, Cleveland Centennial Commission, 1943.

Genealogical information is arranged by counties.

Genealogical Library Master Catalog, CD-ROM.

A multi-library bibliography of genealogical books, microfilms, and other sources. See (www.onelibrary.com).

Gilkey, Elliot Howard. *The Ohio Hundred Year Book.* Columbus: Fred J. Heer, 1901.

Lists of members of the General Assembly, senators, representatives, and biographical sketches. This is a revised and enlarged edition of *Taylor's Ohio Statesmen and Hundred Year Book* (1892).

Goulder, Grace. *Ohio Scenes and Citizens.* 1964. Reprint. Dayton, Ohio: Landfall Press, 1973.

Biographies of prominent Ohio citizens.

Grose, Parlee C., et al. *Biographical and Historical Sketches.* McComb, Ohio: General Publishing Co., 1947.

Hammond, Ernestine, ed. *Huguenot Ancestors of Some Ohioans.* Ohio Huguenot Society, 1996.

Hanna, Charles Augustus. *Ohio Valley Genealogies.* 1900. Reprint. Baltimore: Genealogical Publishing Co., 1989.

Genealogies of families in Belmont, Harrison, and Jefferson counties, Ohio, and three Pennsylvania counties.

Harris, C.H. *The Harris History: A Collection of Tales of Long Ago of*

Southeastern Ohio and Adjoining Territories. Athens, Ohio: Athens Messenger, 1957.

Haverstock, Mary Sayre, et al., comps. *Artists in Ohio, 1787-1900: A Biographical Dictionary.* Kent, Ohio: Kent State University Press, 2000.

Hawkins, Cyril. *Sketches, Including Scenes and Incidents of Distinguished "Buckeyes" and Others.* N.p., n.d.

Hayden, Amos Sutton. *Early History of the Disciples in the Western Reserve, Ohio, with Biographical Sketches of the Principal Agents in their Religious Movement.* Cincinnati: Chase & Hall, 1875.

HeritageQuest Online (ProQuest). Online subscription available at large research libraries. Images of books and personal name index to some 25,000 family and local histories. Researchers may search by People (personal names), Places, and Publications. Also, census schedules and census indexes (www.heritagequestonline.com).

Hildreth, Samuel Prescott. *Biographical and Historical Memoirs of the Early Pioneer Settlers of Ohio, with Narratives of Incidents and Occurrences in 1775.* Cincinnati: H.W. Derby & Co., 1852.
Biographical sketches of early Ohioans. 1854 edition has the title *Memoirs of the Early Pioneer Settlers of Ohio, with Narratives of Incidents and Occurrences in 1775* (Cincinnati: H.W. Derby & Co., 1854). See *Index* compiled by Marilyn Sims Vadakin (Marietta, Ohio: It's My Business, n.d.).

_____. *Pioneer History: Being An Account of the First Examinations of the Ohio Valley and the Early Settlement of the Northwest Territory.* Cincinnati: H.W. Derby & Co., 1848.

Hissong, Clyde. *Ohio Lives: The Buckeye State Biographical Record.* Hopkinsville. Ky.: Historical Record Association, 1968.
Detailed sketches of prominent Ohioans, and some portraits.

Historical and Genealogical Records of West Central Ohio. Bowie, Md.: Heritage Books, 1997. CD-ROM.

History of Hocking Valley, Ohio. 1883. Reprint. Mt. Vernon, Ind.:
      Windmill Publications, 1991.

History of Lower Scioto Valley, Ohio. Chicago: Interstate Publishing
      Co., 1884.

*History of the Upper Ohio Valley, with Family History and Biogra-
      phical Sketches.* 2 vols. Madison, Wisc.: Brant & Fuller, 1890.
      Includes many biographical sketches for this area.

Hood, Marilyn G., ed. *The First Ladies of Ohio.* Columbus: Ohio
      Historical Society, 1970.

Hooper, Osman Castle. *Ohio Journalism Hall of Fame.* Columbus:
      Ohio State University Press, 1929-32.

Houck, George Francis. *History of Catholicity in Northern Ohio and in
      the Diocese of Cleveland from 1749 to December 31, 1900.* 2 vols.
      Cleveland: Savage, 1903.
      Volume 1 historical background; volume 2 contains biographical
      sketches.

Howe, Henry. *Historical Collections of Ohio.* 2 vols. Cincinnati: State
      of Ohio, 1904. (Publisher varied).
      See "Index to Historical Collections of Ohio," index compiled by
      Fresno Genealogical Society, Fresno, Calif. Typescript, WRHS,
      and "Index to Historical Collections of Ohio by Henry Howe,"
      typescript index compiled by Sandra Hudnall Day (Steubenville,
      Ohio: Jefferson County Chapter, Ohio Genealogical Society, 1990)
      (www.hti.umich.edu/cgi/b/bib/bibperm?q1=aja2910).

Hutslar, Donald A. *Gunsmiths of Ohio, 18th & 19th Centuries.* Edited
      by Nancy Bagby. York, Penn.: George Shumway, Publisher, 1973.
      Brief biographical sketches of gunsmiths alphabetically arranged
      by surname under each county name.

Izant, Grace Goulder. *Ohio Scenes and Citizens.* Cleveland: World
      Publishing Co., 1964.

Kennedy, William S. *The Plan of Union, or, A History of the*

Presbyterian and Congregational Churches of the Western Reserve with Biographical Sketches of the Early Missionaries. Hudson, Ohio: Pentagon Steam Press, 1856.

Lake Shore & Michigan Southern Railway System and Representative Employees. Buffalo, N.Y.: Biographical Publishing Co., 1900.

Leahy, Ethel Carter. *Who's Who on the Ohio River and Its Tributaries.* Cincinnati: E.C. Leahy Publishing Co., 1931.

Lester, Annie Jopling, comp. *Ohio State History of the Daughters of the American Revolution.* Greenfield, Ohio: Greenfield Printing & Publishing Co., 1928.

Lewis, Thomas William. *History of Southeastern Ohio and the Muskingum Valley, 1788-1928.* 3 vols. Chicago: S.J. Clarke Publishing Co., 1928.
Volume 3 contains biographical sketches and portraits.

Mansfield, E.D. *Personal Memories: Social, Political, and Literary, with Sketches of Many Noted People, 1803-1843.* Cincinnati: Robert Clarke & Co., 1879.

Marshall, Carrington Tanner, ed. *A History of the Courts and Lawyers of Ohio.* 4 vols. New York: American Historical Society, 1934.
Biographical sketches of prominent Ohio lawyers and judges; includes many portraits.

Memoirs of the Lower Ohio Valley: Personal and Genealogical with Portraits. 2 vols. Madison, Wisc.: Federal Publishing Co., 1905. Evansville, Ind.: Unigraphic, 1971.
Portraits and biographical sketches of prominent Ohio citizens. See typescript index at FHL.

Memoirs of the Miami Valley, edited by John C. Hover. 3 vols. Chicago: R.O. Law Co., 1919.

Memorial Record of the Counties of Delaware, Union, and Morrow, Ohio. Chicago: Lewis Publishing Co., 1895.

Men of Ohio. Cleveland: Cleveland News and Cleveland Leader, ca.

1914.
Intended as a newspaper office reference source. Portraits and brief biographical sketches of prominent Ohio citizens. Online: (www.cwru.edu/UL/DigiLib/CleveHist/MenOfOhio/Men.html).

Men of Ohio in Nineteen Hundred. Cleveland: Benesch Art Publishing Co., 1901.
A collection of portraits of 1,068 representative men of Ohio in 1900; shows their occupation.

Mercer, James Kazerta.*Ohio Legislative History, 1909-1913.* Columbus: Press of Edward T. Miller Co., n.d.

_____. *Representative Men of Ohio, 1884-1885.* Columbus: James K. Mercer, 1885.

_____and C.N. Vallandigham. *Representative Men of Ohio, 1896-1897.* Columbus: Mercer & Vallandigham, 1896.

_____and Edward K. Rige. *Representative Men of Ohio, 1900-1903.* Columbus: James K. Mercer, 1903.

_____. *Representative Men of Ohio, 1903-1908.* Columbus: Press of Fred J. Heer, 1908.

_____. *Representative Men of Ohio, 1904-1908.* Columbus: Press of Fred J. Heer, 1908.

Moore's Who Is Who in Ohio, 1961. Los Angeles, Calif.: Moore's Who Is Who Publications, 1961.

Neely, Ruth, ed. *Women of Ohio: A Record of their Achievements in the History of the State.* 3 vols. S.J. Clarke Publishing Co., n.d.
Biographical sketches and portraits of many prominent Ohio women.

Neff, William B., ed. *Bench and Bar of Northern Ohio: History and Biography.* Cleveland: Historical Publishing Co., 1921.
Biographical sketches and portraits of attorneys in Northern Ohio.

Newton, Jim. *Our Most Famous Buckeyes.* Hamilton, Ohio: Fort Hamilton Press, 1963.

Ohio. Chicago: American Historical Society, 1925.

Biographical sketches and portraits of prominent citizens.

Ohio Biographical Dictionary: People of All Times and All Places Who Have Been Important to the History and Life of the State. Wilmington, Del.: American Historical Publications, 1986.

Nineteenth and twentieth century biographical sketches of prominent Ohioans, alphabetically arranged by surname.

Ohio Biographical Dictionary. 2nd ed. 2 vols. St. Clair Shores, Mich.: Somerset Publishers, 1999.

Includes biographical sketches of many prominent Ohioans.

Ohio Biographies. (OPLIN). Online:

(www.oplin.lib.oh.us/index.cfm?ID=3-58-241)

Ohio Biographies Project. Online:

(http://homepages.rootsweb.com/~usbios/Ohio/mnpg.html).

Ohio Genealogical Society. *Ancestor Charts of Members of the Ohio Genealogical Society*. Mansfield, Ohio: The Society, 1987.

Pedigree charts submitted to OGS by its members. This is a major reference source and finding aid for Ohio genealogists.

_____. *First Families of Ohio Roster, 1964-2000*, edited by Sunda Anderson Peters and Kay Ballantyne Hudson. Mansfield, Ohio: Ohio Genealogical Society, 2001.

_____. *First Families of Ohio*. Collection on microfilm, FHL.

Ohio. General Assembly. *Biographical Directory, General Assembly, Ohio, 1929-1930*. Columbus: F.J. Heer Printing Co., 1931.

_____. *Biographical Notices of State Officers and Members of the Fifty-ninth General Assembly of the State of Ohio*. Columbus: John Wallace, 1871.

_____. *Political Directory Containing Biographical Sketches of the State Officials of Ohio*. Columbus: L.G. Thrall & Co., 1879.

Ohio Obituaries and Biographical Sketches. 7 vols. Columbus, 1908.

Bound newspaper clippings housed at the State Library of Ohio,

Columbus.

Ohio Historical Society. *The Governors of Ohio.* Columbus: The Society, 1954.

Ohio's Progressive Sons, A History of the State: Sketches of Those Who have Helped to Build up the Commonwealth. Cincinnati: Queen City Publishing Co., 1905.

Biographical sketches and portraits of prominent Ohioans.

Ohio Society, Colonial Dames XVII Century. *Our Ancestors' Families.* The Society, 1988.

A monumental collection of family group records. Indexed.

Ohio Society, Sons of the American Revolution. *Centennial Register, 1889 to 1989.* Dayton, Ohio: The Society, 1988.

Ohio Women's Policy and Research Commission. *Women of the Ohio General Assembly, 1922-1996.* Columbus: The Commission, 1996.

Pearson, Francis Bail and J.D. Harlor. *Ohio History Sketches.* Columbus: Press of Fred J. Heer, 1903.

Portrait and Biographical Record of Auglaize, Logan, and Shelby Counties, Ohio. 1892. Reprint. Evansville, Ind.: Unigraphic, 1977.

Portrait and Biographical Record of Fayette, Pickaway, and Madison Counties, Ohio. Chicago: Chapman Bros., 1892.

Portrait and Biographical Record of Marion and Hardin Counties, Ohio. Chicago: Chapman Publishing Co.,1895.

A Portrait and Biographical Record of Mercer and Van Wert Counties, Ohio. 1896. Evansville, Ind.: Unigraphic, 1971.

A Portrait and Biographical Record of Portage and Summit Counties, Ohio. Logansport, Ind.: A.W. Bowen & Co., 1898.

Portrait and Biographical Record of the Scioto Valley, Ohio. Chicago: Lewis Publishing Co., 1894.

Progressive Men of Northern Ohio. Cleveland: Plain Dealer Publishing Co., 1906.

Portraits and brief biographical sketches of prominent citizens of

Northern Ohio; indexed.

Randall, Emilius Oviatt and Daniel J. Ryan. *History of Ohio: The Rise and Progress of An American State*. 6 vols. New York: Century History Co., 1912-15.

Volume 6 includes biographical sketches.

Reed, George Irving, et al., eds. *Bench and Bar of Ohio: A Compendium of History and Biography*. 2 vols. Chicago: Century Publishing and Engraving Co., 1897.

Detailed biographical sketches and many portraits of Ohio lawyers.

Reid, Whitelaw. *Ohio in the War: Her Statesmen, Her Generals, and Soldiers*. 2 vols. Cincinnati: Robert Clarke Co., 1895.

History of Ohio regiments during the Civil War, rosters of soldiers, biographical sketches, and history of military organizations. Illustrated.

Reno, W.W. and Frank R. Whitzel, eds. *The Ohio Blue Book: Leaders in Ohio Politics for the Year 1898*. Montpelier, Ohio: Hann & Adair Printers, 1898.

Representative Men of Ohio, 1884-85. Columbus: James K. Mercer, 1885.

Rice, Harvey. *Sketches of Western Life*. Boston: Lee and Shepard, 1887.

Rust, Orton Glenn. *History of West Central Ohio*. 3 vols. Indianapolis: Historical Publishing Co., 1934.

Volume 3 and part of volume 2 include biographical sketches.

Ryan, Daniel Joseph. *A History of Ohio, with Biographical Sketches of Her Governors and the Ordinance of 1787*. Columbus: A.H. Smythe, 1888.

Scamyhorn, Richard and John Steinle. *Stockades in the Wilderness: The Frontier Defenses and Settlements of Southwestern Ohio, 1788-1795*. Dayton, Ohio: Landfall Press, 1986.

Smith, William Ernest. *History of Southwestern Ohio: The Miami Valleys*. 3 vols. New York: Lewis Historical Publishing Co., 1964.

Volume 3 contains biographical sketches and is subtitled *Family and Personal History*. Indexed.

Southern Ohio and Its Builders: A Biographical Record of Those Personalities Who by Reason of their Achievements Have Merited a Permanent Place in the Story of Twentieth-Century Southern Ohio. Southern Ohio Biographical Association, 1927.
Biographical sketches and portraits of prominent citizens.

Stagg, Abraham. *Biographical Sketches of the Fifty-sixth Ohio House of Representatives, Convened January 4th, 1864*. Columbus: Glenn & Heide, 1865.

Stevens, Harry Robert. "A Study of Notable Ohioans." *Ohio State Archaeological and Historical Quarterly* 47 (1938): 159-67.

Stewart, John Struthers. *History of Northeastern Ohio*. 3 vols. Indianapolis: Historical Publishing Co., 1935.
Volumes 2 and 3 contain biographical sketches of prominent citizens of Northeastern Ohio.

Stille, Samuel Harden. *Ohio Builds A Nation: A Memorial to the Pioneers and the Celebrated Sons of the "Buckeye" State*. 5th ed. Chicago: Arlendale Book House, 1962.
Biographical sketches of Ohioans and Ohio local history.

Stivison, David V., comp. *The Lord's Shepherds in the Ohio Hills: Biographies of 175 Ministers and Wives of the Southeastern Ohio Conferences of the United Brethren and the Evangelical United Brethren Churches, 1901-1974*. Philadelphia: privately printed, 1987.

Summers, Ewing, comp. *Genealogical and Family History of Eastern Ohio*. New York: Lewis Publishing Co., 1903.
Detailed biographical sketches and some portraits. See name index compiled by Mrs. Howard W. (Bernice H.) Simon, *Name Index for Genealogical and Family History of Eastern Ohio* (Chagrin Falls, Ohio, 1973).

Taylor, C.W., Jr. *Bench and Bar of Ohio, 1939-1940.* San Francisco: C.W. Taylor, Jr., 1939.

Taylor, William Alexander. *Ohio in Congress from 1803 to 1901, with Notes and Sketches of Senators and Representatives.* Columbus: Century Publishing Co., 1900.

_____. *Ohio Statesmen and Hundred Year Book, from 1788 to 1892 Inclusive.* Columbus: Westbote Co., 1892.

University of Akron. College of Law. "Ohio Judges: A Biographical Index." 1967. Typescript at Ohio Historical Society.

Upton, Harriet Taylor. *History of the Western Reserve.* 3 vols. Chicago: Lewis Publishing Co., 1910.
Volumes 2 and 3 contain biographical sketches and portraits. This work is one of the major regional histories of the Western Reserve.

Van Tassel, Charles Sumner, comp. *Familiar Faces of Ohio: A Souvenir Collection of Portraits and Sketches of Well-known Men of the Buckeye State.* Bowling Green, Ohio: C.S. Van Tassel Publisher, 1896.
Portraits and sketches of prominent Ohioans.

_____. *Men of Northwestern Ohio: A Collection of Portraits and Biographies.* Bowling Green, Ohio: C.S. Van Tassel, 1898.

_____, comp. *The Ohio Blue Book, or Who's Who in the Buckeye State: A Cyclopedia of Biography of Men and Women of Ohio.* Norwalk, Ohio: American Publishers' Co., 1917-18; Toledo, Ohio: C.S. Van Tassel, 1917-18.
Brief biographical sketches of prominent Ohio residents. Also has the title *Who's Who in the Buckeye State.*

_____. *Story of the Maumee Valley, Toledo, and the Sandusky Region.* 4 vols. Chicago: S.J. Clarke Publishing Co., 1929.
Volumes 3 and 4 contain biographical sketches and portraits.

Van Tassel, David D. and John J. Grabowski, eds. *The Dictionary of Cleveland Biography.* Bloomington, Ind.: Indiana University

Press, 1996.

Vietzen, Raymond Charles. *Yesterday's Ohioans*. Elyria, Ohio: Indian Ridge Museum, 1973.

Walden, Blanche L. *Pioneer Families of the Midwest*. 1939. Reprint. Baltimore: Clearfield, 1998.

Brief genealogical sketches of Ohioans and other Mid-westerners.

Wheeler, Kenneth W. *For the Union: Ohio Leaders in the Civil War*. Columbus: Ohio State University Press, 1968.

Who Is Who in and from Ohio. Cincinnati: Queen City Publishing Co., 1912.

Who's Who in Ohio: A Biographical Dictionary of Leading Men and Women of the Commonwealth. Chicago: Larkin, Roosevelt & Larkin, Ltd., 1947.

Who's Who in Ohio: A Compilation of Biographical Information on Outstanding Citizens of the State of Ohio. N.p., 1974.

Who's Who in Ohio: Those Who Have Achieved Prominence in their Respective Lines of Endeavor. Cleveland: Biographical Publishing Co., 1930.

Brief biographical sketches of prominent Ohioans.

Williamson, C.W. *History of Western Ohio and Auglaize County, with Illustrations and Biographical Sketches of Pioneers and Prominent Public Men*. Columbus: W.M. Linn, 1905.

Winter, Nevin Otto. *A History of Northwest Ohio: A Narrative Account of Its Historical Progress and Development from Its First European Exploration of the Maumee and Sandusky Valleys and the Adjacent Shores of Lake Erie, down to the Present Time*. 3 vols. Chicago: Lewis Publishing Co., 1917.

Volumes 2 and 3 contain biographical sketches and portraits.

Wright, George Frederick. *Representative Citizens of Ohio: Memorial, Biographical*. 7 vols. Cleveland: Memorial Publishing Co., 1914-26.

Detailed biographical sketches of prominent Ohio residents, includes many portraits.

Young American Patriots: The Youth of Ohio in World War II. Richmond, Va.: National Publishing Co., 1947.

Churches and Religious Organizations

Allbeck, Willard D. *A Century of Lutherans in Ohio.* Yellow Springs, Ohio: Antioch Press, 1966.

Amstutz, P.B. *Historical Events of the Mennonite Settlement in Allen and Putnam Counties, Ohio.* 1925. Reprint. Toronto, Ontario, 1978.

Backman, Milton V., Jr. *The Heavens Resound: A History of the Latter-day Saints in Ohio, 1830-1838.* Salt Lake City: Deseret Book Co., 1983.

Barker, John Marshall. *History of Ohio Methodism: A Study in Social Science.* Cincinnati: Curts & Jennings, 1898.

Beachy, Leroy. *Cemetery Directory of the Amish Community in Eastern Holmes and Adjoining Counties in Ohio.* N.p., 1975.

Beggs, S.R. *Pages from the Early History of the West and Northwest, Embracing Reminiscences and Incidents of Settlement and Growth and Sketches of the Material and Religious Progress of the States of Ohio, Indiana, Illinois, and Missouri, with Especial Reference to the History of Methodism.* Cincinnati: Methodist Book Concern, 1868.

Bell, Raymond Martin, et al. *Methodism on the Upper Ohio before 1812.* Washington, Penn.: R.M. Bell, 1963.

_____. "More on Early Methodist Circuits on the Upper Ohio." Washington, Pa., 1983. Typescript. WRHS.

Berry, Ellen Thomas and David A. Berry. *Our Quaker Ancestors: Finding Them in Quaker Records.* Baltimore: Genealogical Publishing Co., 1997.

Bowers, Roy E. "The Historic Rural Church." *Ohio Archaeological and Historical Society Quarterly* 51 (June 1942): 89-100.

Brien, Lindsay Metcalfe. *Abstracts from History of the Church of the*

Brethren in Ohio. Fort Wayne, Ind.: Allen County Public Library, 1983. Typescript.

Brown, James Haldane. "United Church Work in Ohio." *Journal of the Presbyterian Historical Society* 30 (June 1952): 73-94.

Burke, James L. and Donald E. Bensch. "Mount Pleasant and the Early Quakers of Ohio." *Ohio History* 83 (Autumn 1974): 220-25.

_____. *Mount Pleasant and the Early Quakers of Ohio*. Columbus: Ohio Historical Society, 1975.

Burton, Katherine. *Make the Way Known: The History of the Dominican Congregation of St. Mary of the Springs, 1822 to 1957*. New York: Farrar, Straus & Cudahy, 1959.

Church Histories of Tri-State Conference, the Ohio District, the American Lutheran Church 1812-1984. N.p., Tri-State Conference, 1984. WRHS.

Cowles, Henry. *A Defence of Ohio Congregationalism and of Oberlin College*. N.p., n.d.

Davis, Eileen A. and Judith S. Ireton. *Quaker Records of the Miami Valley of Ohio*. Owensboro, Ky.: McDowell Publications, 1981.

Denlinger, Carolyn Teach. *Every Name Index for History of the Church of the Brethren of the Southern District of Ohio*. Dayton, Ohio: Southern Ohio District, Church of the Brethren Historical Committee, 1982.

Diehm, Edgar G., ed. *The Church of the Brethren in Northeastern Ohio*. Elgin, Ill.: The Brethren Press, 1965.

Dolle, Mrs. Percy A., comp. *Ohio Churches: Their Incorporation Dates As Shown in the Laws of Ohio*. Columbus: Mrs. P.A. Dolle, 1957.

Doyle, Joseph Beatty. *The Church in Eastern Ohio*. Steubenville, Ohio: H.C. Cook, 1914.

Dunlevy, A.H. *History of the Miami Baptist Association*. Cincinnati: George S. Blanchard & Co., 1869.

Durnbaugh, Donald F. "Strangers and Exiles: Assistance Given by the

Religious Society of Friends to the Separatist Society of Zoar in 1817-1818." *Ohio History* 109 (Winter-Spring 2000): 71-92.

Eaton, S.J.M. *History of the Presbytery of Erie*. New York: Hurd and Houghton, 1868.

Ebeling, Harry. *The Diocese of Southern Ohio*. Cincinnati: Diocese of Southern Ohio, Communications Office, 1988.
A history of the Episcopal Church in Southern Ohio.

Eberly, William R. *The History of the Church of the Brethren in Northwestern Ohio, 1827-1963*. Hartville, Ohio: Northern Ohio District, 1982.

Eby, Lela, comp. *Every Name Index, Church of the Brethren in Southern Ohio*. Mill Valley, Calif.: The compiler, 1955.

Edwards, Martha L. "Ohio's Religious Organizations and the War." *Ohio Archaeological and Historical Quarterly* 28 (1919): 208-24.

Eltscher, Susan M. *The Records of American Baptists in Ohio, and Related Organizations*. Rochester, N.Y.: American Baptist Historical Society, 1981.

Ernsberger, C.S. *A History of the Wittenberg Synod of the General Synod of the Evangelical Lutheran Church, 1847-1916*. Columbus: Lutheran Book Concern, 1917.

Finley, James Bradley. *Sketches of Western Methodism: Biographical, Historical and Miscellaneous, Illustrative of Pioneer Life*. Edited by W.P. Strickland. Cincinnati: Methodist Book Concern, 1856.

The First Regular Baptist Church and Other Baptist Churches of Columbus and Central Ohio, 1825-1884. Abstracted by Genevieve M. Obetz. Ed. Margaret Hiles Scott. Columbus: Franklin County Genealogical Society, 1984.

Fortman, Edmund J. *Lineage: A Biographical History of the Chicago Province*. Chicago: Loyola University Press, 1987.
The Chicago Province, Society of Jesus; includes Ohio.

The Friends Church. Ohio Yearly Meeting. *Observing Our 150th Yearly*

Meeting. Damascus, Ohio, 1962.

Gill, Charles Otis and Gifford Pinchot. *Six Thousand Country Churches.* New York: Macmillan Co., 1919.

Gray, Elma E. and Leslie Robb Gray. *Wilderness Christians: The Moravian Mission to the Delaware Indians.* Toronto: Macmillian Co., 1956.

Hall, Barbara Yoder. *Born Amish.* Randolph, Ohio: Jacbar Publications, 1980.

Hamilton, Albert. *The Catholic Journey through Ohio.* Columbus: Catholic Conference of Ohio, 1976.

Harter, Frances D., comp. *Guide to the Manuscripts of Early Ohio Methodism: United Methodist Church of Ohio.* Delaware, Ohio: United Methodist Archives Center, Ohio Wesleyan University, 1981.

Hayden, Amos Sutton. *Early History of the Disciples in the Western Reserve, Ohio, with Biographical Sketches of the Principal Agents in their Religious Movement.* Cincinnati: Chase & Hall, 1875. Indexed by Georgene Morris Sones.

Hildreth, Samuel Prescott. *Contributions to the Early History of the Northwest, Including the Moravian Missions in Ohio.* Cincinnati, 1864.

Hinshaw, William Wade. *Ohio Quaker Genealogical Records*, vols. 4-5 of *Encyclopedia of American Quaker Genealogy.*6 vols. 1936-50. Reprint. Baltimore: Genealogical Publishing Co., 1969.
Volumes 4 and 5 cover Ohio Quaker meetings. This is one of the major reference sources for Quaker genealogy.

Historical Records Survey (Ohio). *Inventory of the Church Archives of Ohio Presbyterian Churches.* Columbus: Ohio Historical Society, 1940.
Original records at the Presbyterian Historical Society, Philadelphia. Microfilm, FHL.

History of the Central Ohio Conference of the Methodist Episcopal Church, 1856-1913. Cincinnati: Press of the Methodist Book Concern, n.d.

History of the Church of the Brethren of the Southern District of Ohio. Dayton, Ohio: Otterbein Press, 1920.

See *Every Name Index,* comp. by Carolyn Teach Denlinger (Dayton, Ohio, 1982).

Holmes, John. *Historical Sketches of the Missions of the United Brethren.* Dublin: R. Napper, 1818.

Houck, George Francis. *A History of Catholicity in Northern Ohio and in the Diocese of Cleveland from 1749 to December 31, 1900.* 2 vols. Cleveland: Press of J.B. Savage, 1903.

Volume 1 is historical, volume 2 contains biographical sketches and portraits.

Hynes, Michael J. *History of the Diocese of Cleveland, Origin and Growth (1847-1952).* Cleveland: Diocese of Cleveland, 1953.

Kennedy, William Sloane. *The Plan of Union, or, A History of the Presbyterian and Congregational Churches of the Western Reserve, with Biographical Sketches of the Early Missionaries.* Hudson, Ohio: Pentagon Steam Press, 1856.

Kern, Richard, ed. *A History of the Ohio Conference of the Churches of God, General Conference, 1836-1986.* Nappanee, Ind.: Evangel Press, 1986.

Kimball, Stanley B. "Sources on the History of the Mormons in Ohio, 1830-38." *BYU Studies* 4 (Summer 1971): 524-40.

King, I.F. *Introduction of Methodism in Ohio.* Columbus: Ohio Archaeo-logical and Historical Society Publications, 1989.

Krumm, Delbert R. *A History of the Scioto, Southeast, and Ohio Southeast Conferences.* Circleville, Ohio: Ohio Southeast Conference, Evangelical United Brethren Church, 1958.

Krumm, John M. *Flowing Like A River.* Cincinnati: Forward Movement

Publications, 1989.

Leedy, Roy B. *The Evangelical Church in Ohio, 1816-1951*. Cleveland: Ohio Conference of the Evangelical United Brethren Church, 1959.

Typescript index compiled by Jana Sloan Broglin.

Leonard, Rev. Delavan L. *A Century of Congregationalism in Ohio, 1796-1896*. Oberlin, Ohio: Pearce & Randolph, 1896.

Lubbers, Ferne Reedy and Margaret Dieringer, eds. *Advent of Religious Groups into Ohio*. Mansfield, Ohio: Clark County Chapter, Ohio Genealogical Society, 1978.

A study of the major religious groups in Ohio; includes useful maps.

MacLean, John Patterson. *Shakers of Ohio*. Columbus: F.J. Heer Printing Co., 1907.

McCormick, Virginia E. and Robert W. McCormick. "Episcopal Versus Methodist: Religious Competition in Frontier Worthington." *Ohio History* 107 (Winter-Spring 1998): 5-21.

McKinney, William Wilson, ed. *The Presbyterian Valley*. Pittsburg: Davis & Warde, 1958.

Manning, Barbara. *Genealogical Abstracts from Newspapers of the German Reformed Church, 1840-1843*. Bowie, Md.: Heritage Books, 1995.

Mechling, George Washington. *History of the Evangelical Lutheran District Synod of Ohio Covering Fifty-three Years, 1857-1910*. N.p., 1911.

Miller, Marcus. *Roots by the River: The History, Doctrine, and Practice of the Old German Baptist Brethren in Miami County, Ohio*. Covington, Ohio: Hammer Graphics, 1973.

Moherman, T.S., et al. *A History of the Church of the Brethren, Northeastern Ohio*. Elgin, Ill.: Brethren Publishing House, 1914.

Monfort, J.G. *Presbyterianism North of the Ohio, Containing a*

Statement of the Planting and Progress of the Presbyterian Church in Ohio from 1790 to 1822. Cincinnati: Elm Street Printing Co., 1872.

Morlan, Charles P., comp. *A Brief History of Ohio Yearly Meeting of the Religious Society of Friends (Conservative).* Barnesville, Ohio: The Representative Meeting, 1959.

Mote, Luke Smith. *Early Settlement of Friends in the Miami Valley.* Edited by Willard Heiss. Indianapolis, 1961.

New Order Amish Directory. Millersburg, Ohio: Abana Books, 1999.

Ohio Church History Society. *Papers of the Ohio Church History Society.* Oberlin, Ohio: The Society, 1890-1901.

Ohio Federation of Churches. *Survey Report of Churches and Communiti.* Columbus, 1921-22.

Ohio Lutheran Church Women. *A Century of Roots of Ohio Lutheran Church Women.* N.p., 1978.

Ohio. Sesquicentennial Commission. Religious Participation Committee. *Churches in the Buckeye Country: A History of Ohio's Religious Groups Published in Commemoration of the State's Sesquicentennial, 1953.* (Columbus): The Commission, 1953.

Ohio State Christian Convention. "Proceedings of the First Ohio State Christian Convention." *The Ohio Convention Reporter* 1 (1870).

Ohio's Religious Groups of Historical Interest. Columbus: Columbus Blank Book Co., 1965.

Parkin, Max H. "Conflict at Kirtland: A Study of the Nature and Causes of External and Internal Conflict of the Mormons in Ohio between 1830 and 1838." M.A. thesis, Brigham Young University, 1966.

_____. "Mormon Political Involvement in Ohio." *BYU Studies* 9 (Summer 1969): 484-502.

Peters, Mildred Hull. *Every Name Index for Church of the Brethren in Southern Ohio, 1955.* Elgin, Ill.: Brethren Publishing House, 1955.

Pike, Kermit J. *A Guide to Shaker Manuscripts in the Library of the*

Western Reserve Historical Society. Cleveland: Western Reserve Historical Society, 1974.

Presbyterian Church in the U.S.A. *Historical Sketch of the Synod of Ohio (New School) from 1838 to 1868*. Cincinnati: Elm Street Printing Co., 1870.

History of Presbyterianism in Ohio.

_____. *One Hundred and Fifty Years of Presbyterianism in the Ohio Valley, 1790-1940*. Cincinnati: N.p., 1941.

_____. *The Churches of Miami Presbytery*. By Virginia Rainey. N.p., 1989.

Rainey, Virginia F. *How Firm a Foundation: A Historical Directory of the Congregations of the Miami Presbytery, Presbyterian Church, USA, 1799-1991*. N.p., 1992.

Reed, John H. *Guide to the Manuscripts of Early Ohio Methodism, United Methodist Church of Ohio*. Delaware, Ohio: West Ohio Conference, United Methodist Church, Commission on Archives and History, 1981.

Reichel, Edward H. *An Historical Sketch of the Church and Missions of the United Brethren, Commonly Called Moravian*. Bethlehem, Pa.: J.&W. Held, 1848.

Includes a history of Brethren missions in Ohio.

Robinson, Elmo Arnold. *The Universalist Church in Ohio*. Akron: Ohio Universalist Convention, 1923.

Includes biographical notes of Ohio ministers.

Robison, Elwin C. *The First Mormon Temple: Design, Construction, and Historic Context of the Kirtland Temple*. Provo, Utah: Brigham Young University Press, 1997.

Rodabaugh, James H. and Mary Jane Rodabaugh. *Schoenbrunn and the Moravian Missions in Ohio*. 3rd ed. Columbus: Ohio Historical Society, 1961.

Sesquicentennial History of the Lancaster-Zanesville Presbytery, 1808-

1958. N.p., n.d.

Shaker Membership Card Index. Western Reserve Historical Society, Cleveland. Microfilm, WRHS, FHL.

Shaw, Henry K. *Buckeye Disciples: A History of Disciples of Christ in Ohio.* St. Louis, Mo.: Christian Board of Publications, 1952.

Sheatsley, C.V. *History of the Evangelical Lutheran Joint Synod of Ohio and Other States from the Earliest Beginnings to 1919.* Columbus: Lutheran Book Concern, 1919.

Sinnema, John R. *German Methodism in Ohio: Its Leaders and Institutions.* Berea, Ohio: American-German Institute of Baldwin Wallace College, 1983.

Smith, Joseph. *Old Redstone, or, Historical Sketches of Western Presbyterianism, Its Early Ministers, Its Perilous Times, and Its First Records.* Philadelphia: Lippincott, Grambo & Co., 1854.

Smith, Ophia Delilah. "The Beginnings of the New Jerusalem Church in Ohio." *Ohio State Archaeological and Historical Quarterly* 61 (July 1952): 235-61.

_____. "The Rise of the New Jerusalem Church in Ohio." *Ohio State Archaeological and Historical Quarterly* 61 (Oct. 1952): 380-409.

Smith, Timothy L. "The Ohio Valley: Testing Ground for America's Experiment in Religious Pluralism." *Church History* 60 (1991): 461-79.

A history of Methodism in early Ohio.

Smucker, Isaac. *History of the Moravian Missions of Ohio, and Sketches of Its Missionaries.* Columbus, 1876.

Smythe, George Franklin. *A History of the Diocese of Ohio Until the Year 1918.* Cleveland: The Diocese, 1931.

A history of the Episcopal Church in Ohio.

Snarr, D. Neil. *Claiming Our Past: Quakers in Southwest Ohio and Eastern Tennessee.* Wilmington, Ohio: D. Neil Snarr, 1992.

Society of Friends. Ohio Yearly Meeting. *Observing Our 150th Yearly*

Meeting: Ohio Quaker Sesquicentennial, 1812-1962. Damascus, Ohio: The Friends Church, Ohio Yearly Meeting, 1962.

Stivison, David V., comp. *The Lord's Shepherds in the Ohio Hills: Biographies of 175 Ministers and Wives of the Southeastern Ohio Conferences of the United Brethren and the Evangelical United Brethren Churches, 1901-1974.* Philadelphia: privately printed, 1987.

Stoltzfus, Grant Moses. *Mennonites of the Ohio and Eastern Conference from the Colonial Period in Pennsylvania to 1968.* Scottdale, Penn.: Herald Press, 1969.

    History of pioneer Mennonite communities in Ohio. Includes a list of congregations and leaders. Concludes with a bibliographical essay for the subject.

Taylor, James W. *History of the State of Ohio, First Period, 1650-1787.* Cincinnati: H.W. Derby & Co. Publishers, 1854.

    Includes a history of early Jesuit Missions.

Terrell, C. Clayton. *Quaker Migration to Southwest Ohio.* N.p., n.d.

Umble, John Sylvanus. *Ohio Mennonite Sunday Schools.* Goshen, Ind.: Goshen College, 1941.

    Historical background of Mennonites in Ohio; includes a map of Amish and Mennonite churches in the state.

United Methodist Archives (Ohio). *Methodist Ministers Card Index, All Ohio Conferences, 1797-1981.* United Methodist Archives Center, Ohio. Microfilm, FHL.

The United Methodist Church 1992 East Ohio Conference Journal. 2 vols. Lakeside, Ohio, 1992.

United Presbyterian Synod of Ohio. *Buckeye Presbyterian.* N.p., 1968.

Vaughan, B.F. *A Centennial History of the Miami Ohio Christian Conference, 1819-1919.* Dayton, Ohio: Christian Publishing Association, 1919.

Versteeg, John M. and John D. Green, eds. *Methodism: Ohio Area*

(1812-1962). Cincinnati: Ohio Area Sesquicentennial Committee, 1962.

A history of Methodism in Ohio; includes official rosters.

Wallen, Ed G. *United Methodism Takes Root in the Black Swamp.* Fremont, Ohio: Lesher Printers, 1981.

Welsh, E.B., ed. *Buckeye Presbyterianism.* United Presbyterian Synod of Ohio, 1968.

A history of seven Presbyterian denominations and their twenty-one synods.

Whitlock, Elias D., et al. *History of the Central Ohio Conference of the Methodist Episcopal Church, 1856-1913.* Cincinnati: Press of the Methodist Book Concern, 1914.

Yeager, Helen F. "The Rise, Spread, and Influence of Religion in Ohio from 1783 to 1815." M.A. thesis, University of Cincinnati, 1942.

Ethnic Sources

Abajian, James de T. *Blacks in Selected Newspapers, Censuses and Other Sources: An Index to Names and Subjects.* Boston: G.K. Hall, 1976.

Black, Lowell Dwight. *The Negro Volunteer Militia Units of the Ohio National Guard, 1870-1954: The Struggle for Military Recognition and Equality in the State of Ohio.* Manhattan, Kansas: Military Affairs/Aerospace Historian Publishing, Kansas State University, 1976.

"Blacks in Ohio in 1870 Who Were Born in Ohio." *The Report* 40 (Winter 2000/2001): 169-76; *The Report* 41 (Spring 2001): 4-10.

Blockson, Charles L. and Ron Fry. *Black Genealogy.* Englewood Cliffs, N.J.: Prentice-Hall, 1977.

A general guidebook for African American genealogical research. Includes many addresses and a bibliography.

Brickner, Barnett Albert. *The Jewish Community of Cincinnati, Historical and Descriptive, 1817-1933.* Ph.D. diss., University of Cincinnati, 1933.

Bunch-Lyons, Beverly A. *And they Came: The Migration of African-American Women from the South to Cincinnati, Ohio, 1900-1950.* N.p., 1995.

Byers, Paula K., ed. *African American Genealogical Sourcebook.* Detroit: Gale Research, 1995.

One of the major guides to African American genealogical research. Discusses migration, genealogical sources, oral history, and related topics. Includes bibliographies and many addresses.

Chyet, Stanley F. "Ohio Valley Jewry during the Civil War." *Bulletin of the Historical and Philosophical Society of Ohio* 21 (1963): 179-87.

Clark, Peter H. *The Black Brigade of Cincinnati, Being a Report of Its Labors and a Muster Roll of Its Members.* 1864. Reprint. New York: Arno Press, 1969.

Dabney, Wendell P. *Cincinnati's Colored Citizens: Historical, Sociological, and Biographical.* 1926. Reprint. New York: Negro University Press, 1970.

Biographical sketches of African Americans in Cincinnati.

Davis, Lenwood G. *Blacks in the State of Ohio, 1800-1976: A Preliminary Survey.* Monticello, Ill.: Council of Planning Librarians, 1977.

Davis, Russel H. *Black America in Cleveland, 1796-1969.* Cleveland: Associated Publishers, 1972.

Encyclopedia of Ohio Indians. 2 vols. St. Clair Shores, Mich.: Somerset Publishers, 1998.

Erickson, Leonard. "Politics and Repeal of Ohio's Black Laws, 1837-1849." *Ohio History* 82 (Summer-Autumn 1973): 154-75.

Evans, William R. *History of Welsh Settlements in Jackson and Gallia Counties of Ohio.* 1896. Reprint. Columbus: Chatham Communicators, 1988.

Fuller, Sara, et al., eds. *The Ohio Black History Guide.* Columbus: Archives-Library Division, Ohio Historical Society, 1975.

Bibliographies, lists of county records, and lists of manuscripts. A useful African American reference source.

Gartner, Lloyd P. *History of the Jews of Cleveland.* 2nd ed. Cleveland: Western Reserve Historical Society, 1987.

Gerber, David Allison. *Black Ohio and the Color Line, 1860-1915.* Urbana, Ill.: University of Illinois Press, 1976.

A scholarly study of African Americans in Ohio—race relations, lifestyle, migration, and similar topics.

Haller, Stephen E. and Robert H. Smith, Jr. *Registers of Blacks in the Miami Valley: A Name Abstract (1804-1857).* Dayton, Ohio:

Wright State University, 1977.

Shows name of slave or free Black, owner's name, date and place of freedom, date and place residing in Ohio, and sometimes date of birth or age.

Henritze, Barbara K. *Bibliographic Checklist of African American Newspapers.* Baltimore: Genealogical Publishing Co., 1995.

Hickok, Charles Thomas. *The Negro in Ohio, 1802-1870.* Ph.D. diss., Western Reserve University, 1896. Reprint. New York: AMS Press, 1975.

Houdek, G. Robert and Michel S. Perdreau. *Black's in Ohio: A Selected Bibliography of Materials in the Alden Library.* Athens, Ohio: Ohio University Library, Reference Department, 1978.

Johnson, Anne E. and Adam Merton Cooper. *A Student's Guide to African American Genealogy.* Phoenix, Ariz.: Oryx Press, 1996.

Joiner, W.A., comp. *A Half Century of Freedom of the Negro in Ohio.* Freeport, N.Y.: Books for Libraries Press, 1972.

Koehler, Llyle. *Cincinnati's Black Peoples: A Chronology and Bibliography, 1787-1982.* Cincinnati: University of Cincinnati, 1986.

A chronology and history of African Americans in Cincinnati.

Laffoon, Polk IV. "Cincinnati's Jewish Community." *Cincinnati Magazine* 10 (April 1977): 46-57.

Litwack, Leon F. *North of Slavery: The Negro in the Free States, 1790-1860.* Chicago: University of Chicago Press, 1961.

McCluskey, John A., ed. *Blacks in Ohio.* Cleveland: New Day Press, Karamu House, 1976.

Slavery in Ohio, flight to freedom, Black memories in Ohio.

McGee, Betty. "Early Black Settlements in Ohio." Dayton, Ohio: Miami Valley Council on Genealogy and History, 1980.

Sound recording (cassette) available at Public Library of Cincinnati and Hamilton County, Cincinnati, Ohio.

McGinnis, Frederick A. *The Education of Negroes in Ohio.* Wilberforce, Ohio, 1962.

Malvin, John. *North Into Freedom: The Autobiography of John Malvin, Free Negro, 1795-1880.* 1879. Reprint. Kent, Ohio: Kent State University Press, 1988.

A biography and history of African Americans in Ohio.

Newman, Debra L., comp. *Black History: A Guide to Civilian Records in the National Archives.* Washington, DC: National Archives Trust Fund Board, 1984.

Nitchman, Paul E. *Blacks in Ohio, 1880.* 10 vols. Decorah, Iowa: Anundsen Publishing; Mansfield, Ohio: Ohio Genealogical Society, 1985-97.

Identifies African Americans and Mulattoes in the 1880 Ohio census. Each volume is separately indexed.

Ohio. Auditor of State. Special Enumeration of Blacks Immigrating to Ohio, 1861-1863. Columbus. Microfilm.

Ohio. Adjutant General's Office. *Official Roster of the Colored Troops of the State of Ohio in the War of the Rebellion.* Microfilm.

Original muster in and muster out rolls of the Civil War.

Ohio. Governor's Commission on Socially Disadvantaged Black Males. *Ohio's African-American Males: A Call to Action.* Columbus: Ohio Office of Black Affairs, 1990.

Philipson, David. "Jewish Pioneers of the Ohio Valley." *Publications of the American Jewish Historical Society* 8 (1900): 43-57.

Phillips, Kimberly L. *Heaven-Bound: Black Migration, Community, and Activism in Cleveland, 1915-1945.* N.p., 1992.

Sarna, Jonathan D. and Nancy H. Klein. *The Jews of Cincin-nati.*Cincinnati: Center for the Study of the American Jewish Experience, Hebrew Union College-Jewish Institute of Religion, 1989.

Streets, David H. *Slave Genealogy: A Research Guide with Case*

Studies. Bowie, Md.: Heritage Books, 1986.

Tanner, Helen Hornbeck, ed. *Atlas of Great Lakes Indian History.* Norman, Okla.: University of Oklahoma Press, 1987.

Turpin, Joan. *Register of Black, Mulatto, and Poor Persons in Four Ohio Counties, 1791-1861.* Bowie, Md.: Heritage Books, 1985.

Varady, David P. "Migration and Mobility Patterns of the Jewish Population of Cincinnati." *American Jewish Archives* 32 (1980): 79-88.

Weisman, Kay, comp. *Selected Bibliography of Black History Sources at the Ohio Historical Society.* Columbus: Ohio Historical Society, n.d.

Wesley, Charles Harris. *Negro-Americans in Ohio: A Sesquicentennial View.* Wilberforce, Ohio: Central State College, 1953.

_____. *Ohio Negroes in the Civil War.* Columbus: Ohio State University Press, 1962.

Weston, Rubin Francis, ed. *Blacks in Ohio History.* Columbus: Ohio American Revolution Bicentennial Advisory Commission, Ohio Historical Society, 1976.

Historical essays regarding the Black experience in Ohio.

Whiteman, Max. "Black Genealogy." *RQ* [*Research Quarterly*] 11 (1972).

Witcher, Curt Bryan. *African American Genealogy: A Bibliography and Guide to Sources.* Ft. Wayne, Ind.: Round Tower Books, 2000.

Woodson, Carter G. *A Century of Negro Migration.* Washington, DC: Association for the Study of Negro Life and History, 1918.

Wright, Richard R. *The Negroes of Xenia, Ohio.* United States Department of Labor Bulletin No. 37. N.p., n.d.

Young, Tommie Morton. *Afro-American Genealogy Sourcebook.* New York: Garland Publishing, 1987.

Identifies sources for African American genealogical research. Includes bibliographies and many addresses.

Guidebooks and Methodology

Balhuizen, Anne Ross. *The History of Your Heritage: Ohio.* Centerville, Utah: Advanced Resources, 1993.

Bell, Carol Willsey. *Ohio Genealogical Guide.* 6th ed. Youngstown, Ohio: Bell Books, 1995.

A summary and description of Ohio genealogical records; illustrated with examples and maps.

_____. *Ohio Guide to Genealogical Sources.* Baltimore: Genealogical Publishing Co., 1988.

A summary of many genealogical records available for each Ohio county, alphabetically arranged by county.

Brannick, John A. "Buried Treasures: Ohio's Unusual County Records." *Preview* (Ohio Historical Society) 5 (Summer 1996): 13-16.

Clark, Donna K. *Ohio State Directory of Genealogical Records.* Arvada, Colo.: Ancestor Publishers, 1986.

Colket, Meredith Bright. *The Widely Known "Western Reserve" of Ohio.* Salt Lake City: Genealogical Society, 1969.

Cuyahoga West Chapter, Ohio Genealogical Society. *Cuyahoga County, Ohio: Genealogical Research Guide.* Fairview Park, Ohio: Cuyahoga West Chapter, 1989.

Douthit, Ruth Long. *Ohio Resources for Genealogists with Some References for Genealogical Searching in Ohio.* Rev. ed. Detroit: Detroit Society for Genealogical Research, 1972.

See *Supplement* edited by Mrs. Carl Main.

Eichholz, Alice, ed. *Ancestry's Red Book: American State, County & Town Sources.* Rev. ed. Salt Lake City: Ancestry Publishing, 1991.

Also available on CD-ROM.

Elliott, Wendy L. *Ohio Genealogical Research Guide.* Rev. ed.

Bountiful, Utah: American Genealogical Lending Library, 1988.

Fenley, Ann. *The Ohio Connection Formula for Finding Elusive Ancestors.* Dayton, Ohio: Ohio Connection, 1985.

_____. *The Ohio Open Records Law and Genealogy: Researching Ohio Public Records.* Dayton, Ohio: Ohio Connection, 1989.

A history of Ohio's open records law and accessing Ohio records; partially outdated.

Gagel, Diane VanSkiver. "Researching in Ohio." *The Genealogical Helper* 45 (January-February 1991): 10-16.

Gilkey, Elliot Howard. *The Ohio Hundred Year Book.* Columbus: Fred J. Heer, 1901.

Lists of members of the General Assembly, senators, representatives, and biographical sketches. This is a revised and enlarged edition of *Taylor's Ohio Statesmen and Hundred Year Book* (1892).

The Handybook for Genealogists. 10th ed. Draper, Utah: Everton Publishers, 2002.

Harter, Mary (McCollom). "Ohio." In American Society of Genealogists, *Genealogical Research: Methods and Sources,* vol. 2. Rev. ed., Kenn Stryker-Rodda, ed. Washington, DC: The Society, 1983, pp. 22-28.

Harter, Stuart. *Ohio Genealogy and Local History Sources Index.* Fort Wayne, Ind.: CompuGen Systems, 1986.

Heisey, John W. *Ohio Genealogical Research Guide.* Indianapolis, Ind.: Heritage House, 1987.

Lists of Ohio sources, bibliographies, and addresses.

Hochstetter, Nancy, ed. *Travel Historic Ohio: A Guide to Historic Sites and Markers.* Madison, Wisc.: Guide Press Co., 1986.

Local history, biography, historical markers, Ohio maps.

Kalette, Linda Elise. *The Papers of Thirteen Early Ohio Political Leaders: An Inventory to the 1976-77 Microfilm Editions.*

Columbus: Ohio Historical Society, 1977.

Khouw, Petta. *Genealogy: Helping You Climb Your Family Tree.* Occasional Paper, series 3, no. 2. Columbus: State Library of Ohio, 1990.

A valuable guide to the genealogy collection of the State Library of Ohio, Columbus, and its services, and an overview of Ohio genealogical sources.

McCay, Betty L. *Sources for Genealogical Searching in Ohio.* Rev. ed. Indianapolis: The author, 1973.

Main, Florence (Mrs. Carl), ed. *Ohio Genealogical Records: A Supplement to Some References for Genealogical Searching in Ohio...Based on Material at the Western Reserve Historical Society.* Cleveland: Genealogical Advisory Committee of the Western Reserve Historical Society, 1968.

Maki, Carol L. "Ohio." In *Ancestry's Red Book: American State, County & Town Sources.* Edited by Alice Eichholz. Rev. ed. Salt Lake City: Ancestry, 1992, pp. 572-88.

An overview chapter describing Ohio genealogical sources; includes a useful county outline map of the state and county information.

Mettle, Suzanne Wolfe, et al., comps. *Genealogical Researcher's Manual: With Special References for Using the Ohio Historical Society Library.* Columbus: Franklin County Chapter, Ohio Genealogical Society, 1981.

National Society of the Colonial Dames of America in the State of Ohio. *A Guide to Historic Houses in Ohio.* 2nd ed. Compiled by Elizabeth P. Allyn, et al. Westerville, Ohio: The Society, 1996.

Neel, Thomas Stephen. *Ohio County Courthouse Guide.* Ashland, Ohio: Ashland County Chapter, Ohio Genealogical Society, 1985.

Ohio Factsheet. Online (www.ancestry.com).

The Ohio Genealogy Guide. Online:

(http://usgenealogyguide.com/ohio).

The Ohio Genealogical Helper: Vital Records Research. Columbus: Maxwell Publications, n.d.

Ohio Genealogical Society. *Guide to Cemetery Preservation.* Mansfield, Ohio: The Society, 1987.

Ohio Public Information Laws. Columbus: Ohio Attorney General.

Ohio Research Outline. Online (www.familysearch.org).
Briefly outlines Ohio genealogical sources and includes some bibliographies. See "Research Helps" at this Internet site.

Parker, Jimmy B. *A Definitive Study of Major U.S. Genealogical Records: Ecclesiastical and Secular, Part I, Ohio.* Salt Lake City: Genealogical Society, 1969.

Reed, John H. *Guide to the Manuscripts of Early Ohio Methodism, United Methodist Church of Ohio.* Delaware, Ohio: West Ohio Conference, United Methodist Church, Commission on Archives and History, 1981.

Research Outline: Ohio. Salt Lake City: Family History Department, 1988.
A valuable overview of Ohio genealogical sources. For an expanded and updated version see (www.familysearch.org).

Schulz, Margaret J., comp. *Sources of Genealogical Help in Ohio.* Burbank, Calif.: Southern California Genealogical Society, 2000.

Schweitzer, George K. *Ohio Genealogical Research.* Knoxville, Tenn.: The author, 1994.
Bibliographies and descriptions of Ohio sources arranged by subject (church records, etc.) and Ohio by counties.

Sperry, Kip. "Genealogical Research in Ohio." *National Genealogical Society Quarterly* 75 (June 1987): 81-104.

_____. "Ohio Research on the Internet." Online:
(www.ancestry.com/library/view/columns/tips/922.asp).

_____. "Finding Your Ohio Ancestors." *Everton's Genealogical*

Helper 52 (1998): 10-15.

Szucs, Loretto Dennis and Sandra Hargreaves Luebking, eds. *The Source: A Guidebook of American Genealogy*. Rev. ed. Salt Lake City: Ancestry Inc., 1997.

This is one of the premier reference sources for American genealogists. Well illustrated.

Terheiden, Connie Stunkel and Kenny R. Burck, comps. *Guide to Genealogical Resources in Cincinnati & Hamilton County, Ohio*. 3rd ed. Cincinnati: Hamilton County Chapter of the Ohio Genealogical Society, 2001.

Wright, David K. *Ohio Handbook*. Emeryville, Calif.: Moon Publications, 1999.

Includes Ohio history, an overview of Ohio's canals, and other state and local information.

History

Abbott, John Stevens Cabot. *The History of the State of Ohio from the Discovery of the Great Valley to the Present Time.* Detroit: Northwestern Publishing Co., 1875.
One of the major early histories of the state. Illustrated. Online: (www.rootsweb.com/~usgenweb/oh/abbot.htm)

Ambler, Charles Henry. *A History of Transportation in the Ohio Valley.* Glendale, Calif.: Arthur H. Clark, 1931.

Andrews, E.B. "The Early History of Ohio." *New Englander* 12 (Aug. 1854): 384-408.

Atwater, Caleb. *A History of the State of Ohio, Natural and Civil.* 2nd ed. Cincinnati: Glezen & Shepard, 1838.
See *Index to A History of the State of Ohio, Natural and Civil*, indexed by Marilyn Sims Vadakin (Marietta, Ohio: Lemon Tree Press, 1993); a personal name, subject, and locality index to this state history.

Aumann, Francis R. and Harvey Walker. *The Government and Administration of Ohio.* New York: Thomas Y. Crowell Co., 1956.

Balhuizen, Anne Ross. *The History of Your Heritage: Ohio.* Centerville, Utah: Advanced Resources, 1993.

Banta, Richard Elwell. *The Ohio Valley: A Students' Guide to Localized History.* New York: Teachers College Press, 1966.
Ohio Valley history and bibliographies.

Barclay, Morgan and Charles N. Glaab. *Toledo: Gateway to the Great Lakes.* Tulsa, Okla.: Continental Heritage Press, 1982.

Barker, Joseph. *Recollections of the First Settlement of Ohio.* Edited by George Jordan Blazier. 1958. Reprint. Marietta, Ohio: Richardson Printing, 1982.

Barnhart, John D. *Valley of Democracy: The Frontier Versus the*

Plantation in the Ohio Valley, 1775-1818. Lincoln: University of Nebraska Press, 1953.

Belote, Theodore Thomas. *The Scioto Speculation and the French Settlement at Gallipolis: A Study in Ohio Valley History.* 1907. Reprint. New York: Lenox Hill, 1971.

Berquist, Goodwin F. and Paul C. Bowers, Jr. *The New Eden: James Kilbourne and the Development of Ohio.* Lanham, Md.: University Press of America, 1983.

Early Ohio state history and migration history.

Bigham, Darrel E. *Towns & Villages of the Lower Ohio.* Lexington, Ky.: University Press of Kentucky, 1998.

A scholarly study of lower Ohio River settlements, with pictures, maps, notes, and a bibliography.

Black, Alexander. *The Story of Ohio.* Boston: D. Lothrop Co., 1888.

An early history of the beginnings of Ohio and the Northwest Territory. Illustrated.

Blanchard, Rufus. *The Discovery and Conquests of the Northwest, Including the Early History of Marietta, Cincinnati, Cleveland.* Chicago, 1880.

Bloom, John Porter, ed. *The American Territorial System.* Athens, Ohio: Ohio University Press, 1973.

Bond, Beverely Waugh, Jr. *The Civilization of the Old Northwest: A Study of Political, Social, and Economic Development, 1788-1812.* New York: Macmillan Co., 1934.

_____. *The Foundations of Ohio.* Columbus: Ohio State Archaeological and Historical Society, 1941.

Booth, Russell H., Jr. *The Tuscarawas Valley in Indian Days, 1750-1797.* Cambridge, Ohio: Gomber House Press, 1994.

Boryczka, Raymond. *No Strength without Union.* Columbus: Ohio Historical Society, 1982.

Bowman, David W. *Pathway of Progress: A Short History of Ohio.*

New York: American Book Co., 1951.

An overview history of the state. Illustrated.

Brennan, Joseph Fletcher. *A Biographical Cyclopaedia and Portrait Gallery of Distinguished Men, with an Historical Sketch of the State of Ohio.* 2 vols. Cincinnati: Yorston, 1879.

Brown, Jeffrey P. "The Ohio Federalists, 1803-1815." *Journal of the Early Republic* 2 (1982): 261-82.

_____ and Andrew R.L. Cayton, eds. *The Pursuit of Public Power: Political Culture in Ohio, 1787-1861.* Kent, Ohio: Kent State University Press, 1994.

Especially useful are the footnotes, historical background, Ohio timeline, and bibliographic essay.

Bryan, John A. *The Ohio Annual Register, Containing a Condensed History of the State.* Columbus: J. Gilbert & R.C. Bryan, 1835.

Buley, R. Carlyle. *The Old Northwest: Pioneer Period, 1815-1840.* Bloomington, Ind.: Indiana University Press, 1978.

A major historical study of the Northwest Territory.

Burke, James L. and Kenneth E. Davison. *Ohio's Heritage Revised.* Salt Lake City: Peregrine Smith Books, 1989.

Ohio history, ethnic composition, state government, and life in Ohio.

Burke, Thomas Aquinas. *Ohio Lands: A Short History.* 9th ed. Columbus: Auditor of State, 1997.

(http://freepages.history.rootsweb.com/~maggie/ohio-lands/ohlands.html)

Burnet, Jacob. *Notes on the Early Settlement of the Northwestern Territory.* Cincinnati: D. Appleton, 1847.

Butler, Joseph G., Jr. *History of Youngstown and the Mahoning Valley, Ohio.* 3 vols. Chicago: American Historical Society, 1921.

Butler, Mann. *Valley of the Ohio.* Frankfort: Kentucky Historical Society, 1971.

Carpenter, Allan. *The Encyclopedia of the Midwest.* New York: Facts On File, 1989.
    Includes brief sketches of Ohio history and biography.
Carpenter, W.H. and T.S. Arthur, eds. *The History of Ohio from Its Earliest Settlement to the Present Time.* Philadelphia: J.B. Lippincott & Co., 1858.
Carter, Clarence Edwin, ed. *The Territorial Papers of the United States.* 26 vols. Washington, DC: Government Printing Office, 1934.
Cayton, Andrew R.L. "Land, Power, and Reputation: The Cultural Dimension of Politics in the Ohio Country." *William and Mary Quarterly*, 3rd series. 47 (1990): 276-82.
_____. *The Frontier Republic: Ideology and Politics in the Ohio Country, 1780-1825.* Kent, Ohio: Kent State University Press, 1986.
    Discusses politics, early settlements in Ohio, and historical background. The footnotes and bibliographic essay are especially helpful for Ohio history. See the useful map, "The Ohio Country."
Chaddock, Robert Emmet. *Ohio Before 1850: A Study of the Early Influence of Pennsylvania and Southern Populations in Ohio.* 1908. Reprint. New York: AMS Press, 1967.
Chater, Melville. "Ohio: The Gateway State." *The National Geographic Magazine* 61 (May 1932): 525-91.
Cherry, Peter Peterson. *The Western Reserve and Early Ohio.* Akron, Ohio: R.L. Fouse, 1920.
Collins, William R. *Ohio: The Buckeye State.* 6th ed. Englewood Cliffs, N.J.: Prentice-Hall, 1980.
Comley, William J. and W. D'Eggville. *Ohio: The Future Great State, Her Manufacturers and a History of Her Commercial Cities, Cincinnati and Cleveland.* Cincinnati: Comley Brothers, 1875.
    Local and manufacturing history, with biographies and portraits.
County and Family Histories: Ohio, 1780-1970. CD-ROM (Family

Tree Maker).

Crout, George C. and W.E. Rosenfelt. *Ohio: Its People and Culture.* Minneapolis: T.S. Denison & Co., 1977.

Ohio history, maps, migration, biographies, pioneer history.

Curtis, Henry B. "Pioneer Days in Central Ohio." *Ohio Archaeological and Historical Publications* 1 (1887-88): 240-51.

Cutler, Julia Perkins. *The Founders of Ohio.* Cincinnati: Robert Clarke & Co., 1888.

Cutler, Manasseh. *An Explanation of the Map of Federal Lands.* 1787. Reprint. Readex Microprint, 1966.

Daughters of the American Revolution. Dolly Todd Madison Chapter. *Ohio: Early State and Local History.* Tiffin, Ohio, 1915.

Dowler, John F., ed. *Centennial History, Ohio State Grange, 1873-1973.* Ashville, Ohio: Ohio State Grange, n.d.

A history of the Grange in Ohio, with biographies and some portraits.

Downes, Randolph Chandler. *Council Fires on the Upper Ohio: A Narrative of Indian Affairs in the Upper Ohio Valley Until 1795.* Pittsburgh: University of Pittsburgh Press, 1940.

_____. *Frontier Ohio, 1788-1803.* Columbus: Ohio State Archaeological and Historical Society, 1935.

An early history of Ohio and its settlers.

_____. *History of Lake Shore, Ohio.* 3 vols. New York: Lewis Historical Publishing Co., 1952.

Volume 3 contains biographical sketches; indexed.

Duff, William Alexander. *History of North Central Ohio, Embracing Richland, Ashland, Wayne, Medina, Lorain, Huron, and Knox Counties.* 3 vols. Topeka-Indianapolis, Ind.: Historical Publishing Co., 1931.

Educational Research Council of America. *The State of Ohio, Part One, Ohio: From Settlement to 1910.* Cleveland, 1970.

Elkins, Stanley and Eric McKitrick. "A Meaning for Turner's Frontier: Democracy in the Old Northwest." *Political Science Quarterly* 69 (1954): 321-53.

Encyclopedia of Ohio: A Volume of Encyclopedia of the United States. St. Clair Shores, Mich.: Somerset Publishers, 1982.
Ohio state history, biographies, gazetteer of Ohio place-names, and descriptions of historical places.

The Evolution of Ohio. Online: (www.oplin.lib.oh.us/products/build/index.html).
For each geographical region in Ohio, this site shows history (chronology), migration, economy, and population.

Fernow, Berthold. *The Ohio Valley in Colonial Days.* Albany, N.Y.: Joel Munsell's Sons, 1890.

Fess, Simeon Davidson. *Ohio: A Four-Volume Reference Library on the History of a Great State.* 5 vols. Chicago: Lewis Publishing Co., 1937.
Historical details for each Ohio county, physical features, first settlements, transportation, economic interests, institutions, notable persons, population statistics, biographies, and portraits. Illustrated.

Fleischman, John. *The Ohio Lands.* San Francisco: Browntrout Publishers, 1995.

Folsom, W.H.C. *Fifty Years in the Northwest, Containing Reminiscences, Incidents and Notes.* Pioneer Press Co., 1888.

Foster, Emily, ed. *The Ohio Frontier: An Anthology of Early Writings.* Lexington: University Press of Kentucky, 1996.
Diaries, letters, travel accounts, and early Ohio history.

Frary, I.T. *Early Homes of Ohio.* New York: Dover Publications, 1970.
Historical background, and some genealogy, along with photographs of homes, courthouses, churches, and other Ohio buildings.

Fry, Mildred Covey. "Women on the Ohio Frontier: The Marietta

Area." *Ohio History* 90 (Winter 1981): 55-73.

Galbreath, Charles Burleigh. *History of Ohio.* 5 vols. Chicago: American Historical Society, 1925.

A detailed and useful history of Ohio. See *Cross Index, Charles B. Galbreath's 1925, 5 Volume, History of Ohio*, 2 vols., comp. by Robertalee Lent (Post Falls, Idaho: Genealogical Reference Builders, 1969) and *Index to Charles B. Galbreath's History of Ohio*, indexed by Fay Maxwell (Columbus, Ohio, 1973).

Garrison, Webb. *A Treasury of Ohio Tales.* Nashville: Rutledge Hill Press, 1993.

A guide to Ohio local history and biography.

Giglierano, Geoffrey J. and Deborah A. Overmyer. *The Bicentennial Guide to Greater Cincinnati: A Portrait of Two Hundred Years.* Cincinnati: Cincinnati Historical Society, 1988.

Gilkey, Elliot Howard. *The Ohio Hundred Year Book.* Columbus: Fred J. Heer, 1901.

Lists of members of the General Assembly, senators, representatives, and biographical sketches. Includes portraits. This is a revised and enlarged edition of *Taylor's Ohio Statesmen and Hundred Year Book* (1892).

Goulder, Grace. *This Is Ohio: Ohio's 88 Counties in Words and Pictures.* Rev. ed. Cleveland: World Publishing Co., 1965.

A brief history of Ohio's counties and regions. Illustrated.

Gregory, William M. and William B. Guitteau. *History and Geography of Ohio.* New edition. Boston: Ginn and Co., 1935.

Griffiths, D., Jr. *Two Years' Residence in the New Settlements of Ohio, North America.* London: Westley and Davis, 1835.

Gruenwald, Kim M. "Marietta's Example of a Settlement Pattern in the Ohio Country: A Reinterpretation." *Ohio History* 105 (Summer-Autumn 1996): 125-44.

Gunckel, John E. *The Early History of the Maumee Valley.* 2nd ed.

Toledo: Henry M. Schmit, 1913.

Hansen, Ann Natalie. *Westward the Winds: Being Some of the Main Currents of Life in Ohio, 1788-1873.* Columbus, 1974.

Harris, Charles H. *The Harris History: A Collection of Tales of Long Ago of Southeastern Ohio and Adjoining Territories.* Athens, Ohio: Athens Messenger, 1957.

See *Surname Index to the Harris History*, indexed by Mrs. Jane Whiteman (Tulsa, Okla., 1978).

Harte, Brian. "Land in the Old Northwest: A Study of Speculation, Sales, and Settlement on the Connecticut Western Reserve." *Ohio History* 101 (Summer-Autumn 1992): 114-39.

Hatcher, Harlan Henthorne. *The Buckeye Country: A Pageant of Ohio.* New York: G.P. Putnam's Sons, 1947.

An illustrated general history of the state.

_____. *The Western Reserve: The Story of New Connecticut in Ohio.* Rev. ed. Cleveland: World Publishing Co., 1966.

Havighurst, Walter. *Ohio: A Bicentennial History.* New York: W.W. Norton & Co., 1976.

A popular and general history of Ohio; illustrated.

_____. *The Heartland: Ohio, Indiana, Illinois.* Rev. ed. New York: Harper & Row, 1974.

Historical background, pioneer settlements, and local history.

Hildreth, Samuel Prescott. *Contributions to the Early History of the Northwest.* Cincinnati: Poe & Hitchcock, 1864.

_____. *Pioneer History: Being An Account of the First Examinations of the Ohio Valley and the Early Settlement of the Northwest Territory.*1848. Reprint. New York: Arno, 1971.

See *Index to Pioneer History*, indexed by Marilyn Sims Vadakin (Marietta, Ohio: It's My Business, n.d.).

Himes, H.E. *A History of Miami-Land, 1770-1990.* Wilmington, Del.: H.E. Himes, 1990.

Hinsdale, Burke Aaron and Mary L. Hinsdale. *History and Civil Government of Ohio and the Government of the United States.* Chicago: Werner School Book Co., 1896.

Hintzen, William. *The Border Wars of the Upper Ohio Valley, 1769-1794.* Manchester, Conn.: Precision Shooting, 1999.

History of Hocking Valley, Ohio. 1883. Reprint. Mt. Vernon, Ind.: Windmill Publications, 1991. *Surname Index* (1980).

History of Lower Scioto Valley, Ohio. Chicago: Inter-State Publishing Co., 1884.

History of the Upper Ohio Valley, with Family History and Biographical Sketches. 2 vols. Madison, Wisc.: Brant & Fuller, 1890-91.

See Leila S. Francy, *Surname Index to History of the Upper Ohio Valley* (Apollo, Pa.: Closson Press, 1993) and Mrs. Jane Whiteman, comp., *Surname Index to History of the Upper Ohio Valley* (Tulsa, Okla., 1978).

Hochstetter, Nancy, ed. *Travel Historic Ohio.* Madison, Wisc.: Guide Press Co., 1986.

Useful for a study of Ohio history, early 1800s to the early 1900s.

Hopkins, Charles Edwin. *Ohio: The Beautiful and Historic.* Boston: L.C. Page & Co., 1931.

Hover, John C., et al., eds. *Memoirs of the Miami Valley.* 3 vols. Chicago: Robert O. Law Co., 1919.

A detailed early history of southwestern Ohio, with biographical details.

Howe, Henry. *Historical Collections of Ohio.* 2 vols. Cincinnati: State of Ohio, 1888-1904. (Publisher varied).

One of the popular histories of the state. See "Index to Historical Collections of Ohio," index compiled by Fresno Genealogical Society (Fresno, Calif.). Typescript. See also *Index to Historical Collections of Ohio by Henry Howe*, compiled by Sandra Hudnall

Day (Steubenville, Ohio: Jefferson County Chapter, Ohio Genealogical Society, 1990). Online:
(www.hti.umich.edu/cgi/b/bib/bibperm?q1=aja2910).

Howe, Robert T. *Ohio: Our State*. Cincinnati: Roblen Publishing Co.,
1992.
Useful for those beginning a study of Ohio history.

Howells, William Cooper. *Recollections of Life in Ohio from 1813 to
1840*. Cincinnati: Robert Clarke & Co., 1895.

Hulbert, Archer Butler, ed. *Ohio in the Time of the Confederation.*
Marietta, Ohio: Marietta Historical Commission, 1918.

_____, ed. *The Records of the Original Proceedings of the Ohio
Company*. 2 vols. Marietta, Ohio: Marietta Historical Commission,
1917.

Hunter, W.H. "The Pathfinders of Jefferson County." *Ohio Archaeological and Historical Society Publications* 6 (1898): 96-313.

Hurt, R. Douglas. *The Ohio Frontier: Crucible of the Old Northwest,
1720-1830*. Bloomington, Ind.: Indiana University Press, 1996.
A scholarly study of early settlements in the state. See Andrew
R.L. Cayton, "The State of Ohio's Early History: A Review
Essay," *Ohio History* 106 (Summer-Autumn 1997): 192-99.

Hutchinson, William Thomas. *The Bounty Lands of the American
Revolution in Ohio*. 1927. Reprint. New York: Arno Press, 1979.

Izant, Grace Goulder. *This Is Ohio: Ohio's 88 Counties in Words and
Pictures*. Rev. ed. Cleveland: World Publishing Co., 1965.

James, John Henry. *Ohio in 1788*. Columbus: A.H. Smythe, 1888.

Johnson, Davis Ben, ed. "Stories of Ohio." N.p., n.d. Typescript.

Jones, Nelson Edwards. *The Squirrel Hunters of Ohio, or Glimpses of
Pioneer Life*. Cincinnati: Robert Clarke Co., 1898.

Jones, Robert Leslie. *History of Agriculture in Ohio to 1880*. Kent,
Ohio: Kent State University Press, 1983.

Jones, William B. *Ohio's Praise in Pictures*. Warren, Ohio: Showcase

Books, 1979.

Kellogg, Louise Phelps, ed. *Early Narratives of the Northwest, 1634-1699.* New York: Charles Scribner's Sons, 1917.

Kennedy, Aileen Elizabeth. *The Ohio Poor Law and Its Administration.* Chicago: University of Chicago Press, 1934.

King, Rufus. *Ohio: First Fruits of the Ordinance of 1787.* 1903. Reprint. New York: AMS Press, 1973.

Kinkead, Charles B. *Ohio Diary: The Saga of Raccoon Valley.* New York: Exposition Press, 1953.

Klauprecht, Emil. *German Chronicle in the History of the Ohio Valley and Its Capital City, Cincinnati in Particular.* Edited by Don Heinrich Tolzmann. Translated by Dale V. Lally, Jr. Bowie, Md.: Heritage Books, 1992.
A German-American history of the Ohio Valley.

Knapp, H.S. *History of the Maumee Valley.* Toledo: Blade Mammoth Printing, 1872.
An early history of the Maumee Valley and early settlements.

Knepper, George W. *An Ohio Portrait.* Columbus: Ohio Historical Society, 1976.
An illustrated general history of Ohio, with historical photos.

_____. *Ohio and Its People.* 2nd ed. Kent, Ohio: Kent State University Press, 1997.
A valuable history of the state. The Ohio maps in this volume are particularly useful.

Kolehmainen, John I. *A History of the Finns in Ohio, Western Pennsylvania, and West Virginia.* Ohio Finnish-American Historical Society, 1977.

Lawyer, J.P. *History of Ohio from the Glacial Period to the Present Time.* 3rd ed. Columbus: Press of Fred J. Heer, 1904.

Lewis, Thomas William. *History of Southeastern Ohio and the Muskingum Valley, 1788-1928.* 3 vols. Chicago: S.J. Clarke

Publishing Co., 1928.

Lieberman, Carl, ed. *Government and Politics in Ohio.* Lanham, Md.: University Press of America, 1984.

Lindsey, David, et al. *An Outline History of Ohio.* Rev. ed. Cleveland: Howard Allen, 1960.

Lossing, Benson J. *A Pictorial Description of Ohio, Comprising a Sketch of Its Physical Geography, History, Political Divisions, Resources, Government and Constitution, Antiquities, Public Lands, etc.* New York: Ensign & Thayer, 1848.

McConagha, John. *Ohio Local History in the Bicentennial Year.* Columbus: State Library of Ohio, 1978.

McConnell, Michael Norman. *A Country Between: The Upper Ohio Valley and Its Peoples, 1724-1774.* Lincoln: University of Nebraska Press, 1992.

A scholarly study of Native Americans and early settlements in the Ohio region; includes valuable maps of the area.

Madison, James H., ed. *Heartland: Midwestern History and Culture.* Bloomington, Ind.: Indiana University Press, 1988.

See especially the chapter, "Ohio: Gateway to the Midwest."

Mahoning Valley Historical Society. *Historical Collections of the Mahoning Valley.* 1876. Reprint. Knightstown, Ind.: The Bookmark, 1977.

Maizlish, Stephen E. *The Triumph of Sectionalism: The Transformation of Ohio Politics, 1844-1856.* Kent, Ohio: Kent State University Press, 1983.

Marshall, Carrington Tanner, ed. *A History of the Courts and Lawyers of Ohio.* 4 vols. New York: American Historical Society, 1934.

Biographical sketches of prominent Ohio lawyers and judges.

Martzolff, Clement Luther. *Fifty Stories from Ohio History.* Columbus: Teacher Publishing Co., 1917.

Marzulli, Lawrence J. *The Development of Ohio's Counties and Their*

Historic Courthouses. Columbus: County Commissioners Association of Ohio, 1982.

A brief history of each Ohio county and their courthouse.

Mathews, Alfred. *Ohio and Her Western Reserve, with a History of Three States.* New York: D. Appleton and Co., 1902.

A regional history of the Western Reserve in Ohio.

Maxwell, Fay, comp. *Irish Refugee Tract Abstract Data & History of the Irish Acadians.* Columbus: Maxwell Publications, 1974.

Michels, Greg, ed. *Governments of Ohio, 1986.* N.p., 1985.

Miller, James M. *The Genesis of Western Culture: The Upper Ohio Valley, 1800-1825.* Columbus: Ohio State Archaeological and Historical Society, 1938.

Mitchener, Charles Hollowell, ed. *Ohio Annals: Historic Events in the Tuscarawas and Muskingum Valleys and in Other Portions of the State of Ohio.* 1876. Reprint. Strasburg, Ohio: Gordon Printing, 1975. Reprint. Bowie, Md.: Heritage Books, 1993.

Moorehead, Warren King. *The Indian Tribes of Ohio Historically Considered.* 1899. Reprint. New York: AMS Press, 1983.

Morrison, Olin Dee. *Ohio, "Gateway State": A History of Ohio, Social, Economic, Political.* 4 vols. Athens, Ohio: E.M. Morrison, 1962.

A typescript general history of the state.

Muller, Edward K. "Early Industrialization in the Ohio Valley: A Review Essay." *Historical Geography Newsletter* 3 (Fall 1973): 19-30.

Murdock, Eugene C. *The Buckeye Empire: An Illustrated History of Ohio Enterprise.* Northridge, Calif.: Windsor Publications, 1988.

Newton, Jim. *Today in Ohio History.* Hamilton, Ohio: Fort Hamilton Press, 1964.

Noble, Allen G., et al. *Ohio: An American Heartland.* Columbus: State of Ohio, Division of Geological Survey, 1975.

Ohio: An Empire within an Empire. 2nd ed. Columbus: Ohio Development and Publicity Commission, 1950.

Ohio History Central: An Online Encyclopedia of Ohio. Online:
   (www.ohiokids.org/ohc/index.html)

Ohio Memory: An Online Scrapbook of Ohio History. Online
   (www.ohiomemory.org)

*Ohio's Progressive Sons, A History of the State: Sketches of Those Who
   have Helped to Build up the Commonwealth.* Cincinnati: Queen
   City Publishing Co., 1905.
   Biographical sketches and portraits of prominent Ohioans.

Ohio Women (OPLIN). Online:
   (www.oplin.lib.oh.us/index.cfm?ID=3-58-2162)

Onuf, Peter S. *Statehood and Union: A History of the Northwest
   Ordinance.* Bloomington, Ind.: Indiana University Press, 1987.
   A scholarly study of Ohio and the Northwest Ordinance.

Overman, William D., comp. *Select List of Materials on Ohio History
   in Serial Publications.* Columbus: Ohio State Archaeological and
   Historical Society, 1941.

Page, Henry Folsom. *The Law of Warrants, Entries, Surveys and
   Patents in the Virginia Military District in Ohio.* Columbus: J.H.
   Riley & Co., 1850.
   Describes the history of Virginia military titles in Ohio.

Particular Places: A Traveler's Guide to Inner Ohio. 2 vols. Wilmington, Ohio: Orange Frazer Press, 1990-93.
   Local history and tours of Ohio.

*Pathways to the Old Northwest: An Observance of the Bicentennial of
   the Northwest Ordinance.* Indianapolis: Indiana Historical Society,
   1988.

Perry, Dick. *Ohio: A Personal Portrait of the 17th State.* Garden City,
   N.Y.: Doubleday & Co., 1969.

Peters, William Edwards. *Ohio Lands and their History.* 3rd ed. 1930.
   Reprint. New York: Arno Press, 1979.

A detailed history of Ohio lands and early settlements in the state. Includes maps of Ohio land divisions.

Phillips, W. Louis. *Jurisdictional Histories for Ohio's Eighty-Eight Counties, 1788-1985.* Bowie, Md.: Heritage Books, 1986.

Pioneer History. Cincinnati: H.W. Derby, 1848.

Randall, Emilius Oviatt and Daniel J. Ryan. *History of Ohio: The Rise and Progress of an American State.* 6 vols. New York: Century History Co., 1912-15.

_____, ed. *Ohio: Centennial Anniversary Celebration.* Columbus: Press of Fred J. Heer, 1903.

Includes lists of Ohioans, judges, and others.

Reichert, W.O. and S.O. Ludd, eds. *Outlook on Ohio.* N.p.,1983.

Rerick, Rowland H. *History of Ohio.* Madison, Wisc.: Northwestern Historical Association, 1905.

_____. *State Centennial History of Ohio.* Madison, Wisc.: Northwestern Historical Association, 1902.

Richards, Wilfrid Gladstone. *The Settlement of the Miami Valley of Southwestern Ohio.* Chicago: N.p., 1948.

Richardson, Robert H. *A Time and Place in Ohio: A Chronological Account of Certain Historical and Genealogical Miscellany in Eastern Ohio.* Smithtown, N.Y.: Exposition Press 1983.

Roberts, Carl H. and Paul R. Cummins. *Ohio: Geography, History, Government.* Laidlaw Brothers, 1961.

Rohrbough, Malcolm J. *The Land Office Business: The Settlement and Administration of American Public Lands, 1789-1837.* New York: Oxford University Press, 1968.

_____. *The Trans-Appalachian Frontier: People, Societies, and Institutions, 1775-1850.* 1978. Reprint. Belmont, Calif.: Wadsworth Publishing Co., 1990.

A scholarly history of the trans-Appalachian frontier, 1775-1850, experiences of the people, rise of societies, social history, and development of institutions. Includes useful maps of the frontier, including Ohio.

Roseboom, Eugene Holloway and Francis Phelps Weisenburger. *A History of Ohio*. 2nd ed. Columbus: Ohio Historical Society, 1969. A popular and well-illustrated history of the state.

Rust, Orton Glenn. *History of West Central Ohio*. 3 vols. Indianapolis: Historical Publishing Co., 1934.

Ryan, Daniel Joseph. *A History of Ohio, with Biographical Sketches of Her Governors and the Ordinance of 1787*. Columbus: A.H. Smythe, 1888.

Santmyer, Helen Hoover. *Ohio Town*. Columbus: Ohio State University Press, 1962.

Scamyhorn, Richard and John Steinle. *Stockades in the Wilderness: The Frontier Defenses and Settlements of Southwestern Ohio, 1788-1795*. Dayton, Ohio: Landfall Press, 1986.
An early history of settlements in southwestern Ohio.

Scheiber, Harry N. *Ohio Canal Era: A Case Study of Government and the Economy, 1820-1861*. Athens, Ohio: Ohio University Press, 1969.

_____, ed. *The Old Northwest: Studies in Regional History, 1787-1910*. Lincoln: University of Nebraska Press, 1969.
Development of the Old Northwest, frontier history, regional history, and studies of migration in the Old Northwest.

Shannon, Timothy J. "The Ohio Company and the Meaning of Opportunity in the American West, 1786-1795." *The New England Quarterly* 64 (1991): 393-413.

_____. "This Unpleasant Business: The Transformation of Land Speculation in the Ohio Country, 1787-1820." In *The Pursuit of Public Power: Political Culture in Ohio, 1787-1861*. Ed. Jeffrey P. Brown and Andrew R. L. Cayton. Kent, Ohio: Kent State University Press, 1994.

Sherman, Christopher Elias. *Original Ohio Land Subdivisions*. 1925. Reprint. Columbus, 1982.

Siebert, Wilbur H. *The Underground Railroad in Ohio*. 1895. Reprint. A.W. McGraw, 1993.

Skaggs, David Curtis, ed. *The Old Northwest in the American Revolution: An Anthology*. Madison, Wisc.: State Historical Society of Wisconsin, 1977.

Slocum, Charles Elihu. *History of the Maumee River Basin*. Defiance, Ohio: The author, 1905.

———. *The Ohio Country between the Years 1783 and 1815*. 1910. Reprint. Bowie, Md.: Heritage Books, 1991.

Smith, Thomas H., ed. *An Ohio Reader: 1750 to the Civil War*. Grand Rapids, Mich.: William B. Eerdmans, 1975.

———, ed. *An Ohio Reader: Reconstruction to the Present*. Grand Rapids, Mich.: William B. Eerdmans, 1975.
The above two volumes are a documentary history of the development of Ohio.

Smith, William Ernest. *History of Southwestern Ohio: The Miami Valleys*. 3 vols. New York: Lewis Historical Publishing Co., 1964. Regional and local history of southwestern Ohio, with many biographies and portraits.

Soltow, Lee. "Inequality Amidst Abundance: Land Ownership in Early Nineteenth Century Ohio." *Ohio History* 88 (Spring 1979): 133-51.

Stewart, John Struthers. *History of Northeastern Ohio*. 3 vols. Indiana-polis: Historical Publishing Co., 1935.

Stille, Samuel Harden. *Ohio Builds a Nation: A Memorial to the Pioneers and the Celebrated Sons of the "Buckeye" State*. 5th ed. Chicago: Arlendale Book House, 1962.
Ohio local history and brief biographical sketches.

Taylor, James Wickes. *History of the State of Ohio, First Period, 1650-*

1787. Cincinnati: H.W. Derby & Co. Publishers, 1854.

Taylor, Robert M., Jr., ed. *The Northwest Ordinance, 1787: A Bicentennial Handbook.* Indianapolis: Indiana Historical Society, 1987.

A detailed history and chronology of the Northwest Ordinance. Includes valuable maps of the region.

Taylor, William A. *Ohio Statesmen and Annals of Progress.* 2 vols. Columbus: Westbote, 1899.

Thwaites, Reuben Gold and Louise Phelps Kellogg, eds. *Frontier Defense on the Upper Ohio, 1777-1778.* Madison: Wisconsin Historical Society, 1912.

Traylor, Jeff and Nadean Disabato Traylor. *The Great Ohio Roundabout.* Monroeville, Ohio: King of the Road Press, 1998.

Ohio local history, settlements, maps, and guides to cemeteries and historical sites.

Utter, William T. *The Frontier State, 1803-1825.* Columbus: Ohio State Archaeological and Historical Society, 1942.

Van Aken, William R. *Buckeye Barristers: A Centennial History of the Ohio State Bar Association.* Ohio State Bar Association, 1980.

Van Fossan, William Harvey. *The Story of Ohio.* New York: Macmillan Co., 1937.

Van Tassel, Charles Sumner. *The Book of Ohio and Its Centennial, or One Hundred Years of the Buckeye State.* 20 parts. Bowling Green, Ohio: C.S. Van Tassel, 1901.

A well-illustrated general history of the state.

_____. *Story of the Maumee Valley, Toledo, and the Sandusky Region.* 4 vols. Chicago: S.J. Clarke Publishing Co., 1929.

Van Tassel, David D. and John J. Grabowski, eds. *The Encyclopedia of Cleveland History.* 2 vols. 2nd ed. Bloomington, Ind.: Indiana University Press, 1996. Online (http://ech.cwru.edu).

Venable, W.H. *Footprints of the Pioneers in the Ohio Valley.* Reprint.

Bowie, Md.: Heritage Books, 1987.

Vexler, Robert I. and William F. Swindler, eds. *Chronology and Documentary Handbook of the State of Ohio*. Dobbs Ferry, N.Y.: Oceana Publications, 1978.

Includes a chronology of events in Ohio from 1669 to 1977, biographies of prominent citizens, and selected documents.

Wade, Richard. *The Urban Frontier: Pioneer Life in Early Pittsburgh, Cincinnati, Lexington, Louisville, and St. Louis*. Cambridge: Harvard University Press, 1959.

Walker, Byron H. *Frontier Ohio: A Resource Guide for Teachers*. Columbus: Ohio Historical Society, 1972.

Ohio history and migration, teaching aids, and social history.

Walker, Richard. *Wolf Creek and the Muskingum: Notes on the Settlement of Southeastern Ohio*. Baltimore: Gateway Press, 1996.

Walker, Timothy. *Discourse on the History and General Character of the State of Ohio*. Columbus, 1838.

Ward, Nahum. *A Brief Sketch of the State of Ohio*. Glasgow: J. Neven, 1822.

Warner, Hoyt Landon. *Progressivism in Ohio, 1897-1917*. Columbus: Ohio State University Press, 1964.

Weisenburger, Francis P. *The History of the State of Ohio*. 3 vols. Ed. Carl Wittke. Columbus: Ohio State Archaeological and Historical Society, 1941.

_____. *The Passing of the Frontier, 1825-1850*. Columbus: Ohio State Archaeological and Historical Society, 1941.

West, A.W. and J.L. Hunt *A Short History of Ohio*. Dayton, Ohio: United Brethren Publishing House, 1888.

Wheeler, Robert A. "The Literature of the Western Reserve." *Ohio History* 100 (Summer-Autumn 1991): 101-28.

_____, ed. *Visions of the Western Reserve: Public and Private Documents of Northeastern Ohio, 1750-1860*. Columbus: Ohio

State University Press, 2000.

Whitaker, William E. "Land Surveys of Ohio, Historically Considered." Master's thesis, Ohio State University, 1901.

Whittlesey, Charles Barney. *Topographical and Historical Sketch of the State of Ohio.* Philadelphia: Jas. B. Rodgers Co., Printers, 1872.

Willard, Eugene B., et al., eds. *A Standard History of the Hanging Rock Iron Region of Ohio.* 2 vols. 1916. Reprint. Marceline, Mo.: Walsworth, n.d.

Williams, W.W., ed. *History of the Firelands, Comprising Huron and Erie Counties, Ohio.* 1879. Reprint, Evansville, Ind.: Unigraphic, 1973.

Williamson, C.W. *History of Western Ohio and Auglaize County.* Columbus: Press of W.M. Linn & Sons, 1905.
See *Index to History of Western Ohio and Auglaize County* (Cridersville, Ohio: Susanna Russell Chapter, DAR, 1974).

Wills, Charles A. *A Historical Album of Ohio.* Brookfield, Conn.: Millbrook Press, 1996.
A summary of Ohio history and facts. Illustrated.

Wilson, Ellen Susan. "Gaining Title to the Land: The Case of the Virginia Military Tract." *The Old Northwest* 12 (1986): 65-82.
_____. "Speculators and Land Development in the Virginia Military Tract: The Territorial Period." Ph.D. diss., Miami University, 1982.

Wilson, Frazer Ells. *Advancing the Ohio Frontier: A Saga of the Old Northwest.* Blanchester, Ohio: Brown Publishing Co., 1937.

Winkle, Kenneth J. *The Politics of Community: Migration and Politics in Antebellum Ohio.* Cambridge: Cambridge University Press, 1988.

Winter, Nevin Otto. *A History of Northwest Ohio.* 3 vols. Chicago: Lewis Publishing Co., 1917.
A detailed history of northwestern Ohio, with many biographical

sketches.

Wittke, Carl Frederick, ed. *The History of the State of Ohio*. 6 vols.1941-44. Reprint. Columbus: Ohio Historical Society, 1968. A detailed history of Ohio; illustrated and includes many maps.

Indexes and Genealogical Sources

The American Genealogical-Biographical Index to American Gene-
alogical, Biographical, and Local History Materials. 206 vols.
Middletown, Conn.: Godfrey Memorial Library, 1952-2000.
Supplement, vols. 1- , 2000- .

Known as AGBI, this is an extensive index to many published
genealogies and other sources. Also available on CD-ROM
(Ancestry.com) and online (www.ancestry.com).

Baldwin, Henry R. *Henry R. Baldwin Genealogical Records Collection.*
75 vols. Youngstown, Ohio: Public Library of Youngstown and
Mahoning County, 1963.

Typescript and handwritten copies of genealogical records for
western Pennsylvania and eastern Ohio, cemetery and church
records, probate records, genealogies, etc. Separately indexed,
Index to the Henry R. Baldwin Genealogical Records, 8 vols.
(Youngstown, Ohio: Public Library of Youngstown and Mahoning
County, 1961-62).

Bell, Carol Willsey, et al., eds. *Master Index, Ohio Society Daughters of*
the American Revolution Genealogical and Historical Records,
Volume 1. Westlake, Ohio: Ohio Society Daughters of the
American Revolution, 1985.

Useful in identifying Ohio DAR records.

_____. *Ohio Divorces: The Early Years.* Boardman, Ohio: Bell Books,
1994.

Identifies many early divorces in Ohio; indexed.

_____. *Ohio Genealogical Periodical Index: A County Guide.* 6th ed.
Youngstown, Ohio: Bell Books, 1987.

_____. *Ohio Wills and Estates to 1850: An Index.* Youngstown, Ohio:
Bell Books, 1981.

One of the major personal name indexes for Ohio researchers.

_____. *Ohio Lands: Steubenville Land Office, 1800-1820*. Youngstown, Ohio: The author, 1983.

Shows name of proprietor, residence in Ohio or elsewhere, year, certificate number, legal description of land.

Berry, Ellen Thomas and David A. Berry. *Early Ohio Settlers: Purchasers of Land in East and East Central Ohio, 1800-1840*. 1989. Reprint. Baltimore: Clearfield, 2000.

_____. *Early Ohio Settlers: Purchasers of Land in Southeastern Ohio, 1800-1840*. Baltimore: Genealogical Publishing Co., 1984.

_____. *Early Ohio Settlers: Purchasers of Land in Southwestern Ohio, 1800-1840*. Baltimore: Genealogical Publishing Co., 1986.

Bowman, Mary L. *Abstracts and Extracts of the Legislative Acts and Resolutions of the State of Ohio, 1803-1821*. Mansfield, Ohio: Ohio Genealogical Society, 1994.

Gives information on individuals mentioned in Ohio's legislative acts and resolutions; provides details on acts and resolutions. This Ohio reference source is indexed. See next volume cited below.

_____. *Abstracts and Extracts of the Legislative Acts and Resolutions of the State of Ohio, Volumes 20 to 29, 1821-1831*. Mansfield, Ohio: Ohio Genealogical Society, 1996.

Brien, Lindsay Metcalfe. *A Genealogical Index of Pioneers in the Miami Valley, Ohio*. Dayton, Ohio: Dayton Circle, Colonial Dames of America in the State of Ohio, 1970.

Shows names of family members, Ohio residence and previous place of residence, dates, and other genealogical details. Covers Miami, Montgomery, Preble, and Warren counties, Ohio. See *Every Name Index to Miami Valley Ohio Pioneers*, indexed by Marjorie Dodd Floyd (Dayton, Ohio, 1980).

_____. *Miami Valley Will Abstracts from the Counties of Miami, Montgomery, Warren & Preble in the State of Ohio, 1803-1850*.

Dayton, Ohio, 1940.

Burton, Conrad and Ann Burton. *Born in Ohio: Living in Southwest Michigan in 1860*. Decatur, Mich.: Glyndwr Resources, 1986.

Caccamo, James F. *Marriage Notices from the Ohio Observer Series, 1827-1855*. Apollo, Penn.: Closson Press, 1994.

Carmean, Barbara J. Carman, comp. *1860 Mortality Schedule, Ohio*. Hillsboro, Ohio: Southern Ohio Genealogical Society, 1983.

Carter, Clarence Edwin, comp. "The Territorial Papers of the United States, Volume III: The Territory Northwest of the River Ohio, 1787-1803." *The Report* 41 (Fall 2001): 131-34.

A Census of Pensioners for Revolutionary or Military Services, 1840. 1841. Reprint. Baltimore: Genealogical Publishing Co., 1967.
Lists of Revolutionary War pensioners residing in Ohio, and elsewhere, arranged by county. Shows name of pensioner, age, name of head of family with whom residing on 1 June 1840, township, and county. See *A General Index to A Census of Pensioners for Revolutionary or Military Service, 1840* (Baltimore: Genealogical Publishing Co., 1965).

Clark, Marie Taylor. *Ohio Lands: Chillicothe Land Office, 1800-1829*. Chillicothe, Ohio: The author, 1984.

_____. *Ohio Lands South of the Indian Boundary Line*. Chillicothe, Ohio: The author, 1984.

Cleveland Public Library. *Index to Family Genealogical Information in Various Books and Periodicals Owned by Cleveland Public Libraries*. 2 vols. Cleveland, n.d.
Photocopies of a card file to genealogies in periodicals and books in the Cleveland Public Library. Arranged by surname. Gives Cleveland Public Library call number.

Colorado Chapter, Ohio Genealogical Society. *County-by-County Research Being Done by Members of the Colorado Chapter of the Ohio Genealogical Society*. Longmont, Colo.: The Society, 1998.

Cunningham, Miriam L. *Every-Name Index: Together with Abstracted Items of Genealogical Interest Found in Ohio Legislature, 1787-1806*. Columbus: The author, 1980.

A name index to *Journals of the House of Representatives, Journals of the Senate, and Acts of Ohio, 1787-1806*.

Daughters of the American Revolution. Ohio Society. *Early Marriage Bonds of Ohio*. N.p., n.d. (published various years).

Typescripts at State Library of Ohio, Columbus, OH. DAR records are cataloged under each individual Ohio county. Title varies; some carry a series title, *Early Vital Records of Ohio*. Many typescript copies of Bible, cemetery, and vital records are housed at the State Library of Ohio, the DAR Library in Washington, DC, and on microfilm at the Family History Library, Salt Lake City. Most volumes indexed.

_____. *Early Vital Records of Ohio: Bible and Cemetery Records*. N.p., n.d. (published various years).

Typescripts available at the Ohio State Library, Columbus, Ohio. DAR records are cataloged under each individual Ohio county.

_____. *Early Vital Records of Ohio: Family Records*. N.p., n.d.

Typescripts at the Ohio State Library, Columbus, Ohio. DAR records are cataloged under each individual Ohio county.

_____. *Early Vital Records of Ohio: Ohio Bible Records*. N.p., n.d.

Typescripts at the Ohio State Library, Columbus, Ohio. DAR records are cataloged under each individual Ohio county.

_____. *Early Vital Records of Ohio: Ohio Cemetery and Church Records*. N.p., n.d.

Typescripts at the Ohio State Library, Columbus, Ohio. DAR records are cataloged under each individual Ohio county.

_____. *Early Vital Records of Ohio: Ohio Family Histories*. N.p., n.d.

Typescripts at the Ohio State Library, Columbus, Ohio. DAR records are cataloged under each individual Ohio county.

_____. Middle Western Section, *Colonial and Genealogical Records
    Committee.* DAR, 1955.

Day, Sandra Hudnall, comp. *Index to Historical Collections of Ohio by
    Henry Howe.* Steubenville, Ohio: Jefferson County Chapter, Ohio
    Genealogical Society, 1990.

Diefenbach, H.B. Mrs., comp. *Index to the Grave Records of Soldiers of
    the War of 1812 Buried in Ohio.* 1945. Ann Arbor, Mich.:
    University Microfilms 1991.

Dyer, Albion Morris. *First Ownership of Ohio Lands.* 1911. Reprint.
    Baltimore: Genealogical Publishing Co., 1969. Online:
    (www.ancestry.com).

Early Ohio Settlers, 1700s-1900s, CD-ROM (Family Tree Maker).

The 1812 Census of Ohio: A Statewide Index of Taxpayers. Miami
    Beach, Fl.: T.L.C. Genealogy, 1992.
    An alphabetical list of all land owners in Ohio as found in the Ohio
    tax duplicates for 1812 (1814 for Wayne County).

Firelands Pioneer Obituary Index, 1857-1909. N.p., n.d.

Gardner, Frank W. "Central Ohio Genealogical Notes and Queries."
    Columbus: Sunday Journal Dispatch, n.d.
    Photocopies available at State Library of Ohio; indexed.

*Genealogical Data Relating to Women in the Western Reserve before
    1840 [1850]*, compiled by Women's Department, Cleveland
    Centennial Commission. Cleveland, 1943. See separate *Index* cited
    below.

Green, Karen Mauer. *Pioneer Ohio Newspapers.* 2 vols. Galveston:
    Frontier Press, 1986.

Hanna, Charles Augustus. *Ohio Valley Genealogies.* New York: J.J.
    Little & Co., 1900.

Harfst, Linda L. *Local History and Genealogy Resources Guide to
    Southeastern Ohio.* Wellston, Ohio: Ohio Valley Area Libraries,
    1984.

Harter, Stuart. *Ohio Genealogy and Local History Sources Index*. Fort Wayne, Ind.: CompuGen Systems, 1986.
Identifies many genealogy and local history sources for Ohio— books, periodical articles, newspaper articles, etc.; arranged by county. Useful for identifying pre-1986 titles.

Index and Abstract of Obituaries for Individuals with Ties to the State of Ohio Published in Colorado Newspapers. Denver: Colorado Chapter of the Ohio Genealogical Society, 1995-.

Index of the Firelands Pioneer from June 1858 to 1937. Norwalk, Ohio: Firelands Historical Society, 1939.

Index to the Henry R. Baldwin Genealogical Records. 8 vols. Youngstown, Ohio: Public Library of Youngstown and Mahoning Co., 1961-62.

Index to the Microfilm Edition of Genealogical Data Relating to Women in the Western Reserve before 1840 (1850). Cleveland: Genealogical Committee, Western Reserve Historical Society, 1976.

Jackson, Ronald Vern, et al., eds. *Index to Ohio Tax Lists, 1800-1810*. 2 vols. Bountiful, Utah: Accelerated Indexing Systems, 1977-85.

_____ and G. Ronald Teeples. *Early Ohio Census Records*. Bountiful, Utah: Accelerated Indexing Systems, 1974.

_____. *Mortality Schedule, Ohio, 1850*. North Salt Lake: Accelerated Indexing Systems International, 1979.

_____. *Ohio Tax Lists, 1800-1810*. 2 vols. North Salt Lake, Utah: Accelerated Indexing Systems, 1985.

Klauprecht, Emil. *German Chronicle in the History of the Ohio Valley and Its Capital City Cincinnati in Particular*. Bowie, Md.: Heritage Books, 1992.

Koleda, Elizabeth Potts. *Some Ohio & Iowa Pioneers: Their Friends and Descendants*. Prineville, Oregon: The author, 1973.

Lee, Susan Dunlap, comp. *The Ohio Genealogical Society Periodicals*

Index: Topical by Location, 1960-2000. Mansfield, Ohio: Ohio Genealogical Society, 2002.

Indexes topics (subjects) in periodicals published by OGS; arranged by localities in Ohio.

McMullin, Phillip W., ed. *Grassroots of America: A Computerized Index to the American State Papers, Land Grants and Claims (1789-1837).* Salt Lake City: Gendex Corp., 1972.

A personal name index to the *American State Papers* (Land Grants and Claims). Includes many references to Ohio lands.

Miami Valley Genealogical Index (Computerized Heritage Association). Online: (www.ogs.org) and (www.pcdl.lib.oh.us/miami/index.htm).

National Society Colonial Dames of the XVII Century. Ohio Society. *Our Ancestors' Families.* N.p., The Society, 1988.

National Society, United States Daughters of 1812. *Burial Places of Ohio Soldiers of the War of 1812.* 20 vols. The Society, 1927.

Volumes housed at the State Library of Ohio, Columbus. Title varied, *Ohio Burial Places of Soldiers of the War of 1812.* See index edited by Phyllis Brown Miller, *Index to the Grave Records of Servicemen of the War of 1812, State of Ohio.*

Northwest Library District (Ohio). *Genealogical Resources Guide: Northwest Ohio Libraries.* Bowling Green, Ohio: Northwest Library District, 1983.

Ohio. Adjutant General's Dept. *The Official Roster of the Soldiers of the American Revolution Buried in the State of Ohio.* 3 vols. Reprint. 1929-59. Kokomo, Ind.: Selby Publishing, 1988.

Ohio Cemetery Records Extracted from the "Old Northwest" Genealogical Quarterly. Baltimore: Genealogical Publishing Co., 1984.

Ohio Company. *The Records of the Original Proceedings of the Ohio Company.* Edited by Archer Butler Hulbert. Marietta, Ohio:

Marietta Historical Commission, 1917.

Ohio Genealogical Society. Ancestor Card File. Mansfield, Ohio. Microfilm, FHL.

_____. *Ancestor Charts of Members of the Ohio Genealogical Society.* Mansfield, Ohio: The Society, 1987.

Pedigree charts of OGS members; with a surname index. A major genealogical reference source for the state.

_____. *First Families of Ohio Roster, 1964-2000.* Edited by Sunda Anderson Peters and Kay Ballantyne Hudson. Mansfield, Ohio: The Society, 2001.

Arranged alphabetically by surname of ancestor and cross-indexed to name of OGS member. This is one of the major personal name finding aids for the state.

_____. *Official Roster of the Soldiers of the State of Ohio in the War with Mexico, 1846-1848.* Mansfield, Ohio: The Society, 1991.

_____. *The Ohio Genealogical Society Periodicals Index, Topical by Location, 1960-2000.* Mansfield, Ohio: The Society, 2002.

A subject index to Ohio genealogical periodicals; arranged by localities and surnames, such as families and names of pensioners.

_____. *Ohio Marriages Recorded in County Courts through 1820: An Index.* Jean Nathan, chairman. Mansfield, Ohio: The Society, 1996.

A monumental index to pre-1820 Ohio marriages. Updated by OGS, *Ohio Marriages, 1821-1830.*

_____. *Ohio Records & Pioneer Families: Ten Year Surname Index, 1985-1994* (and 1960-84). Mansfield, Ohio: The Society, 1996.

_____. *Surname Index of the Ohio Genealogical Society.* Mansfield, Ohio: The Society, 1967-69.

Indexes in this reference source show name of person, year of birth, birthplace (state or country), spouse's name, year married, year of death, and state where buried.

Ohio. Secretary of State. *Annual Report of the Secretary of State to the Governor of Ohio: Appendix B, Return of the Number of Deaf and Dumb, Blind, Insane, and Idiotic Persons, May 1856.* 1856. Reprint. Bowie, Md.: Heritage Books, 1987.

Shows county, township, person's name, nature of affliction (blind, dumb, insane, etc.), age, sex, occupation, birthplace (state or country), parents' names and their birthplace, and other details.

_____. *Annual Report of the Secretary of State to the Governor of Ohio: Jail Reports, 1854 and 1855.* Bowie, Md.: Heritage Books, 1988.

Ohio Society, Daughters of the American Revolution. *Master Index, Ohio Society, Daughters of the American Revolution Genealogical and Historical Records.* 1985.

Ohio Society, Sons of the American Revolution. *Centennial Register, 1889 to 1989.* Dayton, Ohio: The Society, 1988.

Shows name of SAR member, name of his patriot ancestor, date accepted, and SAR membership details.

_____. *Register, Ohio Society Sons of the American Revolution,* comp. by Charles A. Jones. Columbus: F.J. Heer Printing Co., 1956-64.

Ohio Society, United States Daughters of 1812. *Index to the Grave Records of Servicemen of the War of 1812, State of Ohio.* Edited by Phyllis Brown Miller. Huber Heights, Ohio: Ohio Society, United States Daughters of 1812, 1988.

Shows name of soldier, birth and death dates, wife's name, and where buried.

Ohio Source Records from the Ohio Genealogical Quarterly. Baltimore: Genealogical Publishing Co., 1986. Indexed.

Ohio State Journal Index, 1913-40.

WPA card file on microfilm at the Ohio Historical Society, 1913-26 & 1940. Bound index volumes at OHS prepared by Work Projects Administration in Ohio, Columbus.

Ohio Surname Index. Compiled by the Ohio Society of the Daughters of the American Revolution. Columbus: Ohio Historical Society, 1928-36. Microfilm, FHL.

A statewide index to local histories and other Ohio sources. Cards are arranged alphabetically by surname.

Ohio Veteran's Home Death Records, January 3, 1889 through December 31, 1983. Sandusky, Ohio: Erie County Chapter of the Ohio Genealogical Society, 1984.

Ohioans in the California Census of 1850. San Diego: Southern California Chapter of the Ohio Genealogical Society, 1988.

"Oldest Inscriptions, with Revolutionary and War of 1812 Records, of the Cemeteries of Trumbull, Mahoning, and Columbiana Counties, Ohio, and Lawrence, Mercer, and Beaver Counties, Pennsylvania." 7 vols. in 1. 1913. Typescript.

Page, Henry F. *Virginia Military District of the Law of Warrants, Entries, Surveys and Patents in the V.M.D. of Ohio.* Columbus: J.H. Riley & Co., 1850.

Periodical Source Index. Edited by Michael B. Clegg, Curt B. Witcher, et al. Fort Wayne, Ind.: Allen County Public Library Foundation, 1987-Annual. Retrospective volumes dated 1847-1985. Internet, CD-ROM, published volumes, and microfiche.

See especially U.S. Places—OH (Ohio), Research Methodology, and Family Records (surnames). Periodicals indexed are housed in the Genealogy Department, Allen County Public Library, Fort Wayne, Indiana, but copies are available in many other libraries as well. PERSI is a retrospective and annual index to American genealogical periodicals and includes many Ohio titles. It indexes personal names, source records, and methodology. PERSI is available on compact disc, on the Internet (www.ancestry.com), in published volumes, and on microfiche at some libraries.

Petty, Gerald McKinney, comp. *Index of the Ohio Girls Industrial*

School: Inmates' Case Records, 1869-1911. Columbus: Petty's Press, 1984.

_____, comp. *Index of the Ohio Squirrel Hunters Roster.* Columbus: G.M. Petty, 1984.

_____, comp. *Index of the Ohio 1825 Tax Duplicate.* Columbus: Petty's Press, 1981.

_____, comp. *Index of the Ohio 1835 Tax Duplicate.* Columbus: Petty's Press, 1987.

_____, comp. Name Index, 1812 Ohio Tax Duplicate. Microfilm.

_____, comp. *Ohio 1810 Tax Duplicate.* Columbus: G.M. Petty, 1976.

Phillips, W. Louis. *Index to Ohio Pensioners of 1883.* Bowie, Md.: Heritage Books, 1987.

An index to the list of pensioners, male and female, who were residing in Ohio as of 1 January 1883.

_____. *Jurisdictional Histories for Ohio's Eighty-eight Counties, 1788-1985.* N.p., n.d.

Powell, Esther Weygandt, comp. *Early Ohio Tax Records.* 1971. Reprint. Baltimore: Genealogical Publishing Co., 1985.

Reel Index to the Microform Collection of County and Regional Histories of the Old Northwest, Series II, Ohio. New Haven, Conn.: Research Publications, 1975.

Includes an index to atlases, biographies, and histories of Ohio.

Riegel, Mayburt Stephenson, comp. *Early Ohioans' Residences from the Land Grant Records.* Mansfield, Ohio: Ohio Genealogical Society, 1976.

Identifies many pre-1825 Ohio pioneers who purchased land from the federal government at early land offices in Ohio.

A Roster of Honorably Discharged Ex-Pupils of the Soldiers' and Sailors' Orphans' Home, Xenia, Ohio. Xenia, Ohio: Home Weekly Printing, 1898.

Sacchini, Joseph Louis. *Italian Family Genealogy of the Mahoning*

Valley, 1874-1994: A Genealogy Guide. Boardman, Ohio: The author, 1994.

Short, Anita (Mrs. Don R.) and Mrs. Denver Eller. *Ohio Bible Records.* 2 vols. Greenville, Ohio: Fort Greenville Chapter, DAR, 1970-71.

Sherman, Christopher Elias. *Original Ohio Land Subdivisions.* 1925. Reprint. Columbus, 1982.

Simon, Bernice H., comp. *Name Index for Genealogical and Family History of Eastern Ohio.* Chagrin Falls, Ohio: B.H. Simon, 1973.

Smith, Alma Aicholtz. *The Virginia Military Surveys of Clermont and Hamilton Counties, Ohio, 1787-1849.* Cincinnati: The author, 1985.

Smith, Clifford Neal. *Federal Land Series.* 4 vols. Chicago: American Library Association, 1972-86.

See especially volume 4, parts 1 and 2.

Smith, Marjorie, ed. *Ohio Marriages Extracted from the Old Northwest Genealogical Quarterly.* 1977. Reprint. Baltimore: Genealogical Publishing Co., 1980.

Snyder, Michael G., ed. *Ohio Genealogy and Local History: A Resource Guide to the Holdings of Twenty-three Member Libraries.* Mansfield, Ohio: North Central Library Cooperative, 1984.

Society of Colonial Wars in the State of Ohio. *Register.* 1902.

Society of Mayflower Descendants in the State of Ohio. N.p., 1913, 1938.

Southern Ohio Genealogical Society. *Family Bible Records of Southwestern Ohio.* Hillsboro, Ohio: The Society, n.d.

_____. *Surname/Locality Index.* 4 vols. Hillsboro, Ohio: The Society, n.d.

Indexes pedigree charts on file in the library of the Southern Ohio Genealogical Society, Hillsboro, Ohio.

Sperry, Kip. "Published Indexes." In Kory L. Meyerink, ed., *Printed*

Sources: A Guide to Published Genealogical Records. Salt Lake City: Ancestry, 1998, pp. 193-214.

Sprague, Stuart Seely. *Kentuckians in Ohio and Indiana*. Baltimore: Genealogical Publishing Co., 1986.

An index to biographies in local histories of Kentuckians residing in Ohio and Indiana.

_____. *Kentuckians in Missouri, Including Many Who Migrated by Way of Ohio, Indiana, or Illinois*. N.p., n.d.

Stillahn, Marlene. *Surname Index to the Surname File Cards and Five-generation Charts of the Colorado Chapter, OGS*. Longmont, Colo.: Colorado Chapter of the Ohio Genealogical Society, 1996.

Strong, Donald H., comp. *Southeastern Ohio Genealogies: Allied Families*. 2 vols. Preston, Idaho: D.H. Strong, 1992.

Summers, Ewing. *Genealogical and Family History of Eastern Ohio*. New York: Lewis Publishing Co., 1903.

See *Name Index*, comp. by Mrs. Howard W. Simon (1973).

Tolzmann, Don Heinrich. *Ohio Valley German Biographical Index*. Bowie, Md.: Heritage Books, 1992.

An index to several German-American histories and biographies covering the Ohio Valley—Ohio, Indiana, and Kentucky.

Webb, David K., ed. *Ohio Tombstones (Including Adjoining States)*. Chillicothe, Ohio: W.O. Francis, 1936. Incomplete work.

Workman, Jeanne Britton. *1880 Ohio Mortality Records: Counties Adams through Geauga*. North Olmsted, Ohio: S & J Workman, 1991.

An index to 1880 mortality schedules for these counties.

Maps, Atlases, Gazetteers, and Geographical Finding Aids

All About Ohio Almanac. Hartland, Mich.: Instant Information Co., 1995.

Andriot, Jay, comp. *Township Atlas of the United States*. McLean, Va.: Documents Index, 1991.

> Lists minor civil divisions (townships, etc.) and includes a township map for each county in Ohio and other states.

Atlas of Historical County Boundaries, Ohio. Edited by John H. Long, compiled by Peggy Tuck Sinko. New York: Charles Scribner's Sons, 1998.

> Historical maps and chronology of Ohio counties. This atlas is scholarly and well documented.

Atlas of Ohio. Rockford, Ill.: W.W. Hixson & Co., 1925.

> Maps show land ownership by township in 1925.

Atlas of Ohio. Madison, Wisc.: American Publishing Co., 1975.

Bailey, A. *Bailey's Northern Ohio Gazetteer and Directory, 1871-72*. Cleveland: A. Bailey, Publisher, 1871.

Baldwin, C.C. *Early Maps of Ohio and the West*. Western Reserve Historical Society Tract No. 25.

_____. *Geographical History of Ohio*. Cleveland, 1880.

Brown, Lloyd Arnold. *Early Maps of the Ohio Valley: A Selection of Maps, Plans and Views Made by Indians and Colonials from 1673-1783*. Pittsburg: University of Pittsburgh Press, 1959.

Brown, Samuel R. *The Western Gazetteer, or Emigrant's Directory, Containing A Geographical Description of the Western States and Territories...Ohio*. Auburn, N.Y.: H.C. Southwick, 1817.

Burke, Thomas Aquinas. *Ohio Lands: A Short History*. 9th ed. Columbus: Auditor of State, 1997.

(http://freepages.history.rootsweb.com/~maggie/
ohio-lands/ohlands.html)

CitMap Corporation. *The Complete City Maps of Ohio*. Traverse City,
Mich.: CitMap, 1990.
Detailed city maps for Ohio, arranged by city.

Clagg, Sam E. *Ohio Atlas*. Huntington, West Va.: The author, 1959.
Origin of Ohio county names, maps showing population, land
subdivisions, early settlements, forts, railroads, Ohio Court of
Appeals districts, and other useful maps.

Clements, John. *Ohio Facts: A Comprehensive Look at Ohio Today,
County by County*. Dallas: Clements Research II, 1988.

Collins, Charles W. *Ohio: An Atlas*. Madison, Wisc.: American Printing
& Publishing, 1975.
Maps showing physical features, population, economy, and
statistical data.

Cutler, Jervis. *A Topographical Description of the State of Ohio,
Indiana Territory, and Louisiana*. Boston: Charles Williams, 1812.

Cutler, Manasseh. *An Explanation of the Map of Federal Lands*.
Readex Microprint, 1966.

DeLorme Mapping Company. *Ohio Atlas & Gazetteer*. 5th ed.
Yarmouth, Maine: DeLorme Mapping Co., 1995.
Detailed modern maps of Ohio showing cities and townships,
roads, rivers and creeks, county boundaries, and other useful
details.

Dictionary of Ohio Historic Places. 2 vols. St. Clair Shores, Mich.:
Somerset Publishers, 1999.

Downes, Randolph Chandler. *Evolution of Ohio County Boundaries*.
1927. Reprint. Columbus: Ohio Historical Society, 1970.
A historical description of Ohio's eighty-eight counties.

The 1833 Ohio Gazetteer. 11th ed. 1833. Reprint. Knightstown, Ind.:
Bookmark, 1981.

Describes Ohio counties and towns, with early population statistics.

Everts, L.H. & Co. *Illustrated Historical Atlas of Miami County, Ohio, with an Atlas of Ohio.* Philadelphia: L.H. Everts & Co., 1875.

Encyclopedia of Ohio: A Volume of Encyclopedia of the United States. St. Clair Shores, Mich.: Somerset Publishers, 1982.

See "Dictionary of Places—Ohio."

Fess, Simeon Davidson. *Ohio: A Four-Volume Reference Library on the History of a Great State.* 5 vols. Chicago: Lewis Publishing Co., 1937.

Historical details for each Ohio county, physical features, first settlements, transportation, economic interests, institutions, notable persons, and population statistics. Volume 3 entitled *Historical Gazetteer of Ohio.*

Fitak, Madge R., comp. *Place Names Directory: Northeast Ohio.* Columbus: State of Ohio, Department of Natural Resources, 1976.

_____, comp. *Place Names Directory: Southeast Ohio.* Columbus: State of Ohio, Department of Natural Resources, 1980.

_____, comp. *Place Names Directory: Southern Ohio.* Columbus: State of Ohio, Department of Natural Resources, 1986.

Gallagher, John S. and Alan H. Patera. *The Post Offices of Ohio.* Burtonsville, Md.: The Depot, 1979.

Arranged by county. Lists name of post office and date established and discontinued. Indexed by name of post office. Illustrated.

Hargett, Janet L., comp. *List of Selected Maps of States and Territories.* Washington, DC: National Archives and Records Service, 1971.

See especially the Ohio map section.

Hawes, George W., comp. *Ohio State Gazetteer and Business Directory for 1859 and 1860.* Cincinnati: G.W. Hawes, 1859.

_____. *Ohio State Gazetteer and Business Directory for 1860 and 1861.* Indianapolis: G.W. Hawes, 1860.

Lists of professions, trades, etc. arranged by locality. Online: (www.hti.umich.edu/cgi/b/bib/bibperm?q1=aja2907).

Hayes, E.L. *Illustrated Atlas of the Upper Ohio River and Valley, from Pittsburgh, Pa., to Cincinnati, Ohio.* Philadelphia: Titus, Simmons & Titus, 1877.

Hough, B. and A. Bourne. *A Map of the State of Ohio from Actual Surveys.* Chillicothe, Ohio, 1815.

Howison, William L. *Indian Trails & War Records in Southwestern Ohio.* Rev. ed. Columbus: W.L. Howison & Associates, 1980.

Izant, Grace Goulder. *This Is Ohio: Ohio's 88 Counties in Words and Pictures.* Cleveland: World Publishing Co., 1953.

Jenkins, Warren. *The Ohio Gazetteer and Traveller's Guide.* Rev. ed. Columbus: Isaac N. Whiting, 1841.
An early gazetteer of Ohio place-names. The revised edition includes an appendix with the census of Ohio for 1840. Includes a useful list of early Ohio post offices.

Kent, Robert B., et al., eds. *Region in Transition: An Economic and Social Atlas of Northeast Ohio.* Akron, Ohio: University of Akron Press, 1992.

Kilbourn, John. *The Ohio Gazetteer, or Topographical Dictionary.* 11th ed. 1833. Reprint. Knightstown, Ind.: Bookmark, 1978.
An early gazetteer of the state. Continued by Warren Jenkins' *Gazetteer* cited above.

Marzulli, Lawrence J. *The Development of Ohio's Counties and Their Historic Courthouses.* Columbus: County Commissioners Association of Ohio, 1980.

Maxwell, Fay, comp. *Ohio Indian and Revolutionary Trails: Indexes Ohio Counties, Townships and Dates of Erection.* Columbus: Maxwell Publications, 1974.

Miller, Larry L. *Ohio Place Names.* Bloomington, Ind.: Indiana University Press, 1996.

A valuable gazetteer that describes Ohio cities, towns, villages, hamlets, and communities.

Morrison, Olin Dee. *Ohio "Gateway State": A History of Ohio.* 4 vols. Athens, Ohio: E.M. Morrison, 1962.

Volume 3, *Historical Atlas of Ohio*, contains sketch maps of Ohio history, boundaries, and settlements.

―――――. *Ohio in Maps and Charts: A Historical Atlas, Social, Economic, Political.* Athens, Ohio: E.M. Morrison, 1956.

Historical Ohio maps showing early newspapers, emigrant routes, settlements, boundary changes, and other details.

Newberry Library. *Historical Atlas and Chronology of County Boundaries, 1788-1980.* John H. Long, ed. and Stephen L. Hansen, comp. Boston: G.K. Hall, 1984.

See especially the Ohio boundary chronology section and county maps in volume 2. See also *Atlas of Historical County Boundaries.*

The Ohio Almanac: An Encyclopedia of Indispensable Information About the Buckeye Universe. Edited by Michael O'Bryant. Wilmington, Ohio: Orange Frazer Press, 1997.

A detailed gazetteer of Ohio and its counties.

Ohio. Cooperative Topographic Survey. *Final Report (in Four Volumes) Ohio Cooperative Topographic Survey.* By Christopher Elias Sherman. 4 vols. Mansfield, Ohio: Press of the Ohio State Reformatory, 1916-33.

Maps of original Ohio lands, historical background, description of lands in Ohio. See especially volume 3, *Original Ohio Land Subdivisions* (1925; reprint, Columbus, 1982).

Ohio. Department of Highways. *Individual Maps of Ohio's 88 Counties.* Columbus, 1969-70.

Ohio Department of Transportation. *Ohio County Maps.* Columbus, 1983-87.

Maps of Ohio's 88 counties, with principal highways and towns.

Ohio. Development and Publicity Commission. *Ohio: An Empire within An Empire.* 2nd ed. Columbus: Ohio Development and Publicity Commission, 1950.

Ohio Gazetteer. Wilmington, Del.: American Historical Publications, 1985.

A historical gazetteer of Ohio place-names; includes a Biography Index.

Ohio Geographic Names Information System: Finding List. Reston, Va.: U.S.G.S. Topographic Division, Research & Technical Standards, 1984.

Ohio: Her Counties, Her Townships, and Her Towns. Indianapolis: Researchers, 1979.

Ohio Historical Review. *The 88 County Maps of Ohio.* Columbus: Ohio Historical Review, n.d.

Ohio Maps (OPLIN). Online: (www.oplin.lib.oh.us/index.cfm?ID=3-58-2507)

Ohio Place Names, Including Origin of Counties, Creeks, and Rivers, Post Offices, Towns, and Townships in the Western Reserve. Typed by Joanne Rowe. Cleveland, 1975.

The Ohio State Gazetteer, Shippers' Guide, and Classified Business Directory for 1864-1865. Indianapolis: Hawes & Redfield, 1864.

Ohio, Trailways to Highways, 1776-1976. Columbus: Ohio Department of Transportation, 1976.

"100 Largest Townships in Ohio According to the 2000 Census." *OGS Genealogy News* 34 (January/February 2003): 20.

Overman, William D. *Ohio Place Names: The Origin of the Names of Over 500 Ohio Cities, Towns, and Villages.* Akron, Ohio: The author, 1951.

Gives the county and brief history of many Ohio localities.

_____. *Ohio Town Names.* Akron, Ohio: Atlantic Press, 1959.

A description of Ohio towns; includes a list of Ohio towns which changed names.

Overton, Julie Minot. *Ohio Towns and Townships to 1900: A Location Guide*. Edited by Kay Ballantyne Hudson and Sunda Anderson Peters. Mansfield, Ohio: Ohio Genealogical Society, 2000.

A monumental alphabetical listing of Ohio towns and townships before 1900, giving location in county, year founded, and other related information. An essential reference work for Ohio genealogists and librarians. See also Kay Ballantyne Hudson, comp., "Ohio Towns and Townships to 1900, Addendum I." *The Report* 41 (Summer 2001): 87-90.

Peacefull, Leonard, ed. *A Geography of Ohio*. Rev. ed. Kent, Ohio: Kent State University Press, 1996.

A scholarly look at Ohio settlement, land divisions, geography, and cities. Includes valuable maps.

Peters, William E. *Ohio Lands and their Subdivision*. 2nd ed. Athens, Ohio: Messenger Printery Co., 1918.

Phillips, W. Louis. *Jurisdictional Histories for Ohio's Eighty-eight Counties, 1788-1985*. Bowie, Md.: Heritage Books, 1986.

Place Names in Ohio and County of Location. N.p., 1994. Typescript.

Puetz, C.J., comp. *Ohio County Maps*. Lyndon Station, Wisc:. County Maps, 1996.

Sanborn Map Company. *Sanborn Fire Insurance Maps: Ohio*. Teaneck, N.J.: Chadwyck-Healey, 1983. Microfilm.

Original Sanborn Fire Insurance Maps are located in the Geography and Map Division, Library of Congress.

Smith, Thomas H. *The Mapping of Ohio*. Kent, Ohio: Kent State University Press, 1977.

A valuable collection of early Ohio maps, with detailed descriptions and extensive footnotes and bibliographies.

Swanson, Hal, comp. *The Ohio Township Helper: An Aid to Locating Counties and Townships in the State of Ohio*. Longmont, Colo.:

Colorado Chapter, Ohio Genealogical Society, n.d.

State Maps on File, Midwest (Ohio). New York: Facts On File, 1984.

Thorndale, William and William Dollarhide. *Map Guide to the U.S. Federal Censuses, 1790-1920.* Baltimore: Genealogical Publishing Co., 1987.

Thomas Publications. *Ohio County Maps & Recreation Guide.* 1982.

U.S. Geological Survey Map Locations for Ohio Cemeteries.

Vonada, Damaine. *Amazing Ohio.* Wilmington, Ohio: Orange Frazer Press, 1989.

Historical facts about Ohio and Ohioans, and biographical sketches.

_____, ed. *The Ohio Almanac.* Wilmington, Ohio: Orange Frazer Press, 1992-93.

Historical background, education, religion, and profiles of each county giving date established, county seat, and statistics.

Walling, Henry Francis. *Atlas of the State of Ohio.* 1868. Reprint. Knightstown, Ind.: Bookmark, 1983.

One of the major and most useful atlases of Ohio.

Whittlesey, Charles. *Topographical and Historical Sketch of the State of Ohio, with an Historical Map.* Philadelphia: Jas. B. Rogers & Co., 1872.

Williams, C.S. *Williams' Ohio State Register and Business Mirror for 1857.* Cincinnati: C.S. Williams, 1857.

Williams & Company, comp. *Ohio State Directory.* Cincinnati: Williams & Co., 1868-82.

Writers' Program (Ohio). *The Ohio Guide.* New York: Oxford University Press, 1940.

See especially Part II, "Cities."

Migration, Emigration, and Immigration

Allen, Michael. *Western Rivermen, 1763-1861.* Baton Rouge: Louisiana State University Press, 1990.

A socio-cultural history of Ohio and Mississippi River boatmen.

Ambler, Charles H. *History of Transportation in the Ohio Valley.* Glendale, Calif.: Arthur H. Clark Co., 1932.

Aughenbaugh, Gloria L., comp. *Gone to Ohio.* York, Penn.: South Central Pennsylvania Genealogical Society, 1990-96.

A listing of people who migrated from selected Pennsylvania counties to selected Ohio counties. Indexed.

Baldwin, Charles Candee. *Early Indian Migration in Ohio.* Cleveland, 1878.

Banta, Richard Elwell. *The Ohio.* 1949. Reprint. Lexington: University Press of Kentucky, 1998.

The Barn Builders: Pennsylvania Settlers in Ohio. Athens, Ohio: Ohio Landscape Productions, 1989. Videocassette.

Barnhart, John D. "Sources of Southern Migration into the Old Northwest." *Mississippi Valley Historical Review* 22 (June 1935): 49-62.

_____. "The Southern Influence in the Formation of Ohio." *Journal of Southern History* 3 (Feb. 1937): 28-42.

Bell, Margaret Van Horn. *A Journey to Ohio in 1810.* 2 vols. New Haven: Yale University Press, 1912.

Berquist, Goodwin F. and Paul C. Bowers, Jr. *The New Eden: James Kilbourne and the Development of Ohio.* Lanham, Md.: University Press of America, 1983.

A study of migration from Connecticut to Ohio.

Berry, Ellen Thomas and David A. Berry. *Early Ohio Settlers: Purchasers of Land in East and East Central Ohio, 1800-1840.*

Baltimore: Genealogical Publishing Co., 1989.

_____. *Early Ohio Settlers: Purchasers of Land in Southeastern Ohio, 1800-1840*. Baltimore: Genealogical Publishing Co., 1984.

_____. *Early Ohio Settlers: Purchasers of Land in Southwestern Ohio, 1800-1840*. Baltimore: Genealogical Publishing Co., 1986.

Each of the above three volumes give, in addition to the name of the land purchaser, the date and locality, the person's residence, often in another state. Useful in tracing migration.

Betzler, Allen F. *New Jersey Transplants: A Genealogical Record of Some of the Pioneer Families Who Came from New Jersey to Settle in the Miami Valley of Ohio*. Franklin, Ohio, 1982.

Bigham, Darrel E. *Towns & Villages of the Lower Ohio*. Lexington: University Press of Kentucky, 1998.

Billington, Ray Allen and Martin Ridge. *Westward Expansion: A History of the American Frontier*. 5th ed. New York: Macmillan Publishing, 1982.

Blunt, Edmund M. *Traveller's Guide to and through the State of Ohio, with Sailing Directions for Lake Erie*. New York, 1833.

Bogue, Donald Joseph. *A Methodological Study of Migration and Labor Mobility in Michigan and Ohio in 1947*. Oxford, Ohio: Scripps Foundation, Miami University, 1952.

Bond, Beverely Waugh, Jr. *The Foundations of Ohio*. Columbus: Ohio State Archaeological and Historical Society, 1941.

Bradbury, John. *Travels in the Interior of America in the Years 1809, 1810, and 1811, Ohio*. Liverpool: The author, 1817.

Brien, Lindsay Metcalfe. *A Genealogical Index of Pioneers in the Miami Valley, Ohio*. Dayton, Ohio: Dayton Circle, Colonial Dames of America in the State of Ohio, 1970.

Shows names of family members, Ohio residence and previous place of residence, dates, and other genealogical details. Covers Miami, Montgomery, Preble, and Warren counties, Ohio. See

Every Name Index to Miami Valley Ohio Pioneers, indexed by Marjorie Dodd Floyd (Dayton, Ohio, 1980).

Bullock, W. *Sketch of a Journey through the Western States of North America from New Orleans, by the Mississippi, Ohio, City of Cincinnati*. London: John Miller, 1827.

Bunch-Lyons, Beverly A. *And they Came: The Migration of African-American Women from the South to Cincinnati, Ohio, 1900-1950*. N.p., 1995.

Cayton, Andrew R.L. "A Quiet Independence: The Western Vision of the Ohio Company." *Ohio History* 90 (Winter 1981): 5-32.

Chaddock, Robert E. *Ohio Before 1850: A Study of the Early Influence of Pennsylvania and Southern Populations in Ohio*. 1908. Reprint. New York: AMS Press, 1967.
    Discusses westward migration into Ohio, Germans, Quakers, canals in Ohio, social life, and other migration topics.

Cincinnati, Columbus, Cleveland & Erie Railroad Guide. Dayton, Ohio: Landfall Press, 1986.

Clark, Thomas Dionysius. *Frontier America: The Story of the Westward Movement*. 2nd ed. New York: Charles Scribner's Sons, 1969.
    See especially Chapter 6, "The Frontier on the Ohio and Mississippi."

Coomer, James. *Life on the Ohio*. Lexington: University Press of Kentucky, 1997.

Crouse, D.E. *The Ohio Gateway*. New York: Charles Scribner's Sons, 1938.
    Ohio migration trails are described; includes useful maps.

Dana, E. *Description of the Principal Roads and Routes, by Land and Water, through the Territory of the United States*. Cincinnati: Looker, Reynolds & Co., 1819.
    Illustrates roads in Ohio, pp. 97-99.

_____. *Geographical Sketches of the Western Country*. Cincinnati:

Looker, Reynolds & Co., 1819.

See pp. 64-87 for Ohio sketches.

Dannenbaum, Jed. "Immigrants and Temperance: Ethnocultural Conflict in Cincinnati, 1845-1860." *Ohio History* 87 (Spring 1978): 125-39.

Dollarhide, William. *Map Guide to American Migration Routes, 1735-1815*. Bountiful, Utah: Heritage Quest, 1997.

Shows maps of some Ohio rivers, trails, and other migration routes.

Dolle, Mrs. Percy A., comp. *Abstracts of Items of Genealogical Interest to be Found in the Laws of Ohio*. Columbus: Mrs. P.A. Dolle, 1957.

_____. *Geographical Origins of Early Ohioans As Shown in Land Office Records*. Columbus, 1963.

Shows previous place of residence of Ohioans in another state.

Easterlin, Richard. "Population Change and Farm Settlement in the Northern United States." *Journal of Economic History* 36 (March 1976): 53-54.

Ellis, William Donohue. *The Cuyahoga*. New York: Holt, Rinehart and Winston, 1966.

A history of the Western Reserve and the Cuyahoga River.

Evans, William R. *History of Welsh Settlements in Jackson and Gallia Counties of Ohio*. Columbus: Chatham Communications, 1988.

The Evolution of Ohio. Online: (www.oplin.lib.oh.us/products/build/index.html).

For each geographical region in Ohio, this site shows history (chronology), migration, economy, and population.

Eyre, John. *Travels: Comprising a Journey from England to Ohio, Two Years in that State*. New York, 1852.

Feather, Carl E. *Mountain People in a Flat Land: A Popular History of Appalachian Migration to Northeast Ohio, 1940-1965*. Athens,

Ohio: Ohio University Press, 1998.

An illustrated popular history of Appalachian migration into northeastern Ohio.

Finn, Chester E. "The Ohio Canals: Public Enterprise on the Frontier." *Ohio State Archaeological and Historical Quarterly* 51 (Jan.-March 1942): 1-41.

Frost, Sherman L. and Wayne S. Nichols. *Ohio Water Firsts.* Columbus: Water Resources Foundation of Ohio, 1985.

Gard, R. Max and William H. Vodrey, Jr. *The Sandy and Beaver Canal.* East Liverpool, Ohio: East Liverpool Historical Society, 1952.

Gephart, William F. "Transportation and Industrial Development in the Middle West." Ph.D. diss., Columbia University, 1909.

Development of roads, canals, and railways in Ohio and the Midwestern states.

Gieck, Jack. *A Photo Album of Ohio's Canal Era, 1825-1913.* Kent, Ohio: Kent State University Press, 1988.

Ohio maps, photographs, and historical background of canals in the state for the time period 1825-1913.

Grabb, John R. *The Marietta & Cincinnati Railroad, and Its Successor, the Baltimore & Ohio: A Study of This Once Great Route Across Ohio, 1851-1988.* Chillicothe, Ohio, 1989.

Grant, H. Roger. "Erie Lackawanna: An Ohio Railroad." *Ohio History* 101 (Winter-Spring 1992): 5-20.

_____ *Ohio on the Move: Transportation in the Buckeye State.* Athens, Ohio: Ohio University Press, 2000.

Havighurst, Walter. *River to the West: Three Centuries of the Ohio.* New York: G.P. Putnam's Sons, 1970.

Hawley, Zerah. *A Journal of a Tour through Connecticut, Massachusetts, New York, the North Part of Pennsylvania and Ohio.* New Haven, Conn.: S. Converse, 1822.

He, Jian. *Ohio Migration Patterns: State and Counties (1980-1990 and*

1990-1994). Columbus: Ohio Department of Development, Office of Strategic Research, 1996.

Heiser, Alta Harvey. *West to Ohio.* Yellow Springs, Ohio: Antioch Press, 1954.

A major study of migration to Ohio and migration routes.

Hite, Richard. "The Canals of Ohio." *Preview* (Ohio Historical Society) 5 (Summer 1996): 10-13.

Holbrook, Stewart H. *The Yankee Exodus: An Account of Migration from New England.* New York: Macmillan, 1950.

Hood, Marilyn G. *Canals of Ohio, 1825-1913.* Columbus: Ohio Historical Society, 1971.

"How We Came to Ohio." *The Report* 19 (Summer 1979): 61-67.

Hulbert, Archer Butler. "The Methods and Operations of the Scioto Group of Speculators." *Mississippi Valley Historical Review* 1 (March 1915): 502-15 and 2 (June 1915): 56-73.

_____. *The Ohio River: A Course of Empire.* 1906. Reprint. Salem, Mass.: Higginson Book Co., n.d.

A history of migration on the Ohio River; illustrated.

_____. "The Old National Road: The Historic Highway of America." *Ohio Archaeological and Historical Publications* 9 (1901): 405-519.

Jenkins, Warren. *The Ohio Gazetteer and Traveller's Guide.* Rev. ed. Columbus: Isaac N. Whiting, 1841.

Useful as an early migration source for the state.

Jones, R.R. "The Ohio River, 1700-1914." Cincinnati: U.S. Engineers Office, 1914. Typescript.

Jordan, Wayne. "The People of Ohio's First County." *Ohio Archaeological and Historical Society* 49 (Jan. 1940): 1-40.

King, Horace. *Granville, Massachusetts to Ohio: A Story of Migration and Settlement.* Granville, Ohio: Granville Sentinel Publishing, 1989.

A detailed study of migration from Massachusetts to central Ohio. Includes valuable Ohio maps.

Klein, Benjamin F., ed. *The Ohio River: Handbook and Picture Album.* Rev. ed. Cincinnati: Young and Klein, 1969.

Koleda, Elizabeth Potts. *Some Ohio & Iowa Pioneers: Their Friends and Descendants.* Prineville, Oregon: The author, 1973.

Lang, Elfrieda. "Ohioans in Northern Indiana before 1850." *Indiana Magazine of History* 49 (Dec. 1953): 391-404.

Log Cabins & Castles: Virginia Settlers in Ohio. Athens, Ohio: Ohio Landscape Productions, 1991. Videocassette.

Löher, Franz. *Geschichte und Zuständer der Deutschen in Amerika.* Cincinnati: Berlag von Eggers und Wulkop, 1847.
History and account of Germans in America, chiefly Ohio and the west.

Loomis, Linn. *Here and Now, Ohio's Canals: The Background of Ohio's Canal System.* Newcomerstown, Ohio: The author, 1991.

Lubbers, Ferne Reedy and Margaret Dieringer, eds. *Advent of Religious Groups into Ohio.* Mansfield, Ohio: Clark County Chapter, Ohio Genealogical Society, 1978.
A discussion of major religious groups in Ohio, with maps. Useful for tracing migration to Ohio, and reasons for migration.

McClelland, C.P. and C.C. Huntington. *History of the Ohio Canals.* Columbus: Ohio State Archaeological and Historical Society, 1905.

McCormick, Virginia E. and Robert W. McCormick. *New Englanders on the Ohio Frontier: The Migration and Settlement of Worthington, Ohio.* Kent, Ohio: Kent State University Press, 1998.
A well-researched and documented Ohio local history and migration history. Extensive notes and bibliography.

McNeil, David. *Railroad with 3 Gauges: The Cincinnati, Georgetown & Portsmouth RR and Felicity & Bethel RR.* Cincinnati: The author, 1986.

Marchioni, Michael P. "Economic Development and Settlement Patterns in the Flood Plain of the Upper Ohio Valley." Ph.D. diss., University of Cincinnati, 1971.

Discusses the exploration and settlement of the Ohio Valley, internal transportation, and national expansion. Illustrated.

Merk, Frederick. *History of the Westward Movement*. New York: Alfred A. Knopf, 1980.

Michaux, François André. *Travels to the West of the Alleghany Mountains in the States of Ohio, Kentucky, and Tennessee, 1802*. London: B. Crosby & J.F. Hughes, 1805.

Muller, Edward K. "Selective Urban Growth in the Middle Ohio Valley, 1800-1860." *Geographical Review* 66 (April 1976): 178-99.

Ohioans in the California Census of 1850. Los Alamitos, Calif.: Southern California Chapter, Ohio Genealogical Society, 1988.

Ohio Genealogical Society Quarterly. Quarterly of the Ohio Genealogical Society, Mansfield, Ohio.

Formerly *The Report*, many of the issues include articles which identify Ohioians residing in other states, or whose previous place of residence was Ohio, record abstracts, lists, genealogies with an Ohio connection, book notices, and other articles of interest to Ohio genealogists.

Ohio Migration Trails. Internet: (www.infinet.com/~dzimmerm/Gwen/migration.htm).

Ohio State Archaeological and Historical Society. *History of the Ohio Canals*. Columbus: Press of F.J. Heer, 1905.

Ohio State Library. *Ohio Canals*. Comp. by C.B. Galbreath. Springfield, Ohio: Springfield Publishing Co., 1910.

Papers Relating to the First White Settlers in Ohio. Western Reserve Historical Society, Historical and Archaeological Tracts, No. 6.

Cleveland, 1871.

Peacefull, Leonard, ed. *A Geography of Ohio*. Rev. ed. Kent, Ohio: Kent State University Press, 1996.

Discusses settlement patterns and population patterns. Nicely illustrated.

Pearce, John. *The Ohio River*. Lexington: University Press of Kentucky, 1989.

Peck, J.M. *A New Guide for Emigrants to the West, Containing Sketches of Ohio*. Boston: Gould, Kendall, and Lincoln, 1836.

Phillips, Kimberly L. *Heaven-Bound: Black Migration, Community, and Activism in Cleveland, 1915-1945*. N.p., 1992.

Porter, Burton P. "Old Canal Days." Columbus: Heer Printing Co., 1942.

The Report. See *Ohio Genealogical Society Quarterly*.

Riegel, Mayburt Stephenson, comp. *Early Ohioans' Residences from the Land Grant Records*. Mansfield, Ohio: Ohio Genealogical Society, 1976.

Identifies many pre-1825 Ohio pioneers who purchased land from the federal government at early land offices in Ohio.

Rittinger, Martha Gerber. *Ohio and Erie Canal Motor Tour*. Chillicothe, Ohio: Ross County Genealogical Society, 1997.

History and pictures of the Ohio and Erie Canal.

Scheiber, Harry N. *Ohio Canal Era: A Case Study of Government and the Economy, 1820-1861*. Athens, Ohio: Ohio University Press, 1969.

Schneider, Norris Franz. *The National Road: Main Street of America*. Columbus: Ohio Historical Society, 1975.

Siebert, Wilbur Henry. *The Mysteries of Ohio's Underground Railroads*. Columbus: Long's Book, 1951.

Simonis, Louis A. *Maumee River, 1835*. Defiance, Ohio: Defiance County Historical Society, 1979.

Smith, Clifford Neal. *Early Nineteenth-Century German Settlers in Ohio (Mainly Cincinnati and Environs)*. McNeal, Ariz.: Westland Publications, 1984.

Smithson, Christopher T. *Marylanders to Ohio*. Westminster, Md.: Willowbend Books, 2002.

Soltow, Lee and Margaret Soltow. "A Settlement That Failed: The French in Early Gallipolis, an Enlightening Letter and an Explanation." *Ohio History* 94 (Winter-Spring 1985): 46-67.

Sperry, Kip. "Births of British Subjects in Ohio." *The Report* 37 (Fall 1997): 122-24.

Sprague, Stuart Seely. *Kentuckians in Ohio and Indiana*. Baltimore: Genealogical Publishing Co., 1986.
A valuable index to biographies in local histories of Kentuckians residing in Ohio and Indiana.

_____. *Kentuckians in Missouri, Including Many Who Migrated by Way of Ohio, Indiana, or Illinois*.

Steckmessar, Kent L. *The Westward Movement: A Short History*. New York: McGraw-Hill, 1969.

Stover, John F. *Iron Road to the West: American Railroads in the 1850s*. New York: Columbia University Press, 1978.

Terrell, C. Clayton. *Quaker Migration to Southwest Ohio*. N.p., 1967.
A brief study of Quaker migrations and reasons for migration to southwest Ohio.

Thompson, Warren Simpson. *Migration Within Ohio, 1935-40: A Study in the Re-distribution of Population*. Oxford, Ohio: Scripps Foundation for Research in Population Problems, Miami University, 1951.

Trevorrow, Frank W. *Ohio's Canals*. Oberlin, Ohio: The author, 1973.
A collection of articles and maps relating to the Ohio canal system; includes some biographical sketches.

Unruh, John D., Jr. *The Plains Across: The Overland Emigrants and the Trans-Mississippi West, 1840-60.* Urbana, Ill.: University of Illinois Press, 1979.

Vedder, Richard K. and Lowell E. Gallaway. "Migration and the Old Northwest." In *Essays in Nineteenth Century Economic History: The Old Northwest,* edited by David C. Klingaman and Richard K. Vedder. Athens, Ohio: Ohio University Press, 1975.

Weinberg, Daniel E. "Ethnic Identity in Industrial Cleveland: The Hungarians, 1900-1920." *Ohio History* 86 (Summer 1977): 171-86.

Wheeler, Robert A., ed. *Visions of the Western Reserve: Public and Private Documents of Northeastern Ohio, 1750-1860.* Columbus: Ohio State University Press, 2000.

Wilcox, Frank Nelson. *Ohio Indian Trails: A Pictorial Survey of the Indian Trails of Ohio.* Edited by William A. McGill. Kent, Ohio: Kent State University Press, 1970.

History and sketches of Ohio Indian trails. Lists historic Indian towns in Ohio.

_____. *The Ohio Canals.* Edited by William A. McGill. Kent, Ohio: Kent State University Press, 1969.

A well-illustrated discussion of canals in Ohio.

Wilhelm, Hubert G.H. *Log Cabins & Castles: Virginia Settlers in Ohio.* Athens, Ohio: Ohio Landscape Productions, 1991.

Study guide for videocassette discussing Virginia settlers in Ohio.

_____. *The Origin and Distribution of Settlement Groups: Ohio, 1850.* Athens, Ohio: Ohio University, 1982.

A migration analysis of the 1850 United States census taken for Ohio. Useful for nineteenth-century Ohio migration studies.

Winkle, Kenneth J. *The Politics of Community: Migration and Politics in Antebellum Ohio.* Cambridge: Cambridge University Press, 1988.

Examines political life in antebellum Ohio and the relationship between migration and politics. A scholarly study of migration to Ohio, with extensive footnotes, bibliographies, maps, and charts.

Wolf, Donna M. *Irish Immigrants in Nineteenth Century Ohio: A Database.* Apollo, Penn.: Closson Press, 1998.

_____, comp. *Irish Immigrants in Ohio.* N.p., 1996.

Military Records and Military History

Adams, Marilyn, comp. *Index to Civil War Veterans and Widows in Southern Ohio, 1890 Federal Census*. Columbus: Franklin County Genealogical Society, 1986.
Shows names of Southern Ohio Civil War veterans or widows, county and township, and census page numbers.

Alphabetical Index to Ohio Official Roster, Mexican War, 1846-1848. Cleveland: WPA, 1938. Typescript.

Arnold, Gary J., comp. *Civil War Guide Project: Primary Collections at Ohio Historical Society, with Index*. Columbus: Ohio Historical Society, 1996.

Bell, Annie Walker Burns. *Records of Abstracts of Soldiers Who Applied for Pensions While Residing in Ohio*. N.p., n.d.

Bowman, Mary L., comp. *Some Ohio Civil War Manuscripts: A Finding Tool*. Mansfield, Ohio: Ohio Genealogical Society, 1997. Describes many Ohio Civil War manuscripts at major repositories—Ohio Historical Society, and others.

Broglin, Jana Sloan, comp. *Index to Official Roster of Ohio Soldiers in the War with Spain, 1898-1899*. 1989. Reprint. Mansfield, Ohio: Ohio Genealogical Society, 1999.

Carrington,, Henry Beebee. *Ohio in the Civil War*. Columbus, n.d.
History of Ohio during the Civil War, 1861-65.

Clay, Paul, et al., comps. *The Men and Women of Camp Chase*. Columbus: Hilltop Historical Society, 1990.

Clutters, Kathy and Tom Clutters, eds. *Confederate Soldiers Buried in Ohio*. Ironton, Ohio: The authors, n.d.

_____. *Ohio Battle Deaths in the Civil War (1861-1865)*. Ironton, Ohio: The authors, n.d.

_____, eds. *Ohio Casualties in the Civil War*. 3 vols. Ironton, Ohio:

The authors, n.d.

Crow, Amy Johnson. "Researching Civil War Ancestors: Examples from Ohio's State and Local Records." Lecture, Fort Wayne, Indiana, July 2000. Audiotape. Hobart, Indiana: Repeat Performance, 2000.

_____. "The Virginia Military District: A Study in Contradictions." *NGS Newsmagazine* 28 (July/August 2002): 208-209, 246.

Dailey, Mrs. Orville D., comp. *The Official Roster of the Soldiers of the American Revolution Who Lived in the State of Ohio.* Columbus: State Society, Daughters of the American Revolution, 1938.

Daughters of the American Revolution. Cincinnati Chapter. *Index of Patriots, Revolutionary War Heroes and their Families.* Compiled by Jeraldyne Beets Clipson and Katherine Brewer Brinkdopke. Cincinnati, 1983.

Daughters of the American Revolution of the State of Ohio. *Official Roster III, Soldiers of the American Revolution Who Lived in the State of Ohio.* Painesville, Ohio: Painesville Publishing Co., 1959.

_____. *Ohio State History of the Daughters of the American Revolution.* 2 vols. N.p., 1945.

Diefenbach, Mrs. H.B. and Mrs. C.O. Ross, comps. *Index to the Grave Records of Soldiers of the War of 1812 Buried in Ohio.* N.p., 1945.

Dornbusch, C.E., comp. *Military Bibliography of the Civil War.* 4 vols. New York: New York Public Library, 1961-72. Vol. 4, Dayton, Ohio: Morningside House, 1987.

Extensive bibliographies of Civil War unit histories.

Dyer, Frederick Henry. *A Compendium of the War of the Rebellion.* 1908. Reprint. Dayton, Ohio: Morningside Bookshop, 1978.

See especially historical background of Ohio regiments during the Civil War. One of the classic reference books on the Civil War.

Frohman, Charles E. *Rebels On Lake Erie.* Columbus: Ohio Historical Society, 1965.

A history of Civil War Confederates on Johnson's Island, Lake Erie.

Frontier Retreat on the Upper Ohio, 1779-1781, edited by Louise Phelps Kellogg. 1917. Reprint. Bowie, Md.: Heritage Books, 1994.

Funk, Arville L. *The Morgan Raid in Indiana and Ohio (1863)*. Corydon, Ind.: ALFCO Publications, 1971.

Garner, Grace, comp. *Index to Roster of Ohio Soldiers, War of 1812*. Spokane, Wash.: Eastern Washington Genealogical Society, 1974.

Harper, Robert S. *Ohio Handbook of the Civil War*. Columbus: Ohio Historical Society, 1961.

An overview of Ohio in the Civil War.

Hatcher, Patricia Law. *Abstract of Graves of Revolutionary Patriots*. 4 vols. Dallas: Pioneer Heritage Press, 1987-88.

Hutchinson, William Thomas. *The Bounty Lands of the American Revolution in Ohio*. 1927. Reprint. New York: Arno Press, 1979. An Index of Soldiers of the American Revolution Buried in Ohio. Card index available at the Western Reserve Historical Society Library, Cleveland, Ohio. Microfilm.

Index to Roster of Ohio Soldiers in the War of 1812. Indexed by Bill Oliver. Bowling Green, Ohio: Wood County Chapter of the Ohio Genealogical Society, 1997.

Jackson, Ronald Vern, ed. *Ohio Military Land Warrants, 1789-1801*. North Salt Lake, Utah: Accelerated Indexing Systems, 1988.

Jones, Robert Leslie. *Ohio Agriculture during the Civil War*. Columbus: Ohio State University Press, 1962.

Keifer, J. Warren. *Ohio's Contribution, Sacrifice and Service in the [Civil] War*. Springfield, Ohio: Republic Printing Co., 1878.

Kellogg, Louise Phelps, ed. *Frontier Advance on the Upper Ohio, 1778-1779*. Madison: State Historical Society of Wisconsin, 1916.

———. *Frontier Retreat on the Upper Ohio, 1779-1781*. 1917. Reprint. Bowie, Md.: Heritage Books, 1994.

Latham, Allen and B.G. Leonard. *A Roll of the Officers in the Virginia Line of the Revolutionary Army, Who Have Received Land Bounty in the States of Ohio and Kentucky.* Louisville, Ky.: Lost Cause Press, 1969.

Linscott, Jeff A., comp. *An Organized Listing of the Soldiers of Ohio Who Served in the War of 1812.* Colorado Springs, Colo.: J.A. Linscott, 1993.

A List of the Civil War Regimental Histories on Microfilm at the State Library of Ohio. N.p., n.d.

List of Pensioners on the Roll, January 1, 1883: Ohio. Washington: Government Printing Office, 1883.

Luttner, Ken, comp. *Ohio's Virginia Military Tract: Index of 1801 Tax List.* Austin, Minn.: Ohio Genealogy Center, 1991.
    Index of Virginia militiamen who served in the American Revolution; the tract is located west of the Scioto River.

Maxwell, Fay. *Ohio 1840 Census of Revolutionary War Soldiers.* Austin, Minn.: Ohio Genealogy Center, 1985.

Military Records: Civil War Muster Rolls, CD-ROM (Ancestry.com).

Military Records: Ohio Enlistments, 1908-1928, CD-ROM (Ancestry.com).

The Military History of Ohio: Its Border Annals, Its Part in the Indian Wars, in the War of 1812, in the Mexican War and in the War of the Rebellion. New York: H.H. Hardesty, 1887.
    Ohio military history, unit histories, biographies, portraits.

Military Order of the Loyal Legion of the United States. *Ohio Commandery: Roll of Members of the Ohio Commandery.* Cincinnati: The Commandery, 1884.

Miller, Charles D. *Report of the Great Re-union of the Veteran Soldiers and Sailors of Ohio Held at Newark, July 22, 1878.* Newark, Ohio: Clark & Underwood, 1879.

National Society, Daughters of the American Revolution. *DAR Patriot*

Index: Centennial Edition. 3 vols. Washington, DC: The Society, 1994.

Alphabetically arranged by surname. Shows name of patriot ancestor, birth and death dates, state of birth and death, wife's name, rank, state served from (information varies). This is one of the major genealogical indexes for this time period in American history.

_____. *Index of the Rolls of Honor (Ancestor's Index) in the Lineage Books of the National Society of the Daughters of the American Revolution.* 1916-40. Reprint. 4 vols. in 2. Baltimore: Genealogical Publishing Co., 1988.

National Society, Sons of the American Revolution. *Revolutionary War Graves Register.* Comp. and edited by Clovis H. Brake-bill. Dallas: db Publications, 1993.

National Society, United States Daughters of 1812. *Index to the Grave Records of Servicemen of the War of 1812, State of Ohio.* Edited by Phyllis Brown Miller. Huber Heights, Ohio: Ohio Society, United States Daughters of 1812, 1988.

Indexes *Roster of Ohio Soldiers in the War of 1812.*

National Society, United States Daughters of 1812. Ohio Society. *Burial Places of Ohio Soldiers of the War of 1812.* 20 vols. The Society, 1927.

Volumes housed at the State Library of Ohio, Columbus. Title varied, *Ohio Burial Places of Soldiers of the War of 1812.* See index edited by Phyllis Brown Miller, *Index to the Grave Records of Servicemen of the War of 1812, State of Ohio.*

_____. *Index to the Grave Records of Servicemen of the War of 1812, State of Ohio.* N.p., 1969.

_____. *Index to the Roster of Ohio Soldiers in the War of 1812.* N.p., n.d.

The Military History of Ohio: Its Border Annals, Its Part in the Indian

War, in the War of 1812, in the Mexican War, and in the War of the Rebellion. New York: H.H. Hardsty, 1887.

Neill, Michael John. "World War II Draft Cards." *OGS Genealogy News* 33 (July-August 2002): 124-27.

Niedringhaus, David A. "Dress Rehearsal for World War I: The Ohio National Guard Mobilization of 1916." *Ohio History* 100 (Winter-Spring 1991): 35-56.

The Official Roster of Ohio Soldiers in the War with Spain, 1898-1899. Columbus: Edward T. Miller Co., 1916 (www.ancestry.com).
Consult Jana Sloan, Broglin, comp., *Index to Official Roster of Ohio Soldiers in the War with Spain, 1898-1899* (1989, Reprint. Mansfield, Ohio: Ohio Genealogical Society, 1999).

The Official Roster of the Soldiers of the American Revolution Buried in the State of Ohio. 3 vols. Columbus: F.J. Heer Printing Co., 1929-59.

Official Roster of the Soldiers of the State of Ohio in the War of the Rebellion, 1861-1865. 12 vols. Akron, Ohio: Werner Co., 1893, and Norwalk, Ohio: Laning Co., 1895 (publisher varied). Titles varies. Microfilm.
Arranged by unit, shows names of soldiers, rank, age, date entered service, period of service, remarks (date mustered out), appointments, promotions, if wounded or killed, if captured, date of death, and other details). Volume 12 includes a roster of Ohio soldiers in the War with Mexico, 1846-48. Indexed by Works Progress Administration of Ohio, comps., *Alphabetical Index to Official Roster of the Soldiers of the State of Ohio in the War of the Rebellion,* 9 vols. (Cleveland: Works Progress Administration, 1938). See also index by Jana Sloan Broglin (OGS).

Official Roster of the Soldiers of the State of Ohio in the War with Mexico, 1846-1848. 1897. Reprint. Mansfield, Ohio: Ohio Genealogical Society, 1991. Reprint edition is indexed.

Official Roster of the Soldiers of the State of Ohio, Spanish American War. Muster in and muster out rolls. Microfilm.

Ohio. Adjutant General's Dept. *Roster of Ohio Soldiers in the War of 1812*. 1916. Reprint. Baltimore: Genealogical Publishing Co., 1968.

Arranged by company, shows name of soldier and rank. Online: (www.ohiohistory.org/resource/database/rosters.html).

Ohio. Adjutant General's Office. Grave Registrations of Soldiers Buried in Ohio. Microfilm.

This is one of the major personal name finding aids for Ohio.

_____. *The Official Roster of Ohio Soldiers, Sailors, and Marines in the World War, 1917-1918*. 23 vols. Columbus: F.J. Herr Printing Co., 1926-29. Microfilm.

Includes rosters of soldiers, sailors, and marines for World War I.

_____. *The Official Roster of the Soldiers of the American Revolution Buried in the State of Ohio*. 3 vols. Columbus: F.J. Heer Printing Co., 1929-59. Vol. 2 has the title, *The Official Roster of the Soldiers of the American Revolution who Lived in the State of Ohio*.

_____. *Official Roster of the Soldiers of the State of Ohio in the War of the Rebellion*. Microfilm.

Original muster in and muster out rolls of Ohio military organizations in the Civil War. Arranged by regiment.

_____. *Roster of Soldiers of the Ohio National Guard, 1874-1917*. Microfilm.

_____. *Soldiers from Ohio, War of 1812*. Microfilm.

_____. *World War I, Service Cards of the State of Ohio*. Microfilm.

Ohio. Department of Health. Veteran's Records, 1941-1964. Microfilm. Grave reports regarding deceased veterans in Ohio.

"Ohio Roster of Soldiers in the War of 1812." Akron, Ohio, n.d.

Typescript. Indexes *Roster of Ohio Soldiers in the War of 1812*.

Ohio Veteran's Home Death Records, January 3, 1889 through December 31, 1983. Sandusky, Ohio: Erie County Chapter of the Ohio Genealogical Society, 1984.

"Oldest Inscriptions, with Revolutionary and War of 1812 Records, of the Cemeteries of Trumbull, Mahoning, and Columbiana Counties, Ohio, and Lawrence, Mercer, and Beaver Counties, Pennsylvania." 7 vols. in 1. 1913. Typescript at State Library of Ohio, Columbus.

Oyos, Matthew. "The Mobilization of the Ohio Militia in the CivilWar." *Ohio History* 98 (Summer-Autumn 1989): 147-74.

Page, Henry F. *Virginia Military District of the Law of Warrants, Entries, Surveys and Patents in the V.M.D. of Ohio.* Columbus: J.H. Riley & Co., 1850.

Petty, Gerald M. *Index of the Ohio Squirrel Hunters Roster.* Columbus: Petty's Press, 1984.

Phillips, William Louis. *Annotated Bibliography of Ohio Patriots: Revolutionary War & War of 1812.* Bowie, Md.: Heritage Books, 1985.

_____. *Index to Ohio Pensioners of 1883.* Bowie, Md.: Heritage Books, 1987.

Indexes Civil War and War of 1812 veterans and their widows who received federal pensions and were residing in Ohio in 1883.

Pitcavage, Mark. "Burthened in Defence of Our Rights: Opposition to Military Service in Ohio during the War of 1812." *Ohio History* 104 (Summer-Autumn 1995): 142-62.

Piton, Mrs. Phillip. *Confederate Cemeteries in Ohio: Camp Chase & Johnson Island.* Columbus: Franklin County Chapter, Ohio Genealogical Society, 1980.

The Plain Dealer. *Official History of the Ohio National Guard and Ohio Volunteers.* Cleveland: Plain Dealer Publishing Co., 1901.

Lists of soldiers, portraits, history, and biographical sketches.

Poland, Charles A., comp. *Army Register of Ohio Volunteers in the*

Service of the United States. Columbus: Ohio State Journal Printing Co., 1862.

Porter, George. "Ohio Politics During the Civil War Period." *Columbia University Studies in History, Economics, and Public Law* 50 (1911): 18-21.

Reed, Beverly Todd. *Military Pension Applications, 1875-1889, Buchanan & MacGahan Law Firm, Toledo, Ohio.* Toledo: Lucas County Chapter of the Ohio Genealogical Society, 1997.

Reid, Whitelaw. *Ohio in the War: Her Statesmen, Generals, and Soldiers.* 2 vols. 1895. Reprint. Columbus: Bergman Books, 1996. A history of Ohio during the Civil War, 1861-65. Detailed history of Ohio regiments and other military organizations, rosters of soldiers, and biographical sketches. Includes many portraits of soldiers.

A Reprint of Official Roster of the Soldiers of the American Revolution Buried in the State of Ohio. Mineral Ridge, Ohio: Ohio Genealogical Society, 1973.

Rooseboom, Eugene H. *The Civil War Era, 1850-1873.* Columbus: Ohio State Archaeological and Historical Society, 1944.

Roster of Ohio Volunteers in the Service of the United States, War with Spain. Columbus: J.L. Trauger, 1898.

Ryan, Daniel Joseph. *The Civil War Literature of Ohio: A Bibliography with Explanatory and Historical Notes.* 1911. Reprint. Mattituck, N.Y.: Peconic Co., 1994.

_____. *Ohio in Four Wars: A Military History.* Columbus, Ohio: Heer Press, 1917. History of Ohio in the War of 1812, Mexican War, Civil War, and Spanish American War.

Shriver, Phillip R. and Donald J. Breen. *Ohio's Military Prisons in the Civil War.* Columbus: Ohio State University Press, 1964.

Smucker, Isaac. *The Military Expeditions of the Northwest Territory.*

Columbus, 1876.

Society of Mayflower Descendants, State of Ohio. *Mayflower Descendants of Ohio*. N.p., 1913.

Sons of the American Revolution. Ohio Society. *Centennial Register, 1889 to 1989*. Dayton, Ohio: Ohio Society, SAR, 1988.
Shows name of patriot ancestor, member's name, SAR chapter, and state SAR number. Cross indexed by member's name.

_____. *Register, 1922-1928*. Columbus: The Society, 1928.

_____. *Year Book of the Ohio Society of the Sons of the American Revolution*. Columbus: The Society, 1896-1909.

Sons of the Revolution (Ohio). *Year Book of the Ohio Society of the Sons of the Revolution*. Cincinnati: The Society, 1897-.
Includes a history of this Society and biographical sketches of soldiers showing rank, unit, and other details. Microfilm.

Starr, Stephen Z. "The Third Ohio Volunteer Cavalry: A View from the Inside." *Ohio History* 85 (Autumn 1976): 306-18.

Thwaites, Reuben Gold and Louise Phelps Kellogg, eds. *Frontier Defense on the Upper Ohio, 1777-1778*. 1912. Reprint. Millwood, N.Y.: Kraus Reprint Co., 1973.

_____, eds. *The Revolution on the Upper Ohio, 1775-1777*. 1908. Reprint. Bowie, Md.: Heritage Books, 1992.

Two Hundred Years: The Military History of Ohio. New York: H.H. Hardesty, 1886.

United Spanish War Veterans. Department of Ohio. Deaths and Graves Registration, ca. 1900-1980. Microfilm.

United States. Adjutant General's Office. *Index to Compiled Service Records of Volunteer Union Soldiers Who Served in Organizations from the State of Ohio*. Microfilm.

United States. General Land Office. *Registers of Revolutionary War Land Warrants, Act of 1788: Military District of Ohio, 1789-1805*.

United States. *List of Pensioners on the Roll, January 1, 1883*.

Washington, DC: Government Printing Office, 1883. Volume 3 includes Ohio.

United States Sanitary Commission. Soldiers' Aid Society of Northern Ohio, Cleveland. *Our Acre and Its Harvest: Historical Sketch of the Soldiers' Aid Society of Northern Ohio*. Cleveland: Fairbanks, Benedict & Co., 1869.

United States. Selective Service System. *World War I Selective Service System Draft Registration Cards, 1917-1918*. Microfilm.
Cards are arranged by state, county, city, and then by surname.

Waldenmaier, Inez. *Revolutionary War Pensioners Living in Ohio before 1834*. Tulsa, Okla.: The author, 1983.
Alphabetically arranged by surname. Shows age, residence, and military service.

War Department. *World War II Honor List of Dead and Missing, State of Ohio*. Washington, DC, 1946.

Wheeler, Kenneth W., ed. *For the Union: Ohio Leaders in the Civil War*. Columbus: Ohio State University Press, 1968.

White, Virgil D. *Genealogical Abstracts of Revolutionary War Pension Files*. 4 vols. Waynesboro, Tenn.: National Historical Publishing Co., 1990.

_____. *Index to Old Wars Pension Files, 1815-1926*. Rev. ed. Waynesboro, Tenn.: National Historical Publishing Co., 1993.

_____. *Index to Volunteer Soldiers in Indian Wars and Disturbances, 1815-1858*. 2 vols. Waynesboro, Tenn.: National Historical Publishing Co., 1993.

_____. *Index to Volunteer Soldiers, 1784-1811*. Waynesboro, Tenn.: National Historical Publishing Co., 1987.

_____. *Index to War of 1812 Pension Files*. 2 vols. Waynesboro, Tenn.: National Historical Publishing Co., 1992.

Whittlesey, Elisha. *War of 1812 in Ohio*. Western Reserve Historical Society, Historical and Archaeological Tracts, No. 7.

Wolfe, Barbara Schull. *An Index to Mexican War Pension Applications.*
Indianapolis: Heritage House, 1985.

Young American Patriots: The Youth of Ohio in World War II.
Richmond, Va.: National Publishing Co., 1947.

Periodicals and Newsletters

The American Genealogist. David L. Greene, P.O. Box 398, Demorest, GA 30535-0398.

Black Swamp Heritage. Grace Luebke, Martin, Ohio (continues *Sandusky County Heritage*).

Buckeye Californian. Southern California Chapter, Ohio Genealogical Society, El Cajon, CA. Discontinued.

Bulletin of the Historical and Philosophical Society of Ohio. Historical and Philosophical Society of Ohio, Cincinnati. *Cumulative Index* (Cincinnati, 1957). Discontinued.

Cities & Villages. Bimonthly. Ohio Municipal League, 175 South Third Street, Suite 510, Columbus, OH 43215.

County News. Quarterly. County Commissioners Association of Ohio, 37 West Broad Street, Suite 650, Columbus, OH 43215-4132.

Echoes. Bimonthly. Ohio Historical Society, 1982 Velma Ave., Columbus, OH 43211-2497.

The Firelands Pioneer. Firelands Historical Society, 4 Case Ave., Norwalk, OH 44857 (vol. 1, June 1858-).

Gateway to the West. 1967-78. Quarterly. Compiled by Ruth Bowers and Anita Short. Reprint, 2 vols. Baltimore: Genealogical Publishing Co., 1989; Baltimore: Clearfield Co., 2001.
Covers a wide range of genealogical source materials and records. Well-indexed.

Journal of the Historical and Philosophical Society of Ohio. 1838. Reprint. Cincinnati: Robert Clarke & Co., 1872.

The Library News. Western Reserve Historical Society, 10825 East Boulevard, Cleveland, OH 44106-1777.

The Local Historian. Bimonthly. Ohio Association of Historical Societies and Museums, Ohio Historical Society, 1982 Velma

Avenue, Columbus, OH 43211-2497.

National Capital Buckeye Quarterly. P.O. Box 105, Bladensburg, MD 20710-0105. Discontinued.

National Genealogical Society Quarterly. National Genealogical Society, 4527 17th Street North, Arlington, VA 22207-2399.

Northwest Ohio Quarterly. Lucas County/Maumee Valley Historical Society, 1031 River Road, Maumee, OH 43537.

OAH Newsletter. Published 3 times a year. Ohio Academy of History, Youngstown State University, Youngstown, OH 44555-0001.

OGS Genealogy News. Ohio Genealogical Society, 713 South Main Street, Mansfield, OH 44907-1644. (Began publication in January/February 2002 as Volume 33 Number 1.)

Ohio Academy of History Newsletter. Published three times a year by the Ohio Academy of History, Ohio Wesleyan University, Delaware, Ohio.

Ohio Archaeological and Historical Quarterly [*Ohio Archaeological and Historical Publications*]. Established in June 1887. Ohio State Archaeological and Historical Society, Columbus. Continued by *Ohio State Archaeological and Historical Quarterly*, *Ohio Historical Quarterly*, and *Ohio History* (q.v.). Microfiche (University Microfilms). See *Cumulative Table of Contents*, vols. 1-62 (1954).

Ohio Archivist. Semiannual. Society of Ohio Archivists, Ohio Historical Society, 1982 Velma Avenue, Columbus, OH 44195.

Ohio Civil War Genealogy Journal. Quarterly. Ohio Genealogical Society, 713 South Main Street, Mansfield, OH 44907-1644.

Ohio Clues. Maumee Valley Historical Society, 1031 River Road, Maumee, OH 43537.

The Ohio Genealogical Helper. Maxwell Publications, P.O. Box 83, Columbus, OH. 43216. Discontinued.

The Ohio Genealogical Quarterly. 1937-44. Reprinted in *Ohio Source*

Records from the Ohio Genealogical Quarterly (Baltimore: Genealogical Publishing Co., 1986).

The Ohio Genealogical Society Newsletter. Ohio Genealogical Society, Mansfield, Ohio. Discontinued. Replaced by *OGS Genealogy News.*

Ohio Genealogical Society Quarterly. Ohio Genealogical Society, 713 South Main Street, Mansfield, OH 44907-1644. Quarterly.
This is the major genealogical periodical for the state. Includes First Families of Ohio rosters, Society of Civil War Families of Ohio, Ohio source material, compiled genealogies, biographies, family Bibles, members' ancestor charts, lists of Ohioans in other states, ethnic sources, related articles, and book reviews.

Ohio's Heritage. Quarterly. Ohio Department of Aging, 50 West Broad Street, Columbus, OH 43215-3363.

Ohio's Historical Detective. Quarterly newsletter for genealogists researching Ohio. Dukeman Publications Company, 4111 Yellowwood St., Lima, OH 45806-1121.

Ohio History. Ohio Historical Society, 1982 Velma Avenue, Columbus, OH 43211-2497. Online and indexed at the Ohio Historical Society Web site (www.ohiohistory.org).

Ohio-Indiana-Iowa Queries. Pioneer Publications, P.O. Box 1179, Tum Tum, WA 99034-1179.

Ohio Libraries. Published three times a year. Ohio Libraries, 35 East Gay Street, Suite 305, Columbus, OH 43215.

Ohio Magazine, 62 East Broad Street, Columbus, OH 43215.

Ohio Palatine Heritage. Palatines to America, 611 East Weber Road, Columbus, OH 43211-1097.

Ohio Queries. Pioneer Publications, P.O. Box 1179, Tum Tum, WA 99034-1179.

Ohio Records and Pioneer Families. Ohio Genealogical Society, 713 South Main Street, Mansfield, OH 44907-1644. Quarterly.

Available by subscription from Ohio Genealogical Society.

The Ohio Researcher. 4 vols. Murray, Utah: Allstates Research Co., 1962-66. Discontinued.

Ohio Valley History Journal. Cincinnati Museum Center, Cincinnati, OH 45203-1129.

Ohio's Last Frontier. Newsletter. Williams County Genealogical Society, P.O. Box 293, Bryan, OH 43506-0293.

Ohio Records. Edwards Brothers, 2500 South State Street, Ann Arbor, MI 48104-6173.

Ohioana News. Ohioana Library Association, 274 East First Avenue, Columbus, OH 43201

Ohioana Quarterly. Ohioana Library Association, 274 East First Avenue, Columbus, OH 43201.

Ohionetwork. Monthly newsletter of OHIONET, 1500 West Lane Avenue, Columbus, OH 43221-3975.

The Old Northwest: A Journal of Regional Life and Letters. Quarterly. Miami University, Oxford, OH 45056.
Biographies, memoirs, diaries, history of the Old Northwest, social history, book reviews.

The "Old Northwest" Genealogical Quarterly. 15 vols. The "Old Northwest" Genealogical Society, Columbus, Ohio, 1898-1912.
Cemetery records, notes and queries, vital records, genealogies, local history, and biographies. See "Index of the Granville Centennial Issue, the 'Old Northwest' Genealogical Quarterly, 1905." Typescript.

Our Family Heritage: A Journal of Genealogy and History of the Ohio River Valley and Central Kentucky. Genealogical Research, Fairborn, Ohio, 1973-75. Discontinued.

The Palatine Immigrant. Quarterly. Palatines to America, 611 East Weber Road, Columbus, OH 43211-1097.

Preview. Ohio Historical Society. Discontinued.

Describes records and the Ohio Historical Society collections of interest to genealogists.

Quarterly Bulletin. The Historical Society of Northwestern Ohio, 1932-33. Discontinued.

Quarterly Publication of the Historical and Philosophical Society of Ohio. Cincinnati, Ohio. Discontinued.

The Report. See *Ohio Genealogical Society Quarterly.*

The Researcher: A Family Heritage Newsletter. Family Heritage, 3105 Petersburg Rd., Jackson, OH 45640-9210.

Rocky Mountain Buckeye. Colorado Chapter, Ohio Genealogical Society, P.O. Box 470189, Aurora, CO 80047-0189.

Roots & Shoots Quarterly. Southern Ohio Genealogical Society, P.O. Box 414, Hillsboro, OH 45133-0414.

State Library of Ohio News. Monthly. State Library of Ohio, 274 East First Avenue, Columbus, OH 43201.

Timeline. Bimonthly. Ohio Historical Society, 1982 Velma Ave., Columbus, OH 43211-2497.

Towpaths. Quarterly. Canal Society of Ohio, 550 Copley Road, Akron, OH 44320.

The Tracer. Quarterly. Hamilton County Chapter, Ohio Genealogical Society, P.O Box 15865, Cincinnati, OH 45215-0865.

Western Reserve Historical Society Genealogical Committee Bulletin. Western Reserve Historical Society, Genealogy Committee, 10825 East Boulevard, Cleveland, OH 44106-1777.

Western Reserve Historical Society News. Western Reserve Historical Society, 10825 East Boulevard, Cleveland, OH 44106-1777.

Western Reserve Magazine. Western Reserve Magazine, 2101 Superior Avenue, Cleveland, OH 44114. Discontinued.
Northern Ohio and Western Reserve local history, collectibles, antiques.

Ohio Maps

Index to Ohio Maps

1. *Map of the State of Ohio*, by Rufus I. Putnam, January 1804.
2. Early Ohio map, not dated (Ohio Historical Society, Columbus).
3. Early Ohio map, not dated (Ohio Historical Society, Columbus).
4. Ohio [map] to Accompany Rufus King's *Ohio in American Commonwealths*, not dated.
5. Ohio, 1828. Anthony Finley, *A New General Atlas* (Philadelphia: Anthony Finley, 1828).
6. Ohio in 1853 (Jonathan Sheppard Books, Albany, NY).
7. Ohio, Principal Land Grants and Surveys, not dated.
8. *The Ohio Country*, by Robert L. Brewer. In Andrew R.L. Cayton, *The Frontier Republic: Ideology and Politics in the Ohio Country, 1780-1825* (Kent, Ohio: Kent State University Press, 1986). With permission of Kent State University Press.
9. *Original Ohio Land Divisions* (Ohio University Cartographic Center). Permission to reproduce the maps "Original Ohio Land Divisions," and "Frontier Settlement Advance," received from Hubert G.H. Wilhelm, Professor of Geography, Ohio University, Athens, Ohio.
10. *Frontier Settlement Advance* (Ohio University Cartographic Center).
11. *Early Migration Routes to Ohio* (Ohio map, 1803). Permission to reproduce this Ohio map, published with the article "How We Came to Ohio," *The Report* 19 (Summer 1979), p. 61, received from Phyllis Brown Delaney, former president, Ohio Genealogical Society, Mansfield, Ohio.
12. *Map of Ohio Canals* (State Library of Ohio, Columbus).

13.   *Map of the State of Ohio Showing Existing, Abandoned and Proposed Canal Routes and the Lands Granted by the United States to the State of Ohio for Canal Purposes* (Ohio Historical Society, Columbus).

14.   *Road Map of Ohio, 1810* (Survey of Transportation).

15.   *Ohio's Transportation Ties*, ca. 1840. Permission to reproduce this map, published in *The Heavens Resound: A History of the Latter-day Saints in Ohio, 1830-1838*, by Milton V. Backman, Jr. (Deseret Book Co., 1983) received from Deseret Book Company, Salt Lake City, Utah. Rights of this map are owned by Deseret Book Company.

16.   Ohio County Boundary Changes, 1801-1808.

17.   Ohio, ca. 1900.

18.   *Counties of Ohio*. This map was created for the author by the Geography Department, Brigham Young University, Provo, Utah. All rights reserved by Kip Sperry.

19.   Map of Ohio Counties (Ohio Department of Transportation, Columbus, Ohio), not dated.

20.   *Ohio Counties and County Seats*, not dated.

21.   *Ohio Network of American History Research Centers*. This map is adapted and updated from a handout available from the Ohio Historical Society, Columbus. See Ohio Historical Society, Archives/Library Division, "Information Packet." An earlier version of this map was published in the *Western Reserve Historical Society Genealogical Committee Bulletin* (Fall 1993), p. 22, and in other Ohio publications. Consult also: (www.ohiohistory.org/textonly/resource/lgr/networkl.html) (http://homepages.rootsweb.com/~maggieoh/ohionet.html)

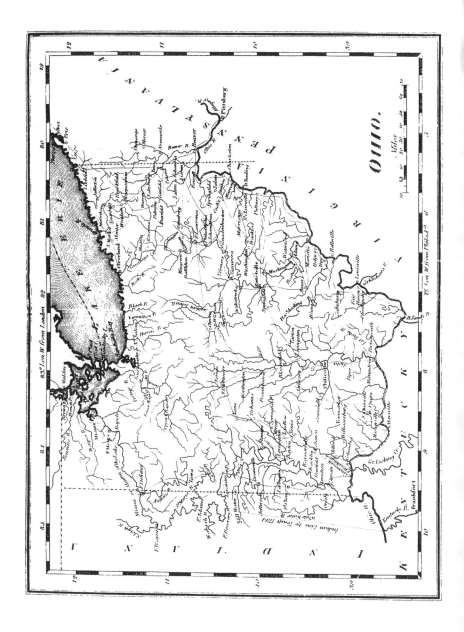

OHIO.

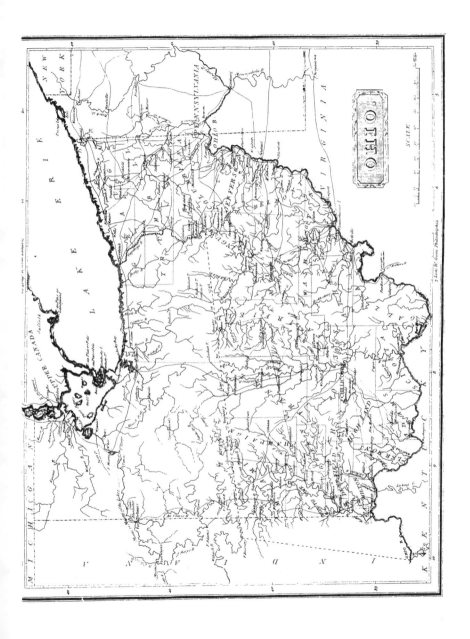

OHIO

J. Lewis Wm. Green Philadelphia

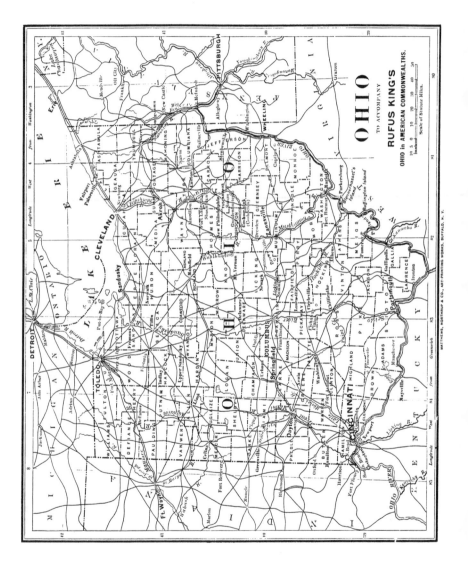

OHIO

TO ACCOMPANY

RUFUS KING'S

OHIO in AMERICAN COMMONWEALTHS.

Scale of Statute Miles.

MATTHEWS, NORTHRUP & CO., ART-PRINTING WORKS, BUFFALO, N.Y.

OHIO

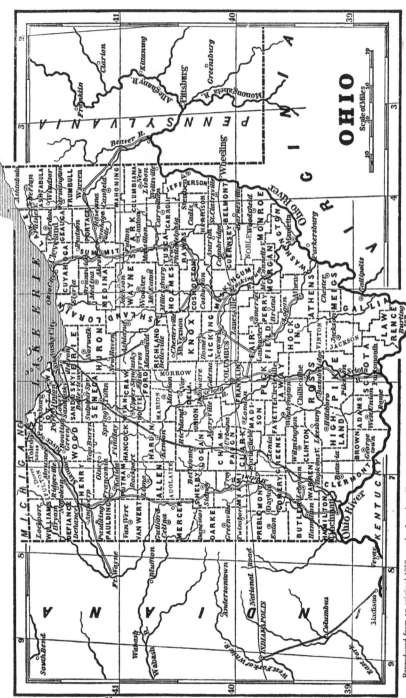

OHIO

Scale of Miles

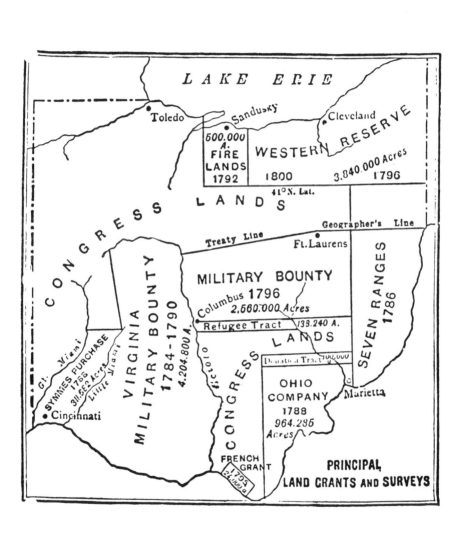

LAKE ERIE

Toledo • Sandusky • Cleveland

500,000 A. FIRE LANDS 1792

WESTERN RESERVE
1800
3,840,000 Acres
1796

CONGRESS LANDS

41° N. Lat.

Geographer's Line

Treaty Line

Ft. Laurens

MILITARY BOUNTY
Columbus 1796
2,560,000 Acres

SEVEN RANGES
1786

VIRGINIA MILITARY BOUNTY
1784–1790
4,204,800 A.

Refugee Tract   139,240 A.

CONGRESS LANDS

Gt. Miami

SYMMES PURCHASE
1788
311,682 Acres

Little Miami

Scioto

Donation Tract 100,000

OHIO COMPANY
1788
964,285
Acres

Marietta

• Cincinnati

FRENCH GRANT
1795
24,000 a.

PRINCIPAL
LAND GRANTS AND SURVEYS

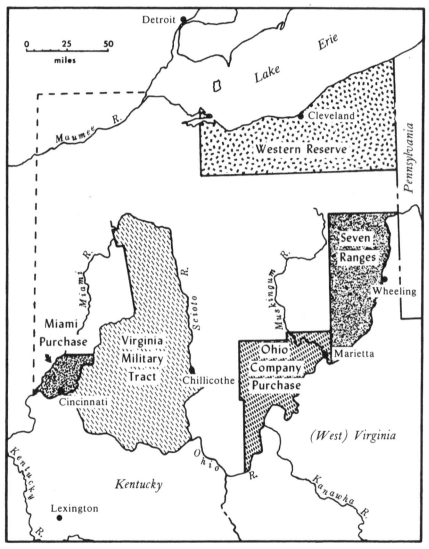

The Ohio Country

Map drawn by Robert L. Brewer.

ORIGINAL OHIO LAND DIVISIONS

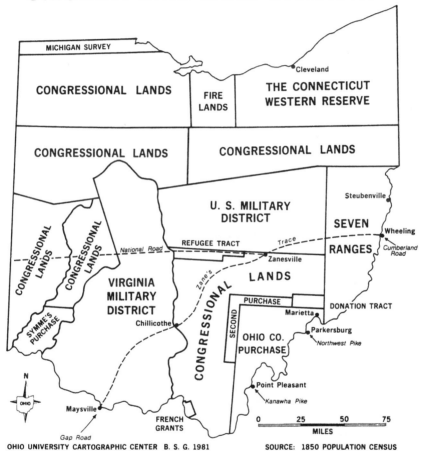

MICHIGAN SURVEY

CONGRESSIONAL LANDS

FIRE LANDS

THE CONNECTICUT WESTERN RESERVE

Cleveland

CONGRESSIONAL LANDS

CONGRESSIONAL LANDS

U. S. MILITARY DISTRICT

Steubenville

SEVEN

RANGES

Wheeling

Cumberland Road

REFUGEE TRACT

Trace

National Road

Zanesville

CONGRESSIONAL LANDS

CONGRESSIONAL LANDS

VIRGINIA MILITARY DISTRICT

LANDS

Zane's

CONGRESSIONAL

SECOND

PURCHASE

DONATION TRACT

Marietta

Parkersburg

Northwest Pike

SYMME'S PURCHASE

Chillicothe

OHIO CO. PURCHASE

Point Pleasant

Kanawha Pike

N

OHIO

Maysville

FRENCH GRANTS

0   25   50   75

MILES

Gap Road

OHIO UNIVERSITY CARTOGRAPHIC CENTER B. S. G. 1981

SOURCE: 1850 POPULATION CENSUS

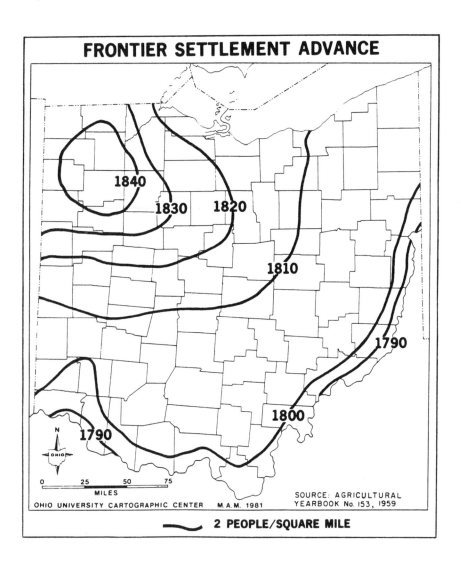

FRONTIER SETTLEMENT ADVANCE

1840
1830 1820
1810
1790
1790
1800

N
OHIO

0   25   50   75
MILES

OHIO UNIVERSITY CARTOGRAPHIC CENTER   M.A.M. 1981

SOURCE: AGRICULTURAL
YEARBOOK No. 153, 1959

2 PEOPLE/SQUARE MILE

Early Migration Routes to Ohio

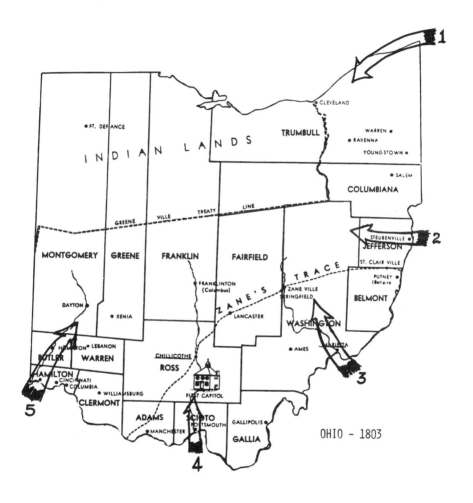

"How We Came to Ohio," The Report 19 (Summer 1979): p. 61
Used with permission of the Ohio Genealogical Society, Mansfield, OH

MAP OF OHIO CANALS.

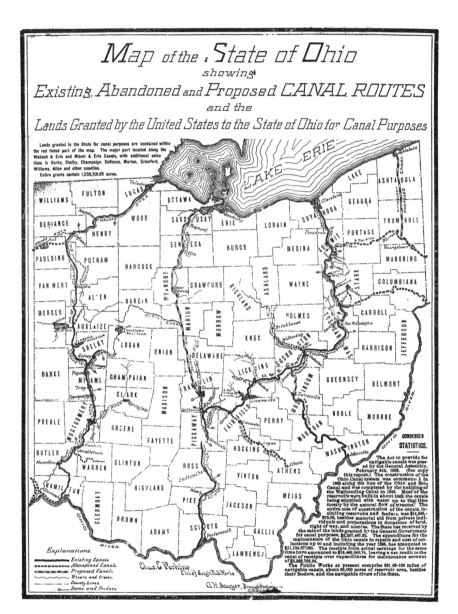

Map of the State of Ohio
showing
Existing, Abandoned and Proposed CANAL ROUTES
and the
Lands Granted by the United States to the State of Ohio for Canal Purposes

Lands granted to the State for canal purposes are contained within the red tinted part of the map. The major part located along the Wabash & Erie and Miami & Erie Canals, with additional selections in Darke, Shelby, Champaign, Defiance, Marion, Crawford, Williams, Allen and other counties.
Entire grants contain 1,230,521.95 acres.

CONDENSED STATISTICS.

The Act to provide for navigable canals was passed by the General Assembly, February 4th, 1825. (See copy this report.) The construction of the Ohio Canal system was commenced in 1825 along the line of the Ohio and Erie Canal and was completed by the building of the Walhonding Canal in 1842. Most of the reservoirs were built in about 1842, the canals being supplied with water up to that time mostly by the natural flow of streams. The entire cost of construction of the canals, including reservoirs and feeders, was $14,840,-973.59, besides material aid from private individuals and corporations in donations of land, right of way, and monies. The State has received by the sale of the lands granted by the General Government for canal purposes, $2,257,487.32. The expenditure for the maintenance of the Ohio canals in repairs and cost of collections up to and including the year 1898, has amounted to $11,104,871.80. The receipts from actual earnings for the same time have amounted to $16,463,640.74, leaving a net credit to the canal of receipts over expenditures for maintenance account of $5,358,768.94.

The Public Works at present comprise 581 89-100 miles of navigable canals, about 30,000 acres of reservoir area, besides their feeders, and the navigable rivers of the State.

Chas. E. Perkins
Chief Engr. Pub. Works

A.H. Sawyer, Draughtsman

Explanations.

- Existing Canals.
- Abandoned Canals.
- Proposed Canals.
- Rivers and Creeks.
- County Lines.
- Dams and Feeders.

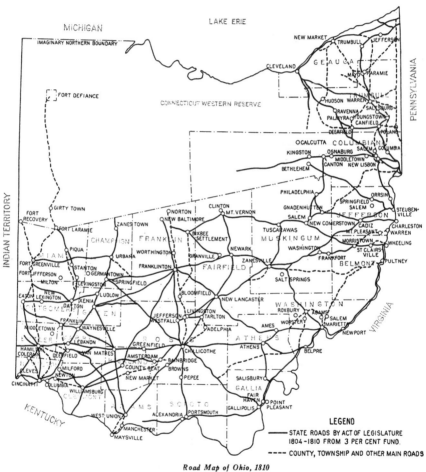

Road Map of Ohio, 1810

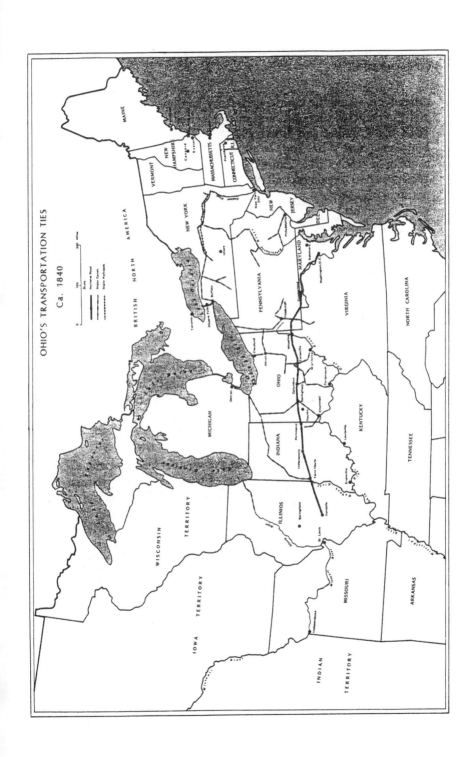

OHIO'S TRANSPORTATION TIES

Ca. 1840

COUNTY BOUNDARY CHANGES

1801

1803
(Statehood granted)

1806

1808

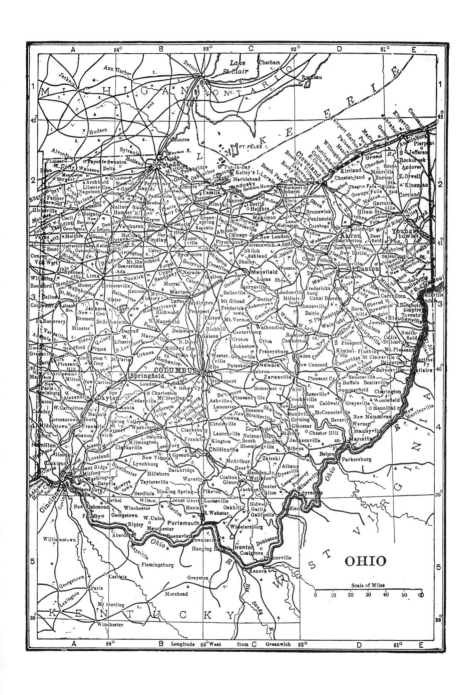

OHIO

Scale of Miles

COUNTIES OF OHIO

MICHIGAN

Lake Erie

Williams | Fulton | Lucas | Ottawa

Defiance | Henry | Wood | Sandusky | Erie | Lorain | Cuyahoga | Lake | Ashtabula | Geauga | Trumbull

Paulding | Putnam | Hancock | Seneca | Huron | Medina | Sum-mit | Portage | Mahoning

Van Wert | Allen | Wyandot | Crawford | Rich-land | Ash-land | Wayne | Stark | Columbiana

Mercer | Auglaize | Hardin | Marion | Morrow | Knox | Holmes | Tusca-rawas | Carroll | Jeffer-son

Shelby | Logan | Union | Delaware | Coshocton | Harrison

Darke | Miami | Champaign | Clark | Madi-son | Franklin | Licking | Muskingum | Guernsey | Belmont

Preble | Mont-gomery | Greene | Fayette | Pickaway | Fairfield | Perry | Morgan | Noble | Monroe

Butler | Warren | Clinton | Ross | Hocking | Athens | Washington

Hamilton | Cler-mont | Highland | Pike | Vinton | Meigs

Brown | Adams | Scioto | Jackson | Gallia

Lawrence

IND.

PENN.

WEST VIRGINIA

KENTUCKY

| 0 | 20 | 40 | 60 | 80 kms |
| 0 | 10 | 20 | 30 | 40 | 50 miles |

BYU Geography Dept.

OHIO DEPARTMENT OF TRANSPORTATION

Ohio Counties & County Seats

OHIO NETWORK OF AMERICAN HISTORY RESEARCH CENTERS

1. University of Akron, Archival Services
    Polsky Bldg.
    Akron, OH 44325-1702
    (216) 972-7670

2. Bowling Green State University
    Center for Archival Collections
    Bowling Green, OH 43403-0175
    (419) 372-2411

3. University of Cincinnati
    Archives and Rare Books Department
    Blegen Library
    Cincinnati, OH 45221-0113
    (513) 556-1959

4. Ohio Historical Society
    Archives-Library Division
    1982 Velma Avenue
    Columbus, OH 43211-2497
    (614) 297-2510

5. Ohio University
    Archives and Special Collections
    Alden Library
    Athens, OH 45701-2978
    (614) 593-2712

6. Western Reserve Historical Society
    10825 East Boulevard
    Cleveland, OH 44106-1788
    (216) 721-5722

7. Wright State University
    Special Collections and Archives
    Paul Laurence Dunbar Library
    Dayton, OH 45435-0001
    (513) 873-2092

8. Youngstown Historical Center
    of Industry and Labor
    P.O. Box 533
    151 West Wood St.
    Youngstown, OH 44501
    (216) 743-5934

General Index